TRAUMA'S LABYRINTH

REFLECTIONS OF A WOUNDED HEALER

LAURA K. KERR

LK KERR
BOOKS

Trade paperback ISBN: 979-8-9857460-1-3

Ebook ISBN: 979-8-9857460-0-6

Edited by Jefferson, FirstEditing

LK Kerr Books
laurakkerr.com
PO Box 27152, San Francisco CA 94127-0152

CONTENTS

Dedicated to those once lost on the journey to themselves

&

to Valentin Y Mudimbe
mentor and friend.

PREFACE

I began writing these essays about psychological trauma in 2010 with a feeling of urgency to communicate the impact of violence on minds, bodies, and societies. At that time, I was practicing psychotherapy, training in somatic psychotherapy and Jungian psychology, and researching trauma's social and cultural consequences. My efforts were regularly undermined by traumas, big and small, that filled my life and the news. Often I felt unsettled, although I was never at a loss for material. Writing has always been how I make peace with what threatens to overwhelm me, and the same was true for these essays. I looked for topics, ideas, and practices that might steer me away from a sense of hopelessness and toward continual engagement. Nevertheless, the themes I explored left me heavy-hearted.

I called this online project *Trauma's Labyrinth*. On a superficial level, the idea of a labyrinth mirrored my personal need for continual adjustments and realignments in my quest for a balanced life. Yet labyrinths are so much more than a practice for centering. They also symbolize the failures and traumas through which we can lose ourselves. Traversing trauma's labyrinth is akin to experiencing a dark night of the soul, when brushes with death—of body or spirit—shatter illusions and pull us into despair, yet there is also an opportunity for transformation and growth.

During the inception of psychiatry as a medical profession —especially the heyday of Sigmund Freud, Carl Jung, Pierre Janet, and Emil Kraepelin—the wounding was still a potential wellspring of knowledge and creativity. Much like shamanism in some cultures, madness held forth the possibility of an initiation into the healing arts—the so-called *journey of the wounded healer*. But the advancement of psychiatry led to an emphasis on diagnoses and fixing a broken brain. Unwittingly, perhaps, a profession of healers emerged that stood separate from those they treated, individuals they perceived as somehow *disordered* rather than lost somewhere in the labyrinth. Instead of a journey of recovery, the boundaries of sanity were erected, and entirely new mazes were created. Granted, we all need help at times, but I never found being pathologized particularly helpful. Lost is the connection between the wisdom found through the wounding and the art of healing. Thus, I also use *Trauma's Labyrinth* to deconstruct what I believe is a false divide between the wounded and the healer.

I've tried to live on both sides of this socially constructed divide, both in communities and my beliefs. It doesn't work. It's a false divide, and like any falsehood about oneself, it is inherently shaming and painful. I grew tired of half-truths, limiting beliefs, and damaging social conventions, especially since they have a way of propagating less-than-ideal solutions and more suffering. And really, how few among us aren't wounded healers? Isn't it just a matter of degree rather than difference? Aren't distinctions between the wounded and the healer just another way of constructing dominance hierarchies and projecting fears of inadequacy—or, alternatively, projecting one's power and idealizations on another? Hence the subtitle of this collection of essays: *Reflections of a Wounded Healer*. Not only does this accurately portray my perspective, but it also supports my assumptions about the eventual direction of the mental health field if it maintains a focus on trauma.

When I live equally as a researcher, healer, and trauma survivor, I believe my best insights come forth. And the greatest insight of all? When the wounded and the healer are integrated *both* within ourselves and our communities, healing is transformative and enduring.

Perhaps as we learn more about trauma, we will discover how best to treat its effects through ages-old wisdom as much as through new, scientific approaches. With *Trauma's Labyrinth*, I have tried to merge the old and new, examining not only how we can heal ourselves but also the increasingly traumatized world in which we live.

THE WORLD I WISH FOR

I wish for a world where we understand what it means to be human among other species, without the pretext of superiority. I wish for a world adapted to our social and emotional needs, not the dominant economic theory. I wish for a world where our most adaptive traits—empathy and creative self-expression—are given ample opportunities to thrive. I wish for a world that is aware of the desire for status yet keeps this drive in check through healthy competition constrained by the needs of communal life.

In the world I wish for, no child will be abused, molested, or neglected. In the world I wish for, people question the sanity of society before labeling a person mentally ill. In the world I wish for, the compulsion to violence startles the would-be offender to seek help, and people are waiting to provide support effectively and nonjudgmentally. In the world I wish for, both people and society are seen as the origins of violence, so assigning blame loses its appeal as a makeshift solution. In the world I wish for, *peace* is a practice rather than an ideal.

RECOVERY FROM TRAUMA

"DEAR SURVIVOR": A LETTER ABOUT THE HARD TRUTHS OF HEALING FROM CHILDHOOD ABUSE

Dear Survivor,

"Because *then* I knew it was over."

That's what most strive to feel about the lingering effects of childhood abuse, though not about the actual events, which are no more than disassociated memories.

Instead, most want to end sleepless nights and startled awakenings. They want to quit feeling like they live in a parallel universe, outside the world inhabited by "normal" people. They want to stop the intrusive images, feelings, and sensations and rid themselves of the desire to drink, smoke, toke, shoot up, or have sex to oblivion. They are tired of avoiding intimacy because of a seemingly endless reserve of anxiety simmering below a brittle surface of civility; or fighting since the rage never seems to dissipate and they just want to push back, because the planet doesn't feel big enough to hold all their hurt, let alone the emotional needs of another person.

At first inkling of the desire to heal, some try to barter with themselves as a way out of this paradoxical life of repetitive chaos. This often begins with a naïve pact with oneself that by being good and trying really hard, one day life will finally, if not miraculously, turn out differently. This is not an easy promise to let go of, even when you fail miserably at keeping it.

Nevertheless, there will still be a part of you that tries to keep the pact. Why? Often because of the secretly held wish that if you finally get it "right," the love that wasn't there will materialize; or your savior will come and magically change everything, releasing you from both effort and responsibility; or an opportunity for revenge will reveal itself, and there you have it: the transformative moment you have waited for has arrived.

I can tell you such fantasies are a waste of your time and imagination. Even if the perfect love, the ideal savior, or the opportunity for the most humiliating payback comes available, you will never become who you might have been had the abuse never happened, nor will you get the time back wasted waiting for your personal Godot.

You might think I am giving you that old song and dance about picking yourself up and off the curb, brushing off the dust of trauma, stomping its dirt from your shoes, and facing up to life's inevitable trials and tribulations. Not at all. Rather, I think childhood abuse is so life-threatening that it might as well be the antimatter to a thriving life. But because I know what it takes to heal—mainly courage, love, and lots of time—I'd rather not see you waste yours.

I grew up in Texas, in the middle of the Bible belt. My early mind stewed in New Testament ideology. It was impressed upon me—with great fear, I might add—to avoid sin at all costs. As children in Sunday school, we learned to hold our breath when we did something wrong, to look around and make sure no one was watching, to produce the image of being good for fear of reprisal, sanctions, and shaming. If your childhood was anything like mine, it's no wonder only the strictest diet of goodness gives hope of salvation. But the truth is, the abuse wasn't your fault, and no matter how good you were or become, it still would have happened. Start loving yourself now.

Sometimes it helps to acknowledge a few ghosts hover about that interfere with overcoming the impact childhood abuse has had on your life. Who are these ghosts? The person who hurt you. The one who didn't love you. The savior who didn't come. The bully you are still afraid of. We all fight battles in our heads that our bodies could never defend against. Some of these battles are our own; others, we've inherited from our parents and other relatives and ancestors. Sometimes, simply through the act of belonging to a group, we inherit ghosts. Humans are pack animals. Our psyches are permeable and inseparable. Sorting out what is yours and what is theirs is a big part of the process.

You know trauma by how it changes you. There is a story I often tell about how the body responds to fear—the amygdala gets activated, the frontal lobes shut down, and a lot of other stuff gets tripped up—which is all true and matters if you want to get your life back on track.

But what lingers long after the traumatic stress becomes manageable is the confrontation with good and evil that childhood abuse initiates. What do you do with the reality that people can be so damn thoughtless, selfish, and cruel? What do you do with the reality that, because you were abused, you, too, have acted in ways you are not so proud of and sometimes deeply ashamed about?

For it isn't until we can hold our own humanity in its widest sense and acknowledge the potential for good and evil in everyone, do the effects of childhood abuse fully relinquish their hold. When you can accept this, you are also able to give yourself the unconditional love that is your birthright, and you will know that, whatever happened, you managed to save your soul.

HOW CHRONIC TRAUMATIZATION INTERFERES WITH GOALS AND COMPLETING ACTIONS

Trauma-related stress reveals itself in many ways: flashbacks, nightmares, emotional overwhelm, shame, obsessive thoughts, decreased concentration, apathy, and loss of sense of self. When trauma-related stress is chronic, which is a common outcome of early-life abuse and neglect, these symptoms become a way to live without actively recalling the past. As one researcher remarked, "Trauma survivors have symptoms instead of memories."[1] Thus, the memories of past traumas may fade, but their impact continues. The longer trauma-related symptoms occur, the more likely they start to feel like the norm—as if they are the "real" you (but they're not). Over time, they can interfere with harnessing the mental energy needed to meet goals and complete desired actions.

Typically, when people think about overcoming a history of chronic traumatization, they imagine confronting the memories they have avoided. Although this can be an important aspect of posttraumatic growth, it's usually not the best place to start. Rather, learning how to live productively in the present is a rewarding first step, one that involves creating safety and stability not only in the external environment but also in the internal environment of the mind and body. Many of us feel safe and stable when we regularly meet goals and follow through on meaningful projects. Indeed, this is often a sign that the grip of a past trauma is beginning to subside.

In their book, *The Haunted Self*, Onno van der Hart, Ellert R. S. Nijenhuis, and Kathy Steele focused on both *mental energy* and *mental efficiency* as central aspects of healing chronic traumatization and living with greater awareness of present needs:

> Survivors often have trouble starting or completing actions, whether they are mental or behavioral. They can plan, but not begin; or they can begin, but not finish; or their actions may lack adequate quality. Such problems indicate that an individual does not have sufficient mental energy or adequate ability to focus that energy for successful completion of various mental and behavioral actions.[2]

Problems with mental efficiency and energy (neither too high nor too low for the task at hand) can be seen in:

- Difficulty starting and completing goals.
- Difficulty sorting through information to choose direction or focus.
- Difficulty taking breaks when involved in ongoing projects.
- Impulsive actions.
- Lack of satisfaction with efforts.

Work habits that seem chaotic or haphazard can often be traced to how we learned as children to cope and get needs met. What began as strategies for surviving early chronic traumatization now interfere with harnessing mental energy and directing that energy efficiently.

The Role of Character Strategies for Meeting Goals and Completing Actions

Ron Kurtz, the founder of the Hakomi Method, identified several *character strategies* people use to meet emotional needs and reach developmental milestones. We all develop character strategies. We come into the world as unique beings that must adapt to our environments in order to meet our inborn needs for nourishment and love, which are necessary for reaching our full potential. The strategies we use to get our needs met become part of our character.

Sensorimotor psychotherapy, a somatic-based approach to trauma treatment, elaborated on Kurtz's strategies to show how they function as both protective defenses and relational styles within maladaptive or traumatic family conditions. One potential indicator of adverse childhood environments is the extent to which infants and children must adapt themselves to fit the limitations of their caregivers. By adapting needs, beliefs, and behaviors, a developing child potentially increases access to limited emotional, if not also physical, resources in the family.

The character strategies developed for meeting attachment needs in childhood continue in our adult lives and influence more than relationships. They also impact impact how goals are reached and actions completed. Character strategies can unconsciously activate early-life beliefs and defenses that may have been necessary for maladaptive circumstances in the past yet potentially interfere with effectively and efficiently responding to present conditions. Thus, they contribute to how mental energy and efficiency get gummed up.

The Action Cycle

Kurtz identified four stages that contribute to completing actions and reaching goals—what he called *the action cycle*.

These stages are internal states that relay the worthiness of a project and meaningfulness of our actions, including if they feel nourishing and give a sense of completion once the action is done or the goal reached. These stages are:

1. Insight
2. Response
3. Nourishment
4. Completion

When problems with *insight* occur, there is often difficulty identifying the intention or meaning behind actions. Without sufficient insight, it's easy to lose interest in goals. Some call *insight* "knowing your *why*."

If you find it difficult to identify internal *responses* to your efforts to reach a goal, you might be cut off from authentic emotional expression. This can make it hard to feel confident in your choice of actions taken toward goals.

If you have difficulty with *nourishment*, identifying which actions contribute to feelings of fulfillment or accomplishment may be challenging.

Finally, if you have problems with *completion*, you might not feel that stopping to reward or replenish yourself is a deserved aspect of meeting a goal, or you may be unable to identify when an action has reached its endpoint.

Using Kurtz's action cycle, Pat Ogden's sensorimotor psychotherapy addresses how character strategies that were once useful in maladaptive or traumatizing conditions can later interfere with completing actions and reaching goals.[3] Here are some scenarios (by no means an exhaustive list) of how early-life character strategies can interfere with goals later in life:

• If you had to constantly seek attention and approval to feel loved or safe in your family, listening to internal cues about your authentic desires and needs may not be a well-developed skill. This could lead to problems with *insight* and the capacity to be mindfully aware of your needs while also maintaining the belief that you have an inherent right to have your needs met.

• If you were often blamed and punished in childhood, it may be challenging to identify your natural responses to situations and gauge how you feel about goals and actions. This barrier to *response* occurs because obedience was prioritized over self-expression, which can result in difficulties connecting to authentic reasons for wanting to achieve a goal instead of acting on learned *shoulds* and *shouldn'ts*.

• If there was violence in the household or a continual sense of threat (e.g., chronic substance abuse or domestic violence), there can be an underlying sense that life is inherently dangerous or even the belief that you don't have the right to exist. The child learns it's not safe to be known or witnessed (or know what's *really* happening in the home), which can influence attempts to clarify goals and general direction in life. The sense that *nourishment* is both deserved and a possibility may not even be recognized.

• If the message taken in as a child was that you had to perform to feel loved, or you must hide abuse in the home by presenting a "perfect" self to the world—what family systems therapy identifies as the *star child* who draws attention away from family problems—there can be a tendency toward compulsive achieving and a fear of relaxing. This character strategy can create a barrier to *completing actions* or savoring a job well done. There can also be a tendency to seek perfection that interferes with completing projects or feeling satisfied with your efforts.

Sensorimotor psychotherapy identifies "missing experiences" that support meeting goals and completing actions but are often absent from maladaptive and traumatizing households:

- Feelings that can't be expressed (e.g., sadness, anger, joy)
- Body sensations that can't be acknowledged (e.g., a tightness in your chest that if it could speak might say, *No, I don't want to do that!*)
- Boundaries that can't be asserted (e.g, saying no to tasks that keep you from committing to what really matters to you)
- Beliefs that should be true for every child (see below)

These universal, feel-good beliefs include:

- It's okay to be vulnerable.
- It's okay to take care of my needs.
- It's okay to have fun.
- It's safe to feel.
- It's safe to rely on others.
- It's safe to be loved.
- It's safe to be witnessed.
- I can get my needs met and be loved.

For some, it helps to treat these beliefs like mantras and reminders of the universal rights of all children and the adults they become.

Small, incremental steps are often needed to gain footing in the present after a history of chronic childhood traumatization. This isn't necessarily a bad thing and is probably a good goal. Childhood trauma causes people to grow up too fast. They learn to prioritize external demands over internal needs and desires. Learning to proceed at your own pace and relish what is being experienced according to your own internal barometer —or reject it—may be one of the most rewarding ways to experience life without traumatic stress.

The following quote is from Martha Graham. I think she takes the point of honoring the inner drive to create to its most beautiful extreme:

> There is a vitality, a life force, an energy, a quickening that is translated through you into action, and because there is only one of you in all time, this expression is unique. And if you block it, it will never exist through any other medium and it will be lost. The world will not have it. It is not your business to determine how good it is or how valuable nor how it compares with other expressions. It is your business to keep it yours clearly and directly, to keep the channel open.

This is a worthy goal for all of us, and vital to ending the effects of chronic traumatization.

WE CAN DO BETTER THAN DESENSITIZATION AS THE GOAL OF TRAUMA TREATMENT

David J. Morris, a former Marine infantry officer and reporter in some of the most violent regions of the Iraq war, blacked out while watching a movie and ran out of the theater, only to regain awareness in the lobby as he anxiously scanned other patrons for improvised explosive devices (IEDs). Morris's girlfriend later told him an explosion in the movie had precipitated his flashback.

While in Iraq, Morris was nearly killed by an IED, and he saw two National Guardsmen killed by them. He was almost shot down while riding in a helicopter, and with fellow Marines, he withstood shelling for seven days. He had many reasons to be triggered by an explosion, even an imaginary one in a movie.

When Morris sought treatment for posttraumatic stress disorder with the Veterans Administration (VA), they recommended *prolonged exposure therapy*, a form of trauma treatment that attempts to help people like Morris become desensitized to their trauma triggers. In his *New York Times* article, Morris gave the following description of prolonged exposure therapy:

The promise of prolonged exposure is that your response to your trauma can be unlearned by telling the story of it over and over again. The patient is asked to close his eyes, put himself back in the moment of maximum terror and recount the details of what happened. According to the theory, the more often the story is told in the safety of the therapy room, the more the memory of the event will be detoxified, stripped of its traumatic charge and transformed into something resembling a normal memory.[1]

Morris expected the therapy to work: "Given enough time and enough story 'reps,' when I opened my eyes again, I wouldn't feel forever perched on the precipice of a smoke-wreathed eternity. I wouldn't feel scared anymore."

Just the opposite happened. Instead of an "unlearned" traumatic stress response and becoming desensitized to reminders of war, Morris was overwhelmed by the therapy:

But after a month of therapy, I began to have problems. When I think back on that time, the word that comes to mind is "nausea." I felt sick inside, the blood hot in my veins. Never a good sleeper, I became an insomniac of the highest order. I couldn't read, let alone write. I laced up my sneakers and went for a run around my neighborhood, hoping for release in some roadwork; after a couple of blocks, my calves seized up. It was like my body was at war with itself. One day, my cellphone failed to dial out and I stabbed it repeatedly with a stainless steel knife until I bent the blade 90 degrees.

Morris was told prolonged exposure therapy worked for about 85 percent of the VA patients who used it. However, in his book *The Body Keeps the Score*, Bessel van der Kolk discussed a study conducted in the early 1990s that contradicts the VA's statistics. In this study, led by psychiatrist Roger Pitman,

Vietnam veterans were asked to repeatedly talk about their wartime experiences. However, Pitman had to stop the study prematurely. He explained:

> Many veterans became panicked by their flashbacks, and the dread often persisted after the sessions. Some never returned, while many of those who stayed with the study became more depressed, violent, and fearful; some coped with their increased symptoms by increasing their alcohol consumption, which led to further violence and humiliation, as some of their families called the police to take them to the hospital.[2]

Van der Kolk also shared:

> A 2010 report on 49,425 veterans with newly diagnosed PTSD from the Iraq and Afghanistan wars who sought care from the VA showed that fewer than one out of ten actually completed the recommended treatment. As in Pitman's Vietnam veterans, exposure treatment, as currently practiced, rarely works for them. We can only 'process' horrendous experiences if they do not overwhelm us. And that means that other approaches are necessary.[3]

I am not a fan of exposure therapy. I think it's too risky, as these studies suggest. I feel certain it would have caused flooding for me had it been used to treat my flashbacks of childhood sexual abuse. After one session, I would have never returned and likely would have lost trust in psychotherapy and the support I needed to heal.

Humans are impressively resilient and adaptive. We can manipulate ourselves and our bodies in extraordinary ways, even detrimentally, and continue to survive. At birth, our brains are profoundly underdeveloped, but they increase in size by

300 percent over the next two decades of life.[4] Maturation involves gaining the biological, psychological, and behavioral capacities that allow us to continually adapt to physical and social environments that are also malleable and ever-changing.

Because we are "plastic" by nature, I think it is safe to assume there are many ways we can alter ourselves to overcome the fallout of traumatic events. Exposure therapy is only one option among many available for dealing with the after-effects of trauma, albeit one that may work for some people. However, because we are malleable and adaptable, there can be numerous reasons to use a treatment, not just that it works for some people—and there can be other reasons to treat trauma than to stop flashbacks.

For example, instead of making the primary criteria for success be that a treatment "works," we could also think about how treatment alters people and, in turn, impacts the social fabric of our communities. We might ask what kind of people we become when we are desensitized to traumatic reminders. We might wonder if, from an evolutionary standpoint, it is even safe to become hardened to memories of war, rape, and abuse. We might also wonder if there is an implicit assumption at work here—that overwhelming fear is the central problem to address rather than the conditions that lead to war, rape, and abuse. We might ask, "If we become desensitized to our fear, do we also become desensitized to violence?" We might ask, "What is more powerful than profound emotions and visceral reactions when it comes to motivating us to seek meaningful change?" How we treat trauma likely has a greater impact than "just" reducing individual experiences of traumatic stress.

I strongly believe trauma treatments should protect our capacity for vulnerability and empathy while also helping us regain the ability to modulate our defense reactions. We are likely most resilient and wise when we can defend ourselves and loved ones when the need arises and the rest of the time (preferably *most* of the time) live peaceful, engaged, and meaningful lives. We need trauma treatments that can help us regain this full expression of our humanity after traumatic events or conditions.

Two Views of the Nature of Traumatic Stress

Two main views of the nature of traumatic stress seem to guide trauma treatment. One view, which informs treatments such as prolonged exposure therapy, focuses on regulating emotions and sensations. People are seen as needing help with controlling overwhelming emotions and the reactions they cause, such as Morris running out of the movie theater, engulfed by fear. This is a reasonable view and partially correct. Most people who deal with ongoing traumatic stress are frequently overwhelmed by their emotions and body sensations. However, when controlling emotional reactions becomes the sole focus of treatment, the whole person is neither considered nor addressed. Van der Kolk observed:

> Desensitization may make you less reactive, but if you cannot feel satisfaction in ordinary everyday things like taking a walk, cooking a meal, or playing with your kids, life will pass you by.[5]

The other main view of traumatic stress focuses on the loss of the integrative capacity of mind and body that trauma causes. High arousal and shutdown at the time of a traumatic event result in fragmented memories and dissociative splitting. As psychologists Pat Ogden, Kenkuni Minton, and Claire Pain pointed out in their book, *Trauma and the Body*, "Under conditions of arousal that are either too high or too low, traumatic experiences cannot be integrated."[6] Consequently, trauma often leads to compartmentalization of experience and a fragmented sense of self.

When integration is the goal of treatment, split-off memories, emotions, and sensations are mindfully brought back into awareness, contributing to a sense of self as whole again. Increasing emotional regulation is also central to regaining integrative capacity, though it's not the primary goal. Rather, treatment begins with *modulating* arousal, which helps reduce the need to avoid internal and external reactions to traumatic reminders.

The shift in focus from desensitizing emotional reactions to increasing integrative capacity may seem new. However, in the 19th century French psychologist Pierre Janet, a pioneer of trauma treatment, identified integration as the focal point of trauma treatment. Janet advocated *phase-oriented treatment*, which integrates traumatic memories in ways that contribute to a wholistic sense of self. He established three stages of treatment, which are still used today:

1. Symptom reduction and stabilization
2. Treatment of traumatic memory
3. Personality integration

Similar to exposure therapy, phase-oriented treatment begins with improving emotional regulation. Yet when integration is the treatment goal, emotional regulation is gained by increasing a sense of safety (Phase 1) rather than becoming desensitized to emotions, memories, and body sensations.

Exposure to memories of past traumas is still a significant part of treatment (Phase 2). However, the goal is to experience these memories within a window of tolerance that increases the likelihood of their integration with non-traumatic memories and non-traumatic self-states (Phase 3).

Phase-oriented treatment decreases the likelihood of dysregulation by helping clients to establish:

- Body safety and control of the body.
- A safe environment.
- Emotional and autonomic (arousal) stability.

Central to the integrative approach is developing mindful awareness of the conditions that contribute to high arousal or shutdown, along with identifying resources that can help reduce arousal when *hyper*aroused or increase arousal when *hypo*aroused. Resources include skills, practices (e.g., yoga, mindfulness), objects, relationships, services, etc., that support a sense of stability and safety. With this approach, a person learns how to direct energy toward full living through greater awareness of self, relationships, and environment. This is a fundamentally different outcome than exposure therapy. As van der Kolk observed, "Desensitization to our own or to other people's pain tends to lead to an overall blunting of emotional sensitivity."[7]

At times, there are benefits to desensitization. Whether trauma has been chronic, acute, or undertreated (if treated at all), survivors will sometimes try to deal with feelings of overwhelm by avoiding the situations that might trigger them, which, depending on the person and the conditions of their life, can lead to a very circumscribed existence. Thus, in the beginning stages of treatment, people sometimes need to desensitize themselves to overwhelming emotions and sensations as the first step toward a more active life. This level of desensitization is sometimes accomplished with medications—an approach I and many others generally don't encourage. However, I know from experience that people who lack resources and support for an extended period often do well in the beginning stages of treatment with some medications in combination with Phase I work. A better approach than medications is to adapt services to fit the needs of the most vulnerable, such as providing more frequent sessions, including in their homes or through technologies such as Skype, Zoom, or any other virtual platform that allows for contact without forcing clients to endure conditions that might trigger high arousal or shutdown.

Desensitization can also be beneficial when a person is aware that intense reactions are out of proportion to the situation and she has already identified ways to resource herself when overwhelmed. For instance, in dialectical behavior therapy, one exercise, *opposite to emotion action*, encourages a person to take action when she notices her anticipated emotional reaction to a situation is unjustified, otherwise causing her to avoid that circumstance and unnecessarily limit her life. For example, if a person anticipates feeling frightened at the dentist but knows she will be safe, she is encouraged to override her emotional response and keep the appointment. The goal is not to ignore emotions but mindfully be open to the possibility of having a new experience when using methods learned for regulating traumatic stress.

Sometimes we must be less sensitive than we would like or endure conditions we would rather avoid to live full, meaningful lives. But the operative word here is *sometimes*. Most of the time, we should aspire to live a life that is open to a variety of experiences and relationships and have confidence in our ability to tolerate, adapt, learn, and grow, which is the opposite of fear-based, defensive living. In the best of worlds, we feel responsible for developing our capacities for both resilience and compassion.

THE SENSORIMOTOR APPROACH TO STORYING TRAUMA

Far too often, getting on with everyday life requires avoiding the impact of traumatic stress on body, mind, and spirit. This self-imposed desensitization to one's own suffering can lessen how empathetic we are to others' misfortune, including their stories of trauma. Much like the Twitter feeds, Facebook updates, and blog aggregates that keep us aware of current events without demanding much engagement, stories of trauma can cause the same disconnection, if not compassion fatigue, in which only the most horrific and peculiar receive much of an emotional response. Hoping not to hurt, we can risk not feeling much at all.

The lack of emotional engagement with stories of trauma may have increased the last hundred years—an era overrun with world wars, genocides, community and family violence, poverty, natural disasters, and environmental devastation. What may distinguish the current era from past periods of upheaval and destruction are not only the number of people impacted but also how television, the internet, and other communication technologies have led to solitary engagement with stories of trauma. Rather than listening to trauma stories with a group of people who share our concerns and emotions, we often read about trauma when alone. These communication technologies also primarily engage thoughts, perceptions, and hearing, thus leaving our bodies largely inert as we passively watch stories unfold on screens or in print. Similarly, clients in psychotherapy traditionally have been expected to tell their stories of trauma with minimal or no awareness of their bodies.

This is a bit mind-boggling since our bodies are the source of our emotions. Furthermore, recovering from trauma typically requires re-integrating split-off emotions that once threatened to overwhelm at the time of the traumatic event and are triggered by unconscious reminders. Perhaps unwittingly (or in an unconsciously avoidant state of mind), we've sought communication technologies that allow us to connect to each other and be aware, but also to choose our level of emotional engagement—or disengagement, should that be preferred. (At the very least, this has been an unintentional consequence.)

At the beginning of the twentieth century, German author Franz Kafka wrote, "A literary work must be an ice axe to break the sea frozen inside us," which speaks to the expectation that stories should somehow transform us by stirring deeply felt emotions.[1] More recently, American novelist Deb Olin Unferth stated, "Fiction is not natural. It imitates nothing but itself. More than resembling what we see, it expresses what is absent, what we dimly desire. Fiction is everything that life is not."[2] Olin Unferth's account of fiction reflects the disengagement and muted emotions that seem more common today than when Kafka lived. When I read her words, I think of disillusionment, lack of hope, and disbelief that what we imagine is on some level also real—an attitude I do not attribute to Olin Unferth but to a more general resistance to the power of story to transform that is prevalent today.

I believe the lack of faith in the transformative power of story is related to how we passively consume stories (both factual and fictional), including our own, especially stories of trauma. In particular, the lack of connection between the body and the *imaginal*—the images, fantasies, memories, and reveries that take up so much of our mental life—suppresses stories' impact and their power to transform.

This disconnect between the imaginal and the body also plagues the treatment of trauma and *re-storying* the past. It is difficult to heal from trauma and learn from it—*to grow despite it*—without somehow bringing the body and the imaginal together. To overcome the dissociative splits between body, mind, and spirit caused by trauma, what we imagine, fantasize, and remember must be reconnected with the intense emotions that led to memories and images being split off in the first place. But this also means reconnecting with the body.

In the following section, I use *sensorimotor psychotherapy*—a mindfulness-based, somatic-focused form of psychotherapy developed for the treatment of trauma—as an example of how psychotherapy can facilitate transformative experiences that emerge when the story of trauma is told through the body *and* the imaginal.

Basic Goals and Tenets of Sensorimotor Psychotherapy

When the body is the focus of treatment, the role of the trauma story changes. In fact, telling the trauma story can become an impediment. To resolve past traumas, we need to directly experience their effects on our body, mind, and spirit in the present moment, as doing so allows us to address how they continue to impact us. As psychiatrist Daniel Siegel observed, "Without the balance of our non-linguistic world of images, feelings, and sensations, the seduction of words and ideas can keep us from direct experience."[3]

Rather than focusing on retelling the story of past traumas, sensorimotor psychotherapy directs attention toward becoming mindfully aware of how experience is organized in the present moment. This involves tracking what are called *core organizers of experience*—the thoughts, emotions, five-sense perceptions, movements, and inner sensations that co-occur with remembrances of past traumas. Thus, instead of mastering the trauma story—for example, remembering every detail as done with exposure therapy—clients become aware of how traumatic memories organize their sense of personhood. They pay attention to memories held in the body that speak not only of what happened but also of what the body wanted to do—what psychiatrist Pierre Janet called *acts of triumph*—the scream that was suppressed, the punch held back, the desire to run not acted upon. This mindful awareness of what did not transpire —what the body wanted to happen but could not do— becomes a central part of the new story about the trauma, though this story exists in bodily awareness and the imaginal.

According to Pat Ogden, Kenkuni Minton, and Claire Pain, the first goal in the treatment of trauma is:

> To restore the clients' capacity to tolerate and integrate their own thoughts, feelings, and bodily sensations, to bear witness to their own experience, to be able to process significant life events—past and present, painful and pleasurable, ordinary and traumatic—within a window of tolerance.[4]

The window of tolerance is gauged in part by how well a person maintains social engagement without activating the body's defense responses, such as fight, flight, or freeze states. Within the window of tolerance, we can be mindfully aware of our thoughts, feelings, and body sensations while also engaging with awareness of others and their experiences. In sensorimotor psychotherapy, tracking the body and other core organizers of experience is key to understanding the extent to which someone is within the window of tolerance or has moved either into a state of *hyper-* or *hypo*arousal, thus lessening their ability for present-focused, socially engaged thoughts and actions.

People who habitually activate traumatic defenses often become either avoidant of traumatic memories or preoccupied with them. Consequently, opportunities for an "everyday life" of relationships, work, and play are superseded by an often unconscious need to defend against the possibility of retraumatization. Sensorimotor psychotherapy attempts to disrupt the activation of traumatic defenses by challenging the rigid division that gets constructed between needing to protect oneself and being able to relax into the activities of daily life. Engaging in play is an integral part of recovery, including in the relationship between therapist and client. Ogden and colleagues wrote:

> In the context of curious, nonjudgmental exploration, significant moments of playfulness between therapist and client often unfold spontaneously. The goal in treatment is to improve upon the adaptive functioning of all action systems and to mitigate the unfettered arousal of the defensive system so that it is activated only when needed, no longer disrupting the functioning of other systems.[5]

When a person no longer lives defensively, they can focus on developing aspects of who they want to become while maintaining the supportive, safe relationships they deserve and desire.

The Sensorimotor Approach and Outcome

How does sensorimotor psychotherapy work? Well, it's taken me several years of training, assisting with trainings, and working with clients to understand the process, yet so much still feels ineffable—and extraordinary—about the approach. Perhaps this is because sensorimotor psychotherapy is specifically directed toward transformation. The body implicitly guides the process. Furthermore, event-bound conceptions of time, space, and memory often lose their grasp during moments of transformation.

An example comes from my own experience of practicing sensorimotor techniques with one of my peers. During our practice session, I recalled a pivotal moment in my childhood when awareness of my mother's deepening depression was particularly acute and joined with an awareness of the loss of her protection. Rather than focusing on the details of my memory—the story of that day when my mother and I were picking out wallpaper for my bedroom—my peer partner tracked my body, paying attention to the sense of heaviness in my shoulders as I recounted snippets of memory. We explored the tingling in my feet, which I came to perceive as my previously unconscious (and unexpressed) desire to run. We also discussed what I needed to believe was true to regain a sense of safety.

With my peer partner's support, and through the integration of memories, images, and body sensations (all part of a sequenced protocol taught in the trainings), I told a new, transformative story of that time with my mother, one that included the narratives of my body and the imaginal aspects of my psyche. This story was less organized around fear, and hence, the need for defense, and more organized around a sense of wholeness and safety. I challenged the unconscious, organizing belief that the loss of a safe attachment necessitates a threat to safety. Sometimes I am just sad or afraid. When I am mindful, I try to stay with what I am feeling, watching how it shows up in my body and naturally dissipates, without getting caught in old stories and defenses.

Through the therapeutic process of sensorimotor psychotherapy, triggers that the body once unconsciously reacted to are less likely to be activated. New ways of responding to memories and events are identified. By changing how the past is remembered, a new sense of oneself also emerges.

For transformation to occur, we must sometimes be willing to let go of the quest to find the truths of our pasts and instead trust the body's wisdom and our capacity to imagine a different outcome from what originally occurred. This isn't wish fulfillment but rather an acknowledgment of unmet needs and a letting go of defenses that no longer serve who we are becoming. There is often grief at such moments of transformation, which sensorimotor psychotherapy identifies as the *grief of relief*, but this grief is well worth the sadness since it also signals the release of attachment to past circumstances that no longer contribute to growth.

When no longer driven by the need to defend against unconscious reminders of danger or threat, everyday life can occur within the window of tolerance so that present-focused awareness of self and others is possible. Within this range of experience, we feel the transformative effects of both life and story without the need to suppress their potential impact on us.

KNOW YOUR HABITUAL
DEFENSE RESPONSES AND
LIVE WITHIN YOUR WINDOW
OF TOLERANCE

Here's the scenario:

You are moving across the country, driving from Los Angeles, California, to Sarasota, Florida. Everything you own is in your car. *Everything.* You need to make it to Sarasota *Fast.* You start a new job in less than a week. You've given yourself three days to drive there—at most!—and two days to settle in your new place before the job starts.

You are alone, except for your cherished pet, Kitty.

(Okay, maybe you have a dog.)

Luck is not on your side. You are passing through Louisiana one day after a major hurricane, and the highway patrol puts you on a detour through the state's backroads. You spot tornadoes funneling across flat stretches of land. You drive on roads where water covers your wheels. You pass raccoons, deer, and possums, their eyes glowing with that blank, in-the-headlights stare. You think of them as kindred spirits, mirroring the hollow feeling in your frightened soul.

It's now evening and still storming.

You decide enough with the crazy push to cross the entire country in less than three days and stop in a roadside motel. (Think Bates Motel or something out of a David Lynch movie, not the Ritz Carlton.) Tired, you leave your things in the car, though you don't feel safe about the decision. You take Kitty in the room with you.

A bit spooked, Kitty curls up in a corner, trying to make herself small. You climb in the lonely bed and try to fall asleep, but startle when you hear something rustling in the corner opposite Kitty. You turn on the lights, and *OMG! There's a poisonous snake!*

What would you do?

1. Look for something to use to kill the snake?
2. Crunch your legs up and push your body hard against the headboard while screaming uncontrollably?
3. Even though your heart's racing, pick up the phone and, in a relatively calm voice, tell the woman at the front desk you need, *um, some assistance, please,* and start whispering about the snake?
4. Bolt out of the room and hope Kitty follows you out the open door?
5. Grab Kitty and *then* bolt out the room?
6. Grab your phone and take a photo of the snake, maybe even a selfie, before running out the door, calling, *Here, Kitty, Kitty,* once you're far, far away?
7. Just sit there. *Frozen.*

How you imagine dealing with this scenario might tell you something about yourself and your "go-to" defenses during times of stress. Are you someone who usually tries to fight your way out of problems? When you get scared, do you avoid relying on others? Blinded by your fear, do you forget there is anyone or anything else? Do you rely too much on others to get you out of jams? Do you get caught in minutia, distractions, or denial? Do you just freeze up? Sometimes, when fear or stress is intense, the problem isn't so much the overwhelmingly scary or stressful thing happening in our lives but how we deal (or don't deal) with it.

Maybe you learned you had to fight your way out of every bad situation on your own, and now you need to learn how to rely more on others. Maybe you've come to see yourself as weak, and you need to break out of "victim" mentality. Perhaps you caretake others so much you don't even know your own needs, let alone how to address them. Maybe you are so emotionally cut off from feeling fear that you treat life-threatening danger like it's a ride at Disneyland.

Ideally, we have access to all possible defense reactions—fight, flight, freeze, submit, attach. The correct defense is the one that most adaptively fits the situation we find ourselves in. But in reality, the defenses we use are largely determined by past traumatic or potentially traumatic situations along with our temperaments and our efforts to adapt to family, cultural, and environmental conditions. Past conditioning inevitably influences how we adapt to present-moment experiences.

For example, people who have had to endure histories of chronic abuse often submit when fighting or fleeing would be a better option. They "over learn" submission as a defense and tend to lack a robust fight response, or at least one that would increase survival when they are no longer subjected to what trauma psychologist Judith Herman categorized as *conditions of captivity*, such as childhood abuse or domestic violence.[1]

In contrast, someone who has had to react quickly and aggressively to survive, such as under conditions of combat, may have more difficulty reaching out for help or running from a threat when these responses would lead to a better outcome.

I doubt many people take the time to contemplate their go-to defenses unless they cause a lot of trouble, but I think it's a wise thing to do. Best-laid plans—not to mention perfectly good relationships—can be destroyed by a lack of awareness of the defenses that get activated in times of threat or intense stress. Furthermore, our go-to defenses also typically come with a costly recovery period. For example, going back to the snake-in-the-motel scenario...

After the snake problem is resolved, what would you do?

1. Go back to bed, thinking, *What's the chance of another snake showing up?*
2. Go back on the road, perhaps in search of a Ritz Carlton?
3. Suffer insomnia as your mind obsessively and uncontrollably continues to envision the snake?
4. Gorge on the $30 worth of vending machine snacks you just bought in the lobby?
5. Buy a six-pack (or 12-pack) from the 7-Eleven down the road and drink yourself numb while watching infomercials with the TV on mute, your ears piqued for the sound of snake?
6. Call someone who can give you support and help calm your nerves?
7. Call someone you wish could give you support but never has and likely never will? Then maybe pick a fight and discharge all that pent-up fear but blame your outburst on their chronic insensitivity?
8. Surf the web until light breaks and then sleep until noon, screwing up your plans for driving the next day?
9. Acknowledge your state of distress and use meditation or physical activity to discharge the tension from your body? (Yeah, right.)

Assuming the snake has been removed and the motel now safe, the best options are #1, completely let the crisis go (You're a Yogi!—or in total denial), #6, seek truly supportive help that you are emotionally prepared to receive, or #9, acknowledge that your body needs attention and care. These responses are the most likely choices if you are some advanced emotional being or are on your way there.

In times of intense fear, most of us regress to our own personal "lesser" selves—that shell beneath the shell of basic functioning. Supposedly, these are the times when we discover our character. In actuality, we're just being our scared selves. It's okay to be scared or stressed, except for the impact chronic fear and stress have on the body (including contributing to the onset of things like dementia, diabetes, fibromyalgia, etc.) and the reverberating impact that intense fear (including its dissociation or complete denial) can have on relationships when we act like selfish jerks—you know, when you act like you're the only person who ever woke up to a cottonmouth in the corner of a motel room. *Please!*

Often, we need to get over ourselves, albeit with compassion, kindness, and nonjudgmental self-awareness. (Most of us really need to stress that nonjudgmental part.)

And the quicker the better.

Disasters, chaos, and uncertainty are the norm, while compassion and emotional calm, like stable weather, are in short supply. We can't help but get scared and stressed these days—and frequently—but we can help ourselves, each other, and the planet when we learn how to bring ourselves quickly back to our higher selves and with minimal damage to our well-being or anyone else's.

Learning the Practice of Continually Returning to the Window of Tolerance

If there is one thing I would want to teach every person on the planet, it's about the window of tolerance and getting back into it. If we all knew about the window of tolerance and treated it as the smaller yet noble star we must always find before reaching our North Star (that truest, enlightened version of ourselves), oh, what a happy planet of beings we would be!

I've written about the window of tolerance elsewhere, but I can't believe I haven't written about it more, seeing as it has become the wind in my sails, the honey to my inner bee, the Toto to my darling Dorothy Self (you get the point). Seriously. I don't even know how to live without it these days. Every disturbance to my inner chill has me resourcing myself back to my window of tolerance, and as a result, people comment on my peaceful presence, and I feel more grounded, too. It's one of the basics of trauma work, but I think it's been ghettoized a bit by this association. It's something we all should learn since we all are continually adapting to conditions that cause stress and fear.

Here's what you need to know about WOT (the acronym for window of tolerance) and how to get back there:

- From what I have been able to learn, the WOT was first introduced by Daniel Siegel, who, in his book *The Developing Mind*, stressed the importance of emotional regulation for mental health.[2]
- The best way to think about the WOT is as an emotional, physical, and social state we can inhabit where we feel capable of attending to the task at hand, along with interacting meaningfully with others, while also attending to our own emotional states and needs.

- The WOT has an upper limit, *hyper*arousal, and a lower limit, *hypo*arousal. These extremes have their associated emotional, physical, and social states, just as the WOT does.
- To live within the WOT requires knowing the signs that you are out of it—either hyperaroused or hypoaroused—and then knowing what to do to get yourself back within the WOT.
- Getting back in the WOT is all about resourcing. Depending on your unique self and approach to living—e.g., your temperament, attachment style, go-to defenses, and other habitual propensities— you resource yourself through your body, thoughts, emotions, or a combination of the three.

Below is a diagram of the WOT and some resourcing tips.[3] The diagram includes the primary signs that you are either in the WOT, hyperaroused, or hypoaroused. The resources are things you can do when you find yourself outside the WOT and ways to widen your habitual WOT and reduce the amount of stress you experience and react to.

I truly believe the more we try to live within the window of tolerance, the safer this world will feel *and* be.

WINDOW OF TOLERANCE: ZONES OF AROUSAL

HYPERAROUSAL ZONE

Sympathetic "Fight or Flight Response"
(Too much arousal)

SIGNS YOU ARE HERE:

- Tension, shaking
- Hypervigilance
- Impulsivity
- Defensiveness
- Anger/Rage
- Obsessive/cyclical thoughts
- Intrusive imagery
- Emotional reactivity
- Emotional overwhelm
- Feeling unsafe
- Racing thoughts

OPTIMAL AROUSAL ZONE

Ventral Vagal "Window of Tolerance"

SIGNS YOU ARE HERE:

- Feel and think simultaneously
- Awareness of boundaries (yours & others)
- Experience empathy
- Reactions adapt to fit the situation
- Feelings are tolerable
- Feel safe
- Present moment awareness –
"Right here, right now"
- Feel open and curious
(versus judgmental and defensive)

HYPOAROUSAL ZONE

Parasympathetic "Immobilization Response"
(Too little arousal)

SIGNS YOU ARE HERE:

- No energy
- Feel 'dead'
- Reduced movement
- Passive
- Ashamed
- Can't defend oneself
- Dulled cognition/"can't think"
- Relative absence of sensation
- Numbing of emotions
- Shut down
- Disconnected
- No feelings
- "Not there"
- Can't say no
- Flat affect

The free guide, "Living Within Your Window of Tolerance," is available at laurakkerr.com.

I. Practices for Being in the "Here and Now"

These exercises take less than a minute to do. They're great when you awaken in the morning, as a break from work, or anytime throughout the day to increase emotional regulation and relaxation.

Centering exercise

Put one hand over your heart and rest your other hand on your belly. Lengthen your spine. Take several full, slow breaths. Notice the fullness of your body as you let your breath come and go.

Grounding exercise

Stand in a relaxed position, focusing attention on the sensations in your feet. Put weight on different areas of your feet: front, back, sides. Then play a bit with movement—bending your knees, moving up and down. Sense the ground through your feet and legs.

Alignment exercise

Take a little time to become aware of how your body aligns in a vertical direction: your ankles on top of your feet, your legs on top of feet and ankles, the pelvis resting on your legs, torso on pelvis, your head supported by shoulders and torso, arms hanging off your torso. Then imagine that you are being lifted by the top of your head. Also imagine the feeling of gravity pulling in the opposite direction on the bottom of your spine. Next, shift from feeling stretched to allowing your spine to collapse. Repeat these two movements several times with the flow of your breath—expand on the inhale and then collapse on the exhale.

Walking exercise

Bring all your attention to your body as you walk (out of your head and worries). Notice how your feet hit the ground, how they roll, the movement in your knees, and corresponding sensations in your hips and shoulders. Play with your usual gait. Practice pushing off with your feet or walking at different paces. Notice the corresponding changes in body sensations.

II. Power of Breath

The following simple breathing exercises are also great to do throughout the day, whether during your commute, while waiting in line, as you transition between work and play, or when giving yourself the ultimate treat—meditation!

Simple breath

Imagine while you are inhaling that your breath is going all the way down to your pelvis. Then let the breath expand in your lower belly. When you exhale, let the breath escape effortlessly. Repeat five to ten times.

Bell jar breath

Inhale a breath. When at the top (or end) of the inhale, imagine a rounded quality. Then let the inhale roll over into the exhale. Notice where the breath rolls—front, back, side to side (wherever it seems to go). Repeat five to ten times. This breath is also useful when feeling hyperaroused.

4 x 4 x 4 breathing

Inhale deeply for four counts, exhale for four counts, and repeat the cycle for four minutes several times a day. I find this a good practice before starting work or appointments and while commuting. It's also a great way to get back in the window of tolerance after stressful experiences. You can use a smartphone to time yourself so you can give full attention to your breath.

III. Getting Back in the Window of Tolerance

The following are ways to calm yourself when you find yourself outside your window of tolerance.

If experiencing overwhelm

Sit in a chair with your feet fully planted on the ground, or stand with your spine fully extended. Then slowly scan the environment, naming the objects within your field of vision.

If shaking or trembling

Take full yet slow and easy breaths. No need to breathe too deeply, though. If you can, sit in a chair or on a sofa and wrap a blanket or comforter around yourself. Some people feel better if they also cover their heads.

If numb

Gently squeeze your forearms with opposite hands. Also increase your awareness by noticing the environment through your five senses. What do you see, hear, smell? If you can, try touching or tasting something mindfully.

If hypervigilant

Lengthen your spine while taking full breaths. Pay attention to the rise and fall of your breath as it alternatively fills and empties your chest and/or belly.

If heart rate is accelerated

Take your attention away from the heart region by paying attention to the sensations in your feet. Notice the feeling of being grounded and connected to the floor or earth beneath you.

If you have a collapsed feeling in your body

Try pushing firmly against the wall with your arms fully extended, your head up, and using your energy to ground down through your feet. Notice the feeling of sturdiness in your body as you push.

If feeling the impulse to hurt yourself or someone else

Push against a sturdy wall without aggression. Focus your awareness on grounding, starting with your feet and then slowly moving up your body. Feel your connection to the earth. Take full breaths and keep bringing your thoughts back to your body sensations and away from the focus of your desperation, anger, or rage.

If feeling disconnected or experiencing depersonalization

Start by slowing the pace of whatever you are doing. Then firmly but gently squeeze the forearms, calves, thighs—whatever feels enlivening to you. Also try the "walking exercise" above.

If feeling frozen or panicked

Sit comfortably in a chair or sofa and wrap yourself in a comforter or blanket. Focus on taking full, slow breaths, continually bringing your thoughts back to the present moment. Create a mantra for such moments, such as "I can be present and watch the waves of energy go by without getting caught in the story."

"Shake off the freeze"

Begin by slowly jumping off the ground. Then shake your arms when your feet land on the ground. Take full breaths, mindfully inhaling when you jump and exhaling fully when your feet land. You can also say something to yourself like, "I'm safe. I'm letting go."

Using thoughts

Name your reaction to yourself as a defense response, reframing the experience. Say to yourself, "This is just a memory," or, "I'm just triggered right now." You might also try saying to yourself, "I can be here—right here, right now."

Mindfully not dealing works, too

Give yourself permission to avoid, dissociate, or disconnect. But when you do, try to be mindful of your need to check out. Also make plans to give yourself needed attention and care (like these exercises) as soon as you can—and follow through!

SEARCHING FOR NIRVANA

Nirvana.

The word conjures a state of perfect peace. It is the endpoint of the spiritual path and marks enlightenment, where there is no more suffering or desire. Scholar and professor Steven Collins wrote the following about the Buddhist journey to nirvana:

> The Path to salvation is...a journey through time from the city of the transient body to the city of timeless and deathless nirvana: the city without fear, as one of the earliest texts to use the image calls it.[1]

The "image" referred to here is of a fire going out, of *fear* being extinguished.

Could it be that the desires we create and the pain we suffer are all responses to fear? When I first read the above quote, I thought, *Maybe nirvana is like being in the optimal physiological state of arousal, the window of tolerance, and on the path to avoiding the physiological states of hyperarousal and hypoarousal—our ingrained reactions to fear.*

Could enlightenment really be that straightforward? It

would explain why mindfulness meditations are so useful for overcoming traumatic stress.

Perhaps, like me, you have heard there are two basic emotions: love and fear. From sensorimotor psychotherapy, I learned to elaborate on this fundamental distinction with the *action tendencies* of defense and daily living. We all must be able to defend ourselves against threats. We all must eat, exercise, work, play, take care of each other, love, sleep, and so on. We must protect *and* nurture ourselves. The less we fear, the more we can love. The window of tolerance may be thought of as the optimal level of arousal where we can maximize our connection to the people and things we love.

Collins also wrote: "Nirvana is the full stop (period) in the Buddhist story, the point at which narrative imagination must cease." Reading this, I thought, *Yeah, if you can just drop the storyline and all the "what if" scenarios and just be with what is, it's easier to extinguish the fear.* We talk a lot about dropping the storyline in the treatment of trauma. Healing trauma involves learning to drop the underlying story told through defenses—that story the body unconsciously tells every time it gets triggered by old traumatic reminders. It's not just the stories we tell about ourselves—those narratives about what we want to avoid as much as who we aspire to become (that old divide between fear and love showing up here, too). It's also the body's continual and unconscious scanning for the possibility of threat—what psychiatrist and neuroscientist Stephen Porges called *neuroception*—that keeps us reproducing fear and imagining danger.[2]

It's nearly impossible to live without fear since fear plays an integral role in keeping us alive. This is why *nirvana* is so profound and rare (and requires so much meditation to reach) —it's the point at which there is no more action tendency toward defense, no more natural, unconscious impetus toward protecting oneself from the inevitability of death and suffering. It's a bit like no longer being human.

I don't think I'm there yet.

But I do like thinking of nirvana as similar to the window of tolerance, an optimal zone within us that lacks the physiological reactions of fear. In trauma recovery, it's the idea of reaching a point where the trauma narrative eventually sloughs off like an outgrown skin because you no longer need to remind yourself there's something dangerous in your past that, the moment you're off guard, will return to haunt you in some new rendition. Dropping that fear—and knowing you will never pick it up again—also sounds a lot like nirvana to me.

I once heard the story of an old, enlightened Buddhist monk who was envied by the government officials in the country where he lived. The officials worried the monk's peacefulness might spread to the people, ending their attachment to fear. Without fear, the government had no control over them. So, one night, the government officials sent some low-level soldiers to kill the monk.

The soldiers broke into the monk's small house and began stabbing him. Although in pain, the monk saw the holes in the soldiers' shoes and their bony, half-starved frames. Wincing from his wounds, the monk told the soldiers where they could find a few coins to buy themselves a meal, maybe even repair their shoes. Overwhelmed by the monk's compassion, the soldiers began to cry and fled without murdering him.

I tell this tale not to give you ideas should you ever have paranoid government officials send soldiers to kill you, but rather to help you imagine the kind of compassion humans are capable of when they no longer feel fear.

That's nirvana.

RESPONDING TO MORAL
INJURY

For too many veterans, serving in the military was a mental health risk. According to the Department of Veteran Affairs (VA), on average 20 veterans commit suicide each day. Veterans account for 18 percent of all suicides in the United States but are less than 9 percent of the population. Approximately 65 percent of all veteran suicides are by individuals 50 years and older who have had little or no exposure to the most recent wars. The diagnosis most often associated with combat, post-traumatic stress disorder (PTSD), cannot sufficiently explain the increased suicide risk associated with military service. However, the idea of moral injury can.

Moral injury has been defined as "the lasting psychological, biological, spiritual, behavioral and social impact of perpetuating, failing to prevent, or bearing witness to acts that transgress deeply held moral beliefs and expectations."[1] In this essay, I elaborate on this definition, identify the causes of moral injury and how it impacts veterans, provide a clinical explanation of moral injury, and share some of the efforts to address it in the clinical setting.

More and more, veterans are writing and speaking about war as a moral injury, especially how it impacts their identities, if not their souls. I share their words—found in memoirs, scholarly books, and articles—to provide a robust and realistic portrayal of moral injury. You might notice some quotes I share are long. However, I hope to convince you that at the core of healing moral injury is the community's willingness to listen to stories of moral injury and veterans' willingness to share their stories.

Moral injury is not a pathological reaction to war. It's certainly not a mental illness, nor is it a weakness. On the contrary, moral injury is evidence of a strong moral sense and a commitment to living in accordance with one's values or spiritual beliefs. Moral injury also marks the beginning of an often uncertain journey toward wholeness after being ruptured by the morally reprehensible experiences that make up war.

Throughout human history, spiritual leaders have been tasked with purifying soldiers' souls after war. Rather than "training down," as we say today—focusing on adjustment and regulating a body rattled by traumatic stress—past societies and cultures attended to the moral needs of soldiers and believed war had the potential to steal a soldier's soul. The Navajo, for instance, have a ceremony called "the Enemy Way" that takes two weeks to perform and is believed to cure the effects of war and other encounters with death, including contact with the corpses of non-Navajo people. This ceremony is still used today by the Navajo to reintegrate US combat veterans back into their communities. Christians in the first millennium also spiritually rehabilitated those who participated in war. Soldiers were quarantined for at least a year and reduced to the status of followers not yet baptized. In effect, they were expected to spend a year regaining their faith.[2]

This idea that the soul needs its own rehabilitation after war is reintroduced with the idea of moral injury. However, the term *moral injury* is neither religious nor spiritual in origin. Instead, it was introduced by Marine veteran and philosopher

Camillo "Mac" Bica to describe the agony he felt on reflection of who he had been during war and the painful self-judgment he felt for what he had done. He wrote:

> Vietnam was the defining experience of my life. Though physical wounds may heal, the psychological, emotional, and moral injuries of war linger and fester. Vietnam forever pervades my existence, condemning me to continually relive and question the past. "Did I do enough?" "Could I have done better?" "Did I make the correct decisions?" Inevitable concerns of those who must take life and whose decisions cause others to die.[3]

Army colonel Herm Keizer, who served as a chaplain in Vietnam, also witnessed a crisis of consciousness arising in the soldiers he ministered to:

> I noticed that my experience was different from those who were combatants, especially those who had taken life or watched innocent people be maimed or killed. I was amazed at their personal shame—not guilt—but profound, searing shame.... Many felt that they had committed a personal affront against God. My religious training helped me see that what they were confronting is what many experience as sin, and I tried to minister to their broken souls.[4]

Moral injury goes to the heart of what our ancestors saw as the spiritual crisis caused by war and killing. Soldiers cannot "train down" from war without addressing moral injury.

Moral injury often starts when veterans finally have the time and energy to reflect on what happened, what they did, what they saw, how they were treated, and who they have become due to being part of war. As veterans begin to speak about their moral injuries, like Bica, we see that for many, recovery from moral injury requires profound emotional fortitude. War pulls from the deepest parts of a soldier, forcing them to confront the nature of their own humanity, if not the very nature of humanity itself. However, the rewards are great for those who commit to spiritual rehabilitation after war. They have the opportunity to become warriors of the heart as they learn to compassionately embrace all of who they are—the soldier *and* the human being. They are great teachers for all of us, but especially for other veterans, showing how to safeguard our souls and recover them when they have been lost.

Many do not believe in a god, gods, or spirituality, and thus, the term "soul" might feel irrelevant or off-putting. For them, one non-religious definition of soul that is useful for thinking about moral injury comes from Jungian analyst James Hillman, who described three distinct ways of understanding what the soul *does*:

> First, "soul" refers to the *deepening* of events into experiences; second, the significance soul makes possible, whether in love or in religious concern, derives from its special *relation with death*. And third, by "soul" I mean the imaginative possibility in our natures, the experiencing through reflective speculation, dream, image, and *fantasy*—that mode which recognizes all realities as primarily symbolic or metaphorical.[5]

Hillman's second meaning of soul—the part of the self that lives beyond death or experiences eternal love—is the least relevant to moral injury. The two other aspects of soul—the deepening of events into experiences and that imaginative part of human nature that takes up so much of our inner life—are central to the experience of moral injury. With these two meanings of soul, we identify how we all regularly turn inward, often to an imaginal state of reverie, in our attempts to make meaning of the events in our lives, reflect on the past and anticipate the future, and determine who we are and our worth as human beings. When this imaginal state is overrun with images and memories of death and destruction, along with feelings of shame, survivor's guilt, or the rage of betrayal that commonly occur with moral injury, we can lose the possibility of an inner world of reprieve from the harshness or banality of reality. We can also have difficulty finding hope in the future or seeing the beauty in our lives or the value in ourselves.

The notion of soul also has a long history of representing the experience of feeling deeply interconnected with others and having the capacity to transcend aloneness. To say that one has lost one's soul is to speak of profound alienation.

Origins of Moral Injury

A core outcome of moral injury is the loss of trust in oneself or others, causing a spiral into negativity and alienation. Depending on the cause of the moral injury, humanity itself can begin to appear corrupt. This loss of trust, or faith, in oneself or others is central to the definition of moral injury and distinguishes it from PTSD. Whereas PTSD is the experience of a loss of safety, moral injury is the experience of a loss of trust.[6]

Several types of events can lead to moral injury, including *feeling betrayed* by leaders, peers, or trusted civilians or *betraying* one's own moral standards; *involvement in or witnessing disproportionate violence*, such as mistreatment of the enemy and acts of revenge; *involvement in or witnessing the mistreatment of civilians*, such as assault or destroying personal property; and *involvement in or witnessing within-rank violence*, such as military sexual trauma, friendly fire, or *fragging*, the deliberate attempt to kill a fellow soldier.[7] However, killing, whether of a combatant, fellow soldier, or civilian, is the greatest predictor of moral injury.

The events that cause moral injury are often divided into three categories: *experiencing betrayal, transgressions committed by others, and transgressions committed by oneself.* Looking at the first category, *experiencing betrayal,* for some, feeling betrayed far outweighs the emotional turmoil of battle. For example, Army Major Jeffrey Hall experienced moral injury when his commanding officer gave orders that disregarded the dignity of the civilians Hall was tasked to take care of, which involved burying the bodies of their family members killed in crossfire:

> You have to understand. My PTS [posttraumatic stress] had everything to do with moral injury. It was not from killing, or seeing bodies severed, or blown up. It was from betrayal, from moral betrayal.[8]

Hall's inability to honorably respond to their loss because of bureaucratic rules and apathetic leaders caused him to feel more trapped and helpless than enemy fire.[9]

Some, like Bica, felt betrayed by the entire enterprise of war:

> We are the victims of politicians' hypocrisy, the scapegoats for the inevitable affront to the national conscience, and the sacrificial lambs sent to slaughter in retribution for our collective guilt and inadequacies. In fact, no one knows the sacrilege of war better than we who must fight it and then have to live with the memories of what we have done and what we have become.[10]

The second category of moral injury is *transgressions committed by others,* witnessing someone else engage in acts perceived as gross moral violations. For intelligence officer Dweylon, just knowing his actions contributed to war was enough to make him feel culpable in killing innocent civilians. According to Rita Nakashima Brock and Gabriella Lettini:

> In his role of organizing communications, he delivered orders to officers who vastly outranked him and provided crucial information to commanders on the frontline. Not wanting to be a weak link in his unit, he worked sixteen-hour days and did his very best to help his unit stay safe. He believes that, though he never had to fire a weapon and kill someone, he is as morally culpable in killing innocent people as those who did. His efforts helped his comrades do their job better and stay alive. He also knows that he does not understand the personal cost of actual killing, but accepts that his role in an immoral war was the same as those who did the killing.[11]

Dweylon remarked:

> I love my country, but no one should be proud of an unnecessary war. There were so many people who got killed and didn't need to get killed, a child and his mother who got up one morning, went out to get some water, and were shot or blown up—so many dead innocent people like that. They stay with you; you can't shake them off or ignore them.[12]

The third category of moral injury involves *transgressions committed by oneself*, including killing another human being. Vietnam veteran Karl Marlantes wrote in his powerful memoir *What It Is Like to Go to War*, "Killing someone will affect you. Part of you will think you've done something wrong. It's drilled in from babyhood."[13] Timothy Kudo, a Marine captain in Iraq and Afghanistan, wrote the following about killing:

> War makes us killers. We must confront this horror directly if we're honest about the true costs of war.... I'm no longer the

"good" person I once thought I was. There's nothing that can change that; it's impossible to forget what happened, and the only people who can forgive me are dead.[14]

Of these three types of transgressions, transgressions committed by others or oneself have the highest correlation with suicide attempts. Furthermore, of all the transgressions, killing another person in war is the greatest predictor that a veteran will take their own life. Captain Josh Mantz, who served in the Iraq War, claimed, "It's the moral injury over time that really kills people. Soldiers lose their identity. They don't understand who they are anymore."[15]

One possible reason for the high number of suicides has been the training of soldiers for what is called *reflexive fire*.[16] In World War II, nearly 75 percent of soldiers would not fire directly at the enemy, even when their own lives were threatened. In response, the military changed how it trained soldiers, conditioning them to shoot before thinking—so-called *reflexive fire training*, which has greatly increased the odds that soldiers will fire their weapons at someone over 90 percent of the time. However, as Major Pete Kilner concedes, "The problem with reflexive fire training is that it does bypass, in some sense, [the soldiers'] moral decision-making process."[17]

That combat often happens in communities rather than isolated battlefields has also increased the likelihood soldiers will kill someone during war, and they are as likely to kill a civilian as an enemy combatant. Because there are no clearly defined battle lines, every situation can threaten survival, including contact with civilians, who are sometimes used as shields. Nakashima Brock and Lettini wrote, "Many veterans recount with anguish stories about shooting reflexively at unarmed civilians in a split second without making a conscious decision to take a life."[18]

Moral injuries of war are exacerbated by the lack of sufficient and appropriate opportunities to reintegrate into civilian life, including lack of time to decompress with other veterans following war. This is a particularly precarious situation for the reservists and National Guard troops, who are more likely to be isolated from other veterans and resources, such as the VA and military bases, where they could find companions who share their experiences. The VA is also regularly accused of failing to adequately attend to the psychological effects of war on soldiers. Anti-war activist and deserter Camilo Ernesto Mejia commented:

> A twenty-minute session centering on the admonition *Don't commit suicide* doesn't do much to ease the anguish of a soldier dealing with the horror, for instance, of having killed a child, just as a group session with a combat stress team isn't much help if your life is at risk twenty-four hours a day.[19]

Moral injury usually starts when the intensity of war begins to wear off, and the juxtaposition of civilian life with memories of war stirs negative self-judgment of the beliefs and actions that made surviving war possible. Nakashima Brock and Lettini described this experience in painful detail:

> When the narcotic emotional intensity and tight camaraderie of war are gone, withdrawal can be intense. As memory and reflection deepen, negative self-judgments can torment a soul for a lifetime. Moral injury destroys meaning and forsakes noble cause. It sinks warriors into states of silent, solitary suffering, where bonds of intimacy and care seem impossible. Its torments to the soul can make death a mercy.[20]

Even when veterans have other veterans to talk with, their dynamics often must change before they can have the types of conversations that support recovering from moral injury. According to Dweylon:

> I was with soldiers in Iraq who didn't have close family ties, and they became much more emotionally attached to other soldiers. But fighting together is a different kind of relationship than having someone to talk to about what you are going through. I had friends at home I could talk to, but I didn't talk to other soldiers about my feelings. There's an unspoken rule that you don't show weakness or emotions like crying to other soldiers. We are trained to bottle them up because if you lose your cool in battle for even one second, people can get killed.[21]

Soldiers also need supportive family and friends to help make sense of what happened during war and discover the person they want to become. We all need others to help us make sense of what we imagine about ourselves and hold silently within. Through relationships, we verify that we actually are the persons we believe ourselves to be. Identity construction is not a private act but requires others to confirm or deny our ideas about ourselves. Psychologist Jerome Bruner wrote, "Don't we, too, have to tell the event in order to find out whether, after all, 'this is the kind of person I really mean to be'?"[22]

Too often, silence meets talk of killing and other actions that contribute to moral injury. Civilians often don't want to hear about the realities of war, and feelings of guilt and shame can keep veterans from sharing what led to their moral injuries. The silence is imposed by both veterans and society, compounding feelings of alienation, shame, and guilt. Marlantes saw the situation this way:

The problem is that the veterans' experiences and feelings remain quarantined from their families and communities. They go to the dark bar at the Legion Club, where children and nonveterans are not allowed. They disappear once a week into the VA outpatient clinic to be "cured." They aren't talking to friends and family; they're talking to bar buddies and therapists.[23]

Recovery from war and moral injury requires a collective effort. Ideally, families and friends of veterans and soldiers have opportunities to learn about the types of events that cause moral injury and the signs that their loved one is suffering from it. Ideally, they have opportunities to learn and practice non-judgmental listening skills so they can help their loved ones make sense of who they are after war, witnessing that the depth of their humanity extends far beyond the events that led to moral injury. Ideally, families and friends of veterans also learn how to take care of themselves when feeling overwhelmed by the realities of war and have places where they can seek support.

Although listening to stories of killing and destruction is not easy, they need to be told and heard. As Marlantes witnessed, listening to stories of war can be difficult but necessary:

What do we do when, in an honest moment, the former pilot looks right into your eyes, completely vulnerable, and says in a near whisper, "I loved it. I lit up the entire fucking valley." One honest reaction is to be appalled. The chances are pretty good that if he lit up the entire fucking valley he probably maimed and killed a lot of innocent people along with the ones who were trying to kill him and he most certainly did vast damage to the natural habitat. But should we condemn him for speaking the truth? At one level, and one he's admitting, he certainly loved it. So did I. At another level he did what his society had asked him to do, and he did so with skill, courage, and even élan. Should that same society now cut him off at the throat or, worse, at the balls? The appropriate response is to get him to keep talking about it. It may just be a bit shocking to find your friend has a wild and savage side that did a lot of harm. And it won't hurt him to find out that you think he did something very harmful and destructive, as long as at the same time he finds out that you won't love him any less for it. This is his great fear, that he won't be accepted back in. So he joins the conspiracy of silence. So do we all.[24]

Responding to Moral Injury

Veterans with religious affiliations may seek their churches, synagogues, mosques, temples, or sanghas to support them in their moral recovery, just as humans have done for centuries. However, some returning veterans may feel cut off from their faith because of what happened in war. They may feel they don't deserve forgiveness or that their god deserted them. These veterans, in particular, may benefit from clinical support until they feel comfortable reconnecting with their faith.

However, many veterans and military service personnel feel more comfortable speaking to chaplains and other ministers of faith, especially given the stigma associated with mental illness in the military and the effect that a diagnosis can have on an enlisted person's career. Some researchers suggest religious leaders learn basic psychological first aid, including familiarizing themselves with the signs of PTSD and methods for regulating traumatic stress, while working with veterans to identify the kinds of services they and their families need to support readjustment to civilian life.[25] The goal is to create places of worship that can provide comprehensive care—addressing the psychological, social, *and* spiritual needs of returning veterans and their families.

Whether support is sought in places of worship or mental health clinics, distinguishing between PTSD and moral injury helps to best tailor services to veterans' needs. Here I share an overview of the symptoms associated with PTSD and contrast them with moral injury.

PTSD is a reaction to an overwhelming event that threatened life or caused severe injury, resulting in an overall sense of lost safety. The cardinal symptoms of PTSD are nightmares, flashbacks, and intrusive memories of the traumatic event. When triggered by reminders of the trauma, defensive reactions, such as hyperarousal, numbing, or avoidance, are activated, making it difficult to get on with daily living. The emotions aroused by PTSD include fear, sometimes rising to the level of terror, and helplessness.

In contrast, moral injury causes an inner turmoil in the imaginal state Hillman associated with the soul and includes feelings of shame, guilt, or worthlessness for the perceived moral transgressions. Like PTSD, moral injury can also involve intrusive memories, avoidance, and numbing, yet moral injury is thought to differ in the amount of self-sabotaging behaviors that occur, including deliberately sabotaging relationships, engaging in self-harm, and attempting suicide.[26] PTSD and moral injury can both be present, hence the importance of taking a thorough assessment when supporting veterans and soldiers.

Research into the clinical treatment of moral injury is relatively recent, although established models for treating trauma are useful for thinking about the psychological consequence of moral injury, including the *model of complex trauma* and the *model of structural dissociation*. After outlining these two models, I share current treatments to address moral injury.

Complex Trauma

Some researchers and clinicians have suggested that the model of complex trauma may be a comprehensive way of looking at the impact of war on veterans.[27] This makes sense to me. After working with veterans and other traumatized populations, I have come to think that some of the difficulties with providing adequate and appropriate clinical support arise in part from an overreliance on the *Diagnostic and Statistical Manual of Mental Disorders* definition of PTSD. The PTSD diagnosis may best explain single-instance traumas and how traumatic stress organizes the body to anticipate similar traumas in the future. In contrast, complex trauma addresses changes caused by prolonged and recurring traumatizing conditions, such as those in war. Chronic traumatization can lead to structural changes in the personality and increase the likelihood of self-harm. The conditions that lead to complex trauma include:

- Random, recurring, and unpredictable traumatic events.
- The inability to escape the traumatizing situation, which causes a sense of captivity.
- Emotions that tend to be invalidated or cannot be expressed without fear of invalidation.[28]

All of the above conditions are observed in war. Furthermore, the presence of interpersonal violence and attachment loss, such as the death of a fellow soldier, increase the likelihood of developing complex trauma.

The structural changes in personality associated with complex trauma can cause a demarcation in veterans and soldiers between who they are at home and who they are in war. Veterans and soldiers can feel haunted by the need to join these often radically different senses of self. Marlantes wrote:

Killing someone without splitting oneself from the feelings that the act engenders requires an effort of supreme consciousness that, quite frankly, is beyond most humans. Killing is what warriors do for society. Yet when they return home, society doesn't generally acknowledge that the act it asked them to do created a deep split in their psyches, or a psychological and spiritual weight most of them will stumble beneath the rest of their lives. Warriors must learn how to integrate the experience of killing, to put the pieces of their psyches back together again. For the most part, they have been left to do this on their own.[29]

He goes on to say:

My problem was that for years I was unaware of the need to heal that split, and there was no one, after I returned, to point this out to me. That kid's dark eyes would stare at me in my mind's eye at the oddest times. I'd be driving at night and his face would appear on the windscreen. I'd be talking at work and that face with its angry snarl would suddenly overwhelm me and I'd fight to stay with the person I was talking with. I'd never been able to tell anyone what was going on inside. So I forced these images back, away, for years. I began to reintegrate that split-off part of my experience only after I actually began to imagine that kid as a kid, my kid perhaps. Then, out came this overwhelming sadness—and healing. Integrating the feelings of sadness, rage, or all of the above with the action [of killing] should be standard operating procedure for all soldiers who have killed face-to-face.[30]

Structural Dissociation

A model that helps understand this sense of being split is the *model of structural dissociation,* which, like complex trauma, identifies the core reaction to chronic traumatization as structural changes in the personality.[31] For veterans struggling with structural dissociation, part of the self can feel exiled as they try to avoid memories, beliefs, and actions associated with who they were during war. Tyler Boudreau, a soldier in Iraq, said of veterans at home:

> There are guys who come home from war and live fifty years without a narrative, fifty years lost. They don't know their own story, never have, and never will. But they're moving amidst the text every day and every long night without even realizing it.... They live inside the narrative like a cell, and their only escape is to understand its dimensions.[32]

Structural dissociation of the personality likely takes advantage of the partitioning of the brain into left and right hemispheres, in which the *corpus callosum* that joins the two hemispheres plays a largely inhibitory role. As a result, humans can split off awareness of emotions and traumatic memories located in the right hemisphere while the left hemisphere, as the seat of analytical reasoning and planning, attempts to function unimpeded by unresolved traumatic memories. This splitting of the hemispheres has made possible surviving war and other conditions like childhood abuse and intimate partner violence that are chronically traumatizing. However, recovering from trauma and moral injury requires reintegrating split-off emotions, memories, and beliefs to create the type of narrative and identity that Boudreau and Marlantes saw as necessary for overcoming the effects of war.

It's important to note that all of us have different parts of ourselves, along with their corresponding memories and emotions, some of which at times we try to avoid. What makes structural dissociation particularly difficult is the *rigidity* of the personality that occurs in response to ongoing trauma. In the model of structural dissociation, the personality is thought to be made up of different systems. When these systems are not divided by chronic traumatization, they work together in cohesive and complementary ways to ensure survival.

As discussed in the previous essay, there is a primary division in the personality structure between action systems that contribute to daily living and the action system of defense. The action systems of daily life lead us to seek what keeps us alive and growing, such as safe attachments, companions, a mate, food, shelter, play, and exploration, while the action system of defense leads to defensive reactions to threats, such as fighting, fleeing, freezing, submission, or crying out for help. After chronic traumatization, these personality systems become less adapted to present conditions. The defense system starts to misread benign stimuli as evidence of a threat. The personality becomes rigid rather than adaptive as harmless situations are repeatedly registered as risky. Getting on with daily life becomes complicated, if not exhausting, as the chronically traumatized person becomes phobic of traumatic reminders and thus begins to withdraw from life.

The creators of structural dissociation describe the traumatized self as divided into at least two parts: the *apparently normal part of the personality*, which takes care of day-to-day living by presenting a façade of normalcy, and an *emotional part of the personality*, which holds the emotions and memories split off at the time of the traumatic or morally injurious event. This distinction was first used to describe "shell-shocked" soldiers in World War I by psychiatrist Charles Samuel Meyers.[33] In veterans, distinctions between the apparently normal part of the personality and the emotional part of the personality have been called the "adaptive self" and the "war self,"[34] respectively.

In chronic traumatization, the emotional parts of the personality organize around the defense reactions of fighting, fleeing, freezing, submission, and attachment crying. These defenses are altered by the need to endure ongoing traumatic conditions. For example, there can be a fight emotional part that, when triggered, tries to protect from further harm by being angry, mistrustful, destructive, devaluing, impulsive, and even suicidal. We can expect that veterans trained in combat have a particularly robust fight part that is activated when intrusive memories threaten to break through. There may also be a flight emotional part that distances from threats through ambivalence, difficulty making commitments, and addictive behaviors. Furthermore, a submit emotional part is associated with depression, shame, self-loathing, passivity, and getting needs met by taking care of others. There may be one emotional part, or there may be many.

Emotions such as shame, guilt, and pride are also thought to be part of a personality system.[35] These emotions contribute to social belonging by maintaining attachments and social positioning. Shame and guilt are potentially adaptive when they motivate us to change behaviors in order to maintain important relationships. But like defenses, such as fight or flight, shame and guilt can also be split off, or dissociated, especially when there is fear of social rejection. However, if we hide what makes us feel shameful or guilty, our need to protect ourselves may increase the likelihood of social withdrawal. We can also cause social rejection when we aggressively defend against the possibility of shame.

Splitting off emotions at the time of the moral injury—such as not dealing with the feelings that killing causes during the intensity of battle and then staying silent about those experiences once back home because of fear of rejection—redoubles the likelihood that some very powerful emotions are not integrated with the rest of the personality and become habitually compartmentalized. It's painful for anyone to regularly feel shame, guilt, and worthlessness, let alone stay engaged in relationships and community when continually flooded by these emotions. So, when these emotions come forth, as they invariably will when there is moral injury, the tendency is to try to avoid them if doing so will increase the likelihood of staying socially engaged. As Tyler Boudreau observed, decades can go by without those split-off feelings and memories ever being dealt with. Billie Grimes-Watson shared about her own moral injury:

> I have all this guilt inside me and I want to let it out but I can't. I want to tell my husband and family what's going on, but I don't. I just put on a happy face until I am alone.[36]

Working with complex trauma through the model of structural dissociation focuses on resolving inner conflicts and integrating the different systems of the personality. Treatment follows Janet's phase-oriented model in which the first phase is devoted to stabilization and symptom reduction, the second to the treatment of traumatic memories, and the third to personality integration and rehabilitation.[37] Nonjudgmental, mindful awareness of inner states is at the core of treatment and the basis for learning to accept all aspects of the self while also living with present-centered awareness.

Treatments for Moral Injury

Recovery from chronic traumatization and moral injury is best thought of as an ongoing process rather than one with an endpoint or cure. Veterans and soldiers suffering from moral injury need to establish and maintain an inner middle ground in which they can accept the past even if they cannot condone it. The harsh inner critic that sees goodness forever out of reach must be replaced with a nuanced understanding of the complexities of war and the limits on their responsibility for what occurred. Strict distinctions between good and evil must be dismantled and replaced with acceptance of the ambiguity that surrounds most human behavior. Psychiatrist Carl Jung wrote about the importance of this middle ground in his autobiography of regaining his own soul, *The Red Book*:

> If the power of growth begins to cease, then the united falls into its opposites. We suspect and understand that growth needs both, and hence we keep good and evil close together. Because we know that too far into the good means the same as too far into the evil, we keep them both together.[38]

I don't believe Jung is referring to actions that are good or evil but to the importance of how we interpret imaginal contents of soul, especially how we imagine ourselves to be. Furthermore, I don't think it is a coincidence Jung was incubating many of the ideas developed in this seminal work while serving in the military (noncombat) during World War I.

Similar to Jung's observations, some of the treatments currently used to address moral injury are directed toward reducing the critical inner voice that convinces veterans and soldiers they can never be "good" again. For example, adaptive disclosure treatment works with what Hillman described as the imaginal contents of soul.[39] In adaptive disclosure, over the course of eight weekly ninety-minute sessions, veterans and soldiers work toward reducing the intensity and rigidity of their memories of moral injury. This involves "imaginal exposure" to the events that led to moral injury, identifying the associated beliefs about the self and what occurred, all in the context of charged emotions that such recall inevitably causes. Participants also imagine having a conversation with the person injured or killed. Rather than condemnation, they imagine the person offering compassion and forgiveness. The veteran or soldier can also practice imagining someone they perceive as having moral authority offering compassion and forgiveness in response to perceived moral transgressions.

Another exercise used in adaptive disclosure involves redistributing the blame to create a more accurate portrayal of the event that led to moral injury, especially sharing responsibility across all the people and institutions involved. In this exercise, anyone who played a role in the circumstances leading up to the morally injurious event is listed and assigned percentages for their part in what happened. Journalist David Wood described how this changes the nature of blame:

> If a Marine shot a child in combat, he might accept 30 percent of the blame. He might award the Taliban 50 percent, the child himself 5 percent and the Marine Corps 5 percent. God, perhaps, 10 percent.[40]

Studies show adaptive disclosure reduces PTSD symptoms, negative self-appraisals, and depression while increasing post-traumatic growth.[41]

The San Diego Naval Medical Center offers a similar program—*a moral injury/moral repair group,* which helps soldiers gain a more balanced appraisal of what they did in war. One of the central goals of this program is to help veterans and soldiers see that what they did in war doesn't define who they are or limit who they can become. Those who participate in the group are expected to resist minimizing what veterans did during war while still affirming they are not evil because of their perceived transgressions. During group, a member will share the event that caused moral injury while other members quietly listen, neither passing judgment nor excusing their actions. One participant said about the group:

> People give you space. And they got a therapy dog in there, and he comes over and wags his tail a little bit, tells you it's

OK, too, you know? Not saying it's OK, but just to say you're not some wicked person.[42]

Many, however, do think they are wicked. Michael Castellana, one of the psychotherapists that leads the group, relayed the story of a soldier rushed by insurgents using women and children as shields, whom he inevitably shot so he could stay alive:

> When he arrived home, coming off the plane, his wife handed him his new baby daughter. She put the baby in his arms and he immediately gave the baby back to her with an almost disgusted look—he almost dropped her. The thing was, his new daughter was so beautiful and perfect and pure that he didn't want his filth to contaminate her.[43]

To alleviate the feeling of being forever tainted by their actions during war, members of the moral injury/moral repair group participate in community service, which becomes an opportunity to witness their own goodness and experience their communities' receptiveness to their acts of kindness. Volunteering also helps validate that they belong, reducing alienation and shame.

Near the end of the moral injury/moral repair group, similar to adaptive disclosure, participants write a letter to themselves or someone compassionate and loving in their lives, such as a spouse, elder, or mentor. They use the letter to imagine sharing the actions that led to moral injury. They imagine the person's compassionate acceptance of them, regardless of what they did. Participants are also given the option of writing a letter to a person they transgressed. Marine staff sergeant Felipe Tremillo wrote a letter to a young Afghan boy he watched tremble with shame and rage as Marines forced his family outdoors while they searched his home for weapons. Tremillo wrote in his letter:

> I told him how sorry I was at how I affected his life, that he didn't have a fair chance to have a happy life based off our actions as a unit." About the letter Tremillo remarked "[It] wasn't about me forgiving myself, more about accepting who I am now."[44]

Both adaptive disclosure and the moral injury/moral repair group get the recovery process started, promoting self-forgiveness and self-compassion, challenging the tendency toward all-consuming self-blame that keeps veterans alienated in guilt, shame, and feelings of worthlessness. Yet treatment of moral injury is not over at the end of eight weeks of adaptive disclosure or eight-weeks of moral injury/moral repair group. Instead, recovery from moral injury requires continually investing in the attitudes and skills these programs encourage: compassionately relating to oneself, accepting the past with self-empathy, relying on community to know oneself, and committing to a purposeful life. Then life becomes meaningful again, possibly more than ever imagined.

Mejia explained:

> Moral injury is painful, yes, but it has also returned a sense of humanity that had been missing from my life for longer than I can remember. I have come to believe that the transformative power of moral injury cannot be found in the pursuit of our own moral balance as an end goal, but in the journey of repairing the damage we have done unto others. There is much to be learned about moral injury.... But if there is one thing I am certain about, it is that in committing great wrongs against others, I committed great wrongs against myself as well. And with the certainty that it will take a lifetime to heal

the injuries within me, I embark on this lifelong journey to heal the injuries of others.[45]

As Mejia shows us, despite the psychological and spiritual devastation caused by moral injury, there is a way out. Like the phoenix rising from the ashes, a path is laid in the direction of one's most compassionate self, what some might call *the warrior of the heart*.

IMAGINING SUICIDE

For nearly two years, I commuted across the Golden Gate Bridge from San Francisco to San Rafael. Each time I crossed, the view consumed me. Whether marveling at the bridge, watching the fog mingle with the Pacific Ocean, or eyeing the cramped San Francisco skyline that signaled the end of my workday, I felt part of the grandeur, one small being contributing to a greater meaning.

Symbolically, bridges represent connection as well as transformation. They end separations and mark new frontiers. J. E. Cirlot wrote in *A Dictionary of Symbols*, "The bridge is always symbolic of a transition from one state to another—of change or the desire for change."[1] According to the *Penguin Dictionary of Symbols*, a bridge is sometimes represented by a sword, highlighting that transitions can be dangerous.[2] Perhaps the sublime beauty of the Golden Gate Bridge, along with the symbolism associated with bridges in general, is why this landmark has become one of the world's top suicide destinations.

Dealing with suicidal thoughts and feelings is the shadow work of psychotherapy. Like most dark and scary places, few ever wish to visit, yet for psychotherapists, facing suicide is not a matter of choice but a matter of *when*. If you are prudent, you stay mindful that anyone can be consumed by darkness.

Part of training as a psychotherapist involves learning how to deal with suicide—establishing if a person has a plan, a means to carry out the plan, a history of suicide attempts or suicidal ideation, a precipitating crisis, and, equally important, a reason to live. However, gathering all this information is never enough to save a soul, although it can keep the heart beating a bit longer. Such information helps decide if emergency intervention is necessary and can also point to deeper conflicts beyond a precipitating crisis. For some, thoughts of suicide provide a sense of safety, much like the possibility of an emergency escape if suffering becomes unbearable.

I once watched a documentary about suicide and the Golden Gate Bridge to understand the experience of survivors of attempted suicide. My gut ached after watching the documentary, *The Bridge*, which included footage of people falling to their deaths. I have come to look at strong somatic responses as indicators of both the impact of an event and the inability to make meaning of what transpired. I could not imagine what was going on in people's minds when they jumped—or rather, I would not let myself imagine; it would have overwhelmed me. All life is precious, but too often, people lose connection to the significance of their lives—that *they* matter, that life matters.

It wasn't until I researched the symbolism of bridges and reflected on the cycles of equilibrium and disequilibrium that are an inevitable part of growth that I began to make sense of what I had seen. In their studies of human development, Frances Ilg and Louise Bates Ames observed that in the first two decades of life, growth alternates between periods of equilibrium and disequilibrium—times when we feel calm and well-integrated in our communities and times when we feel unbalanced, even chaotic, and out of sorts with others and our environment. Which stage a person is in depends in part on whether they are trying to balance personal needs with the outside world (equilibrium) or giving attention more to their internal drive for individuation (disequilibrium).

Like Ilg and Bates Ames, Jungian analyst Michael Fordham theorized the ego develops in response to interactions with surroundings, while another more encompassing aspect of psyche, the *Self*, reacts primarily to unconscious symbolic material. We continually try to integrate these two ways of perceiving and being, and it can be profoundly unsettling when they clash.

However we might theorize this process, human growth and development require continually shifting between states of equilibrium and disequilibrium as we balance our inner lives of memories, imaginings, emotions, and beliefs with outer-world possibilities, limitations, and expectations. We alternate between these states throughout our lives. The transitions can be tricky, which may be when suicide is more likely. Not only must we grapple with changing self-perceptions, but we are tasked with relaying to others that we have changed, which, at times, can feel daunting and cause acute states of aloneness.

Although necessary, states of disequilibrium are rarely easy to go through. Feeling unwelcome, unseen, unheard, confused about what direction to take, sick of the effort, exhausted by longing, and angry at the injustices of life can trigger a downward spiral that is profoundly isolating. A history of trauma or mental illness may make periods of disequilibrium especially difficult when they trigger memories of traumatic event(s) or disordered states (which inevitably, they will).

I also think the current state of the world aggravates and amplifies suffering when it fails to foster the deep, reliable connections that can buoy our spirits during times of distress. Collectively, we are unmoored from recent eras and their sense of community. We are still trying to figure out what it means to be human in this latest round of globalization. Sometimes it feels like we are in a collective state of disequilibrium.

From trainings in sensorimotor psychotherapy, I learned to perceive suicide as a fight response, which differs from traditional thinking of suicide as a response to hopelessness and acute depression, which may also be present. This seems right to me, especially after watching footage of people jumping from the Golden Gate Bridge. Suicide is a fight. It's an attempt to break through feeling trapped in one's life, mind, and sometimes relationships. It's a fight against perceived limits on growth and change. It's a fight against suffering.

Suicide may also be a fight with overwhelming feelings. Or a fight with a perpetually critical inner voice. Or a fight with painful memories. Or a fight with the obsessive looping of one's mind. Or a fight with circumstances. Sometimes it's a fight with others, and then it's often a fight against feeling oppressed or controlled. The reasons for suicide is endless. But whatever the reason, suicide is a failure of the imagination since only one solution is perceived: death.

Perhaps the appeal of the Golden Gate Bridge is that it symbolizes the transformation of suffering into something meaningful—that the bridge is somehow grand enough to both contain and transform an inner sense of aloneness. Perhaps in every suicide attempt there is an unconscious wish for transformation, although channeled into a losing battle.

In self-defense training, I learned to get inside the "donut" when in a fight, physically close to the assailant. This is not easy to do. The instinct is to run from what is threatening and dangerous. But getting close allows the greatest impact. The same principle applies when the assailant is suicide: you must get really close to the person contemplating suicide. It's not a time for polite distance or hesitation. You've got to get inside the imagined "donut" that separates the person from humankind, as well as their desired sense of self, and try to stop their isolating spiral. And it's often a good idea to call 911 or a suicide prevention line. Ultimately, human connection is the bridge that saves lives.

WHEN A WOMAN LEAVES
HER BATTERER

Leaving a batterer is never easy. A woman is at greatest risk for murder when she leaves a physically abusive partner. Her decision to leave is a sign to the batterer that he has lost control, which is what batterers fear the most.

Not loss of love. Not loss of a partner. Not even the loss of a scapegoat or whipping girl for all he perceives as wrong with his life. No. Just loss of control. Over her. Over his fears of abandonment. Over his fears that he is not the omnipotent being he imagines himself to be.

A woman's fear of murder, no doubt, will keep her in an abusive relationship, especially if the batterer has threatened to kill her. Perhaps he has strangled her. Strangulation can be enough to keep her submissive and in a pervasive state of terror. It can also be difficult to detect.[1]

Low self-esteem can also keep a woman in an abusive relationship. Sometimes low self-esteem precedes the relationship with the batterer. Maybe she was abused as a child and never learned to value herself. Maybe she was experiencing hard times when she got together with the batterer or she was in a period of existential self-doubt. For some women, a deep desire for a perfect romantic partner causes them to move too quickly into relationships. These women may not have low self-esteem, but their dreams of perfection keep them naïvely fixated on an ideal, blinding them to subtle warning signs of potential trouble in paradise.

Men who batter can be highly charismatic when they want to be. They are unusually sensitive to the signs of a vulnerable woman who might imagine she needs a knight in shining armor to save her. Batterers readily play the role of knight, at least until they see signs of dependency. For the batterer, dependency signals weakness and is a green light to begin exerting control. In a healthy relationship, dependency is a reason for responding sensitively.

If a woman's self-esteem is robust before entering a relationship with a batterer, it won't be afterward. He will make sure of this. Although "battering" typically refers to physical abuse, many battered women say the psychological and emotional abuse inflicted has the most lasting and damaging effect. Batterers seem to know this. Battering rarely—*if ever*—occurs without a backdrop of unending emotional abuse and degrading remarks. A woman with a broken spirit is less likely to leave her batterer.

Along with fear and low self-esteem, the dreams a woman holds for her partner and the relationship will cause her to stay. According to research conducted by Neil Jacobson and John Gottman, it wasn't until women let go of these dreams that they left their batterers for good.

In their book, *When Men Batter Women: New Insights into Ending Abusive Relationships*, Jacobson and Gottman wrote:

How do women get out of these abusive marriages? What we discovered when we interviewed these women was that this leave-taking was in every case an heroic struggle. These women had emerged from hell, and the journey in every case had required them to overcome major obstacles and make psychological transformations. The first step in their transformation was giving up the dream that kept them loyal to their husbands despite the abuse.[2]

And what were the dreams?

- *She dreams of the batterer as the knight* who once saved her.
- *She dreams of the batterer as undiscovered genius, artist, entrepreneur* (whatever his unfulfilled dreams might be) who, with the right support and love, will reach his potential—and stop battering her.
- *She dreams that if she were "good enough," the abuse would stop.* This is the message women constantly hear from their batterers—essentially that the abuse is their fault.

Jacobson and Gottman shared:

All three of the battered women...Martha, Judy, and Cheryl—initially saw their husbands as damaged little boys whom they would support, take care of, and heal until they became the great husbands and fathers the women were sure they could become. This was the dream. Don, Dave, and Randy were all perceived as men who with a little more loving and a little more kindness would blossom into upstanding family men. Until the women gave up that dream, they were unable to leave.

Dreams of a better partner and relationship contribute to the trauma bond between a woman and her batterer. These dreams are the unconscious undercurrent sealing the relationship, much like a secret handshake clinches an unspoken promise. She suffers the vain hope that he will return to being the knight or eventually become the king of his fantasies of grandeur. He needs her suffering to feed his fantasies of omnipotence and deep emptiness within. While she's looking to him for transformation, he's looking to her to make himself feel invincible. They both dream of futures that will never happen.

Without his partner to hold the dream, the batterer becomes vulnerable to his feelings of inadequacy or fears of abandonment—whichever happens to drive his need for control. Many have these fears, but the batterer dehumanizes his partner in his attempts to avoid them.

The batterer's dependency on his partner is much like a torturer's relationship with his captive. In his book *An Evil Cradling*, Brian Keenan wrote about the psychological immaturity and dependency of the captors who kept him hostage in Beirut, Lebanon, for almost five years. Unlike battered women, Keenan's perceptions weren't clouded by hopes of one day having a good relationship or successful partner. Instead, he could readily identify his captors' fear of being alone, their continual need for distractions, and how they were dependent on the hostages to avoid an internal sense of emptiness. He wrote:

> Cruelty and fear are man-made, and men who perpetrate them are ruled by them. Such men are only half-made things. They live out their unresolved lives by attempting to destroy anything that challenges the void in themselves. A child holds a blanket over its face in fear. A fear-filled man transposes his inadequacy onto another. He blames them, hates them, and hopes to rid himself of his unloved self by hurting, or worse, destroying them.[3]

To leave her batterer, the woman must lose the dream that blinds her to the opposing scripts she and her batterer follow—

namely, where she dreams of love, he dreams of power. She must revoke the secret handshake that once implied it was her responsibility to heal the batterer's internal emptiness, and thus, her responsibility to transform him into the man they both wished he could be—and then leave swiftly, safely, and with support.

A WORLD WITHOUT "NARCISSISTS"

The committee responsible for revising the *Diagnostic and Statistical Manual of Mental Disorders* went back and forth in their deliberations over narcissistic personality disorder but ultimately decided the diagnosis would remain. Not that it matters. Omitting *narcissism* from psychiatry's bible won't curb the common practice of hurling the label at foes and ex-lovers. Blame it on the state of the union, but Americans need a term befitting people who are habitually selfish and destructive and lack remorse for the emotional devastation they cause. The term *narcissist* has become a well-known warning label for would-be victims and a lament by survivors of viperous attacks.

One obvious problem with the term *narcissism* is that it applies to all of us. Supposedly, everyone is narcissistic some of the time, and a certain amount of narcissism is healthy. Still, some people are thought to be narcissistic all the time, especially when they are charming. But if we are all *a bit* narcissistic and some of us are *a lot* narcissistic, what is really being said? That we all lack empathy sometimes and can be self-absorbed but, like eating too much sugar or drinking too much booze, these behaviors become vices when done to excess? The term *narcissist* is also used to label extreme self-preoccupation and grandiose behavior, but given the problem of cruelty on our small and fragile planet, I'm not as troubled by this, other than it takes attention from more pressing matters.

There is also a term for the pathological narcissist: *sociopath*. Here again is a slippery slope. At what point does the narcissist become the sociopath?

Another problem is the belief that labeling hurtful people somehow provides protection—like a sign at the foot of a trail that says, *Caution: Mountain Lions*. But labels are often ineffective at creating the boundaries needed to avoid emotional traps and victimization. More importantly, they fail to change the perpetrator. It is well known that pathologically narcissistic people rarely seek help to change themselves. But they need to change—or be restrained. There are simply too many people for any of us to behave *too* narcissistically.

Typically, when imagining pathological narcissism in another person, the cautious mind only sees trouble. Supposedly, a northern aboriginal group would "accidentally" push their troublemakers off the icy edges bordering their communities. With limited resources and space, perhaps they saw cruelty as the only way to reduce the likelihood of cruelty. There may also be a psychological urge to purge the meanest among us, especially given the high anxiety aroused by having someone lurking about who rages at the slightest threat to their sense of self (hence the phrase, *walking on eggshells*, often used to describe life with an extreme narcissist).

Early in US history, our country was a place to push undesirables. Australia was also a favorite dumping ground. But banishment sits on another slippery slope, with the far end occupied by genocide. In the twentieth century, entire populations were brutally murdered because they were imagined threats, irrespective of reality. This happened with the Nazi victimization of the Jews, the Hutu victimization of the Tutsi, and the Ottoman victimization of the Armenians, as well as other groups.

Yes, there are those among us who threaten our emotional and physical survival, and we deserve to feel safe from them. However, the fear of cruelty causes high anxiety that can also lead to savagery. Because of the capacity to imagine the internal worlds of others, it's not difficult to conjure worst-case scenarios when imagining what's going on in the mind of someone perceived as a threat. The imagination goes wild when fear is present, and fear can make us stupid and mean. Pathological narcissists—those who hang out at the sociopath edge of the spectrum, like Adolph Hitler—use their capacity to imagine other peoples' minds to exploit their fears. And one of the classic ways to imply a population or person is a threat is to point to limited resources, which *is* an increasingly common problem across the planet.

One advantage of narcissism as a diagnosis is the opportunity to treat lack of empathy much like a disease or chronic condition and possibly heal pathological narcissism or manage such behavior. Retaining narcissism as a diagnosis is an implicit commitment to understanding what causes people to lack empathy and exploit others for personal gain. Such knowledge might help change the world in ways that lessen the likelihood of pathological narcissism, but this hasn't happened yet.

Although the exact cause of pathological narcissism isn't certain, there is a pretty good understanding of what increases its likelihood:

- Parents who use their children to boost their own self-image
- Parents who pamper and dote excessively
- Parents who are critical but also permissive
- Neglect
- Abuse

Unfortunately, psychotherapy may not be the best way to cure extreme narcissism. Psychotherapy is more often the place where victims go to heal, not where perpetrators go to reform, which is why pathological narcissism needs a societal-based response until perpetrators are ready to explore their own emotional wounds.

Not long after the Holocaust, Simone de Beauvoir introduced the *ethics of ambiguity*, which is basically the following humanistic principle:

My rights stop where your rights begin, and your rights stop where my rights begin.[1]

Simple enough. We all deserve our boundaries respected and we are all obligated to respect others' boundaries.

You might be thinking, *Well, yeah, of course boundaries are the solution—but they're also the problem since pathological narcissism involves ignoring the rights and boundaries of others. If we wait for "those" people to respect boundaries, we'll be waiting forever.* I agree. However, victims of cruelty often need help with boundaries—both with asserting their rights and maintaining the *right kind of boundaries*.

For example, I learned of a woman in Western Africa who was regularly beaten by her husband. She couldn't defend herself, and the authorities were of no help, so her women friends banded together, working their schedules so someone was always at the abused woman's home and she was never alone with her husband. This intimidated him, and he eventually left.

As this example shows, sometimes we need help asserting boundaries and rights, although doing so may mean relaxing the boundaries we have between our public and private lives. When we unite to defend against injurious behavior in non-injurious ways, we may lose some privacy, but we may also become less vulnerable to abuse. Sometimes preoccupation with privacy (along with benign states of narcissism) keeps many of us from seeking support when battered, bullied, or otherwise victimized. Sometimes the boundaries that protect privacy stand in the way of creating safety from cruelty. Perhaps we all would benefit from stressing there is no shame in being a victim but there is shame in hurting another person.

An ethics of ambiguity could also be extended to boundaries on our thoughts. Most of us, at least some of the time, fail to practice healthy boundaries of mind and worry about what others think, their motives, and even how we might change what they think. Instead of giving attention to ourselves and how we feel when we are with a person, we worry about what that person is thinking and feeling about us. I see this happen often with clients mistreated or battered by their partners. Although imagining what a batterer is thinking is a method for anticipating and possibly avoiding danger, it also contributes to paranoia and staying stuck in the relationship.

When we worry about another person's thoughts, we are more likely to become anxious and ignore our own feelings, which are often the best indicators of the quality of a relationship. If you repeatedly feel bad about yourself when you are with someone or are fearful in that person's company, trust your feelings. Don't worry about the reasons for bad behavior. In healthy and safe ways, leave the relationship if it can't be repaired and get outside support when needed (which is often imperative if being battered), thereby asserting your right to safety and freedom from hurt. This is a much healthier practice than hurling the label *narcissist* once the damage has already been done.

IS IT POSSIBLE TO RECOVER FROM RAPE AND SEXUAL ABUSE? YES AND NO

When she was 22 years old, philosopher Karyn L. Freedman was raped at knifepoint. She narrowly escaped being murdered and her body disposed of, perhaps never to be found. In her memoir, *One Hour in Paris,* Freedman recounted her efforts to heal from this horrifying ordeal. Over 25 years have passed since she was raped, but she has yet to fully recover and doubts she ever will. After years of therapy, support group meetings, and educating rape survivors in Africa about the effects of trauma, Freedman claimed:

> The biological truth of my trauma is anchored in me, but it lives there like a parasite. And as I move in and out of recovery I am reminded that however much work I do, healing from a traumatic experience is never complete. This is one of the most significant facts about psychological trauma. It is permanent. The psychological damage that results from the experience of terrorizing life events over which we have no control is profound. It sticks around for life. It is a chronic condition, which makes recovery from traumatic events an ongoing process.[1]

Freedman's continued struggle is common. Susan J. Brison, also a philosopher who was brutally raped in France as an adult, wrote the following about the lingering impact of her rape:

> People ask me if I'm recovered now, and I reply that it depends on what that means. If they mean, 'am I back to where I was before the attack'? I have to say, no, and I never will be. I am not the same person who set off, singing, on that sunny Fourth of July in the French countryside. I left her — and her trust, her innocence, her joie de vivre — in a rocky creek bed at the bottom of a ravine. I had to in order to survive. I now have my own understanding of what a friend described to me as a Jewish custom of giving those who have outlived a brush with death new names. The trauma has changed me forever, and if I insist too often that my friends and family acknowledge it, that's because I'm afraid they don't know who I am.[2]

Although I have never been raped as an adult, I was sexually abused as a child. I spent years nostalgically imagining the person I might have been had I not been abused and gone through periods haunted by nightmares and flashbacks that kept me reliving my abuse. Still, I consider myself lucky. I have managed to escape being raped as an adult, which happens with appalling regularity to women with histories like mine.

However, as with Freedman and Brison, the impact of sexual abuse persists. Sometimes I fail to see the secureness of my present life because of the protracted shadow of fear cast by all forms of sexual violence. Something startles me, and I am reminded that safety can be eclipsed in a moment. Even now, I am prone to dissociate from my body when I am overwhelmed by fear. I learned to escape in my head from conditions in my environment that were physically inescapable. Some habits can feel nearly impossible to break.

It has taken me a long time to honor these survival responses and acknowledge that sexual abuse is not something I, nor anyone else, fully recovers from, although this is not a reason to give up on recovery. Survivors can and do become strong again—sometimes stronger than they ever imagined—and are often graced with an awareness of the fragile nature of life that deepens their capacity for compassion.

But the process of healing from sexual violence is slow, painful, and expensive. Because I have worked hard for a peaceful mind and body, I am protective of them. I have a low tolerance of toxic attitudes and behaviors that might upend my recovery. Yet I am also quick to stand up to injustices that impact others, and I have witnessed this trait in people like me who are committed to healing their wounds of violence and abuse. We unintentionally become warriors of the heart—protectors of those less fortunate and vulnerable—those we imagine are like we were before we reclaimed our right to dignity and self-preservation, and those we imagine could become victims like we once were.

Not everyone likes the justice-seeking aspect of those recovering from sexual violence and other abuses. Anyone who needs to exert power over another needs someone capable of being a victim. The commitment to heal requires a sustained effort at avoiding becoming a victim again. The changes we make to ensure future safety and integrity can also lead to resisting abuses of power in all aspects of our lives. For the psychological complexes and interpersonal dynamics that lead to subjugation extend well beyond the predator-prey dynamics of sexual violence.

Knowledge is a powerful way to defend against further abuse. In *One Hour in Paris*, Freedman shared her extensive knowledge of PTSD and the treatment of psychological trauma. Obviously, I share her desire to know everything I can about healing. Every textbook I have read on the treatment of trauma has been with double vision: one eye on how to maintain my own recovery and the other on how to help others with theirs. Having fallen victim once, some of us arm ourselves with knowledge to failsafe our recovery and ensure we never fall victim to abuse again. This is a largely untapped resource. The wisdom of recovery can enlighten efforts at creating a society centered on safety, respect, and fairness.

Because of insights gained through recovery, I believe the commitment to heal is a generous act, even though the process means focusing intently on oneself. Individual efforts to heal become the groundwork for equality and respect in relationships, families, communities, work environments, and societies. Healing society really does begin with healing individuals.

Granted, as Freedman and Brison shared, even after an extended period of recovery, suffering still happens. No one ever completely gets over being abused by a sexual predator. Still, with time and effort, the reactions can be managed. In the process, the survivor often gains a stronger spirit, greater integrity, and better self-care that together can foster deep caring for others. Brison wrote:

> But if recovery means being able to incorporate this awful knowledge into my life and carry on, then, yes, I'm recovered. I don't wake each day with a start, thinking: 'this can't have happened to me!" It happened. I have no guarantee that it won't happen again, although my self-defense classes have given me the confidence to move about in the world and to go for longer and longer walks—with my two big dogs. Sometimes I even manage to enjoy myself. And I no longer cringe when I see a woman jogging alone on the country road where I live, though I may still have a slight urge to rush out and protect her, to tell her to come inside where she'll be safe. But

I catch myself, like a mother learning to let go, and cheer her on, thinking, may she always be so carefree, so at home in her world. She has every right to be.

In what follows, I discuss some of the reactions, beliefs, and emotions that interfere with seeking help after sexual violence and thus getting the recovery process started. I have found for myself, and for those I have had the honor of supporting in their recovery, that it is difficult to accept the extent of psychological wounding caused by sexual violence. The tendency is to believe that if you can avoid thinking about the rape or abuse, its impact will fade away. Furthermore, shame, no matter how undeserved, keeps women from seeking help. A trauma-informed perspective can help overcome these obstacles to beginning the recovery process.

Initial Steps toward Healing

After sexual violence, most women want to forget what happened and return to the lives they led before the assault. Naturally, the survivor desires to be who she was before the trauma. She also wants to avoid perceiving herself as irrevocably damaged by rape or sexual abuse. Confusion, humiliation, and hurt are common, contributing to self-doubt and silence.

Women often choose a course of action that will protect them from judgment, which may include avoiding seeking help. And who can blame us? Throughout history, women have been held responsible for the sexual violence perpetrated against them. Remaining silent just may be an archetypal defense response to the anticipated judgment and shaming that, over the millennia, have been the common response to sexually violated women (along with abandonment, forced prostitution, and stoning to death).

Freedman's literal cry for help led to the police's immediate involvement and eventually the prosecution and imprisonment of the man who raped her. (Brison's rapist was also prosecuted and imprisoned.) Freedman's family was supportive and protective of her after the rape. However, like many women, Freedman initially resisted telling the truth about what happened to her and instead said she had been mugged. She also sought only limited professional support:

> Outside of a couple of sessions with a psychologist when I first returned home from Paris (attended at the behest of my parents), I had made no serious effort to come to terms with the experience. I believed—wrongly, as it turns out—that the best way to deal with the trauma of that night was to distance myself from it.

No one can anticipate the impact of sexual violence, although anticipation isn't usually needed since reactions to sexual violence appear rather quickly. In his book, *The Trauma Model,* psychiatrist Colin Ross gave the following composite description of typical reactions to rape:

> She has nightmares of being chased and murdered, which she never had before. She has repeated intrusive recollections of the rape, sometimes including details she could not previously recall. She is tense, keyed up, anxious and fearful much of the time. She scans the environment for detail and has an extreme startle response to stimuli that previously would not have affected her. ...
>
> Because of the nightmares, she loses a lot of sleep. As well, she avoids the nightmares by staying up late. The resulting fatigue begins to affect her concentration and performance at work. She will not let her boyfriend, with whom she previously had frequent, mutually satisfying sexual relations,

touch her. When he tries to touch her, she experiences fearful hyperarousal and has to take a shower. She takes at least three showers a day in order to get rid of the dirt on her body and she can still feel the rapist's semen on her. She develops other psychosomatic symptoms including vaginal pain, painful periods, muscle and joint pains, and diarrhea and nausea. ...

Exhausted from lack of sleep, and overwhelmed with traumatic anxiety, she begins to drink in the evenings and uses alcohol to go to sleep. She becomes tired, drained of energy, overwhelmed and despondent. She has many negative cognitions about herself, men and life in general.[3]

Freedman suffered many of the reactions Ross described. Finding herself living alone six years after the rape—a relationship dissolved due to intimacy problems stemming from her assault—Freedman became overwhelmed by fear:

I had minor convulsions at the slightest unexpected noise, anything from the ringing of a telephone to the slamming shut of a book. My ability to fall and stay asleep, which had been a struggle since the rape, became seriously compromised. I would lie in bed for hours listening to the pounding of my own heart and trying to close off my mind to the unwanted images that flew threw it. These intrusive thoughts are a form of traumatic flashback, although since I wasn't actually thinking (or writing or talking) about the rape at that time in my life, these images weren't usually about me or Robert [the rapist] or the knife grazing lines on my breasts. Instead, the intrusive thoughts were centered on my friends and family, and every possible variation that my mind could configure on each one's violent and imminent demise. In quick, successive flashes, I would imagine one sister or the other trampled by the crush of an uncontrollable mob, or my grandmother's head ripped off by a bus whizzing past her, or a friend flattened to death by a crashing plane. At the time, alcohol was the only thing that gave me some temporary relief from these tormenting thoughts.

At one point, almost eight years after the rape, Freedman visited a psychiatrist, who put her on clonazepam, a medication used to treat insomnia and panic attacks. Freedman never disclosed to her psychiatrist that she had been raped. It also seems her psychiatrist failed to ask if Freedman had a history of trauma:

> By the spring of 1998 I had finally had enough. I decided that I needed to get some help. I went to see a psychiatrist, which is how I first ended up on clonazepam. Remarkably, I saw this doctor once a month for about a year, and not once in that time did I mention to her that I had been raped or almost killed. At the time I wasn't even aware of this omission (I realized it only after I went back to see her following a long hiatus). It wasn't that I had entirely blocked out any memory of the rape, but by this point I had assumed that it was long behind me, and I simply did not connect my wretched inner life with the aftermath of that traumatic experience. The event of August 1, 1990, had fallen off my radar even though I was living it out every day.

Because many women avoid support, get the wrong kind of support, or lack opportunities for support and services, it's vital they learn through other avenues how sexual violence impacts the body and mind. This information is best received as soon as possible after the rape or sexual abuse. Knowing what to expect can decrease self-judgment, especially the belief that *I should be over this already*, which commonly creeps in along with thoughts of self-blame. Such beliefs contribute to a self-persecuting spiral that increases the likelihood of substance abuse/dependency and debilitatingly low self-worth. Furthermore, substance abuse and low self-worth increase the likelihood of sexual revictimization.

Awareness of common reactions to a traumatic event can also help create a healthy distance from body sensations, thoughts, and feelings triggered by reminders of the trauma, including overwhelming fear, which can feel as intense as the terror felt during the assault. Knowing these reactions can help disentangle disorienting and often frightening traumatic reminders from the "going on with ordinary life" part of the self —that "old" self who existed before the rape and whom the survivor initially desires to become again—or for those sexually abused when young, whom they hope to become one day.

Sexual violence "splits" a person's psyche so that, when triggered by reminders of the assault, defense reactions are activated and override efforts to get on with ordinary life— including sleeping, working, meeting goals, playing, and enjoying sexual intimacy. This split between defensive reactions and "ordinary life" is a natural response to threat and overwhelming fear.

Trauma memories are not like regular memories, and the body and mind react to them differently. Traumatic reminders feel intrusive, whether they take the form of images, emotions, or body sensations. This is the startle response Freedman described and the panic attacks, too. There is also that other part of the self, the one that has relationships, holds a job, sets goals, but the capacity to express it is continuously overwhelmed by reminders of the attack or abuse. Healing is about regaining the ability to live from that "ordinary life" part of the self without overwhelming defense responses getting activated at inopportune times. For the survivor of child sexual abuse, establishing a sense of "ordinary life" for the first time can feel safe and life-affirming,

Getting back to "ordinary life" begins with becoming aware

of limiting beliefs, overwhelming emotions, and disruptive sensations as defense reactions while also creating conditions that increase feelings of body safety, emotional safety, and safety in the environment. Some possible reactions to sexual violence include:

- Self-blame
- Depression
- Hopelessness
- Physical aches and pains
- Suicidal thoughts and feelings
- A heightened startle response
- Irritability
- Fear or avoidance of intimacy
- Feelings of mistrust and betrayal
- Sexual promiscuity or risk-taking behavior
- Feeling numb, shutting down, dissociating
- Low self-worth
- Inability to feel safe alone
- Catastrophic and morbid thinking
- Foreshortened sense of the future
- Self-medicating to get to sleep or control anxiety (using alcohol or other substances)
- Overwhelming fear and panic attacks
- Feeling alienated from other people
- Living split—a self presented to the world that hides a part of self that feels vulnerable and ashamed
- Self-silencing because of feelings of shame

Some of these reactions may seem to contradict each other. Contradiction is the nature of posttraumatic stress, which can alternate between avoidance of reminders of the traumatic event and preoccupation with them. Reminders may be either real, like seeing someone who looks like the perpetrator, or symbolic, such as Freedman imagining the catastrophic deaths of family members. The body reacts to both in the same way—as potential threats.

My hope is that when survivors know how mind and body react to traumatic events, they will be less likely to think there is something wrong with themselves and more likely to see such changes as having to do with what *happened* to them. Unfortunately, it is highly probable that all survivors of sexual trauma will experience at least some of these reactions.

The Power of Shame

The hardest part of healing from sexual violence may be overcoming the shame that keeps women and girls silent in their suffering. Shame increases the likelihood that traumatic stress reactions will go unaddressed and instead become the new norm as "ordinary life" becomes increasingly difficult.

For those of us who were sexually abused as children, silence about the abuse is typically how many tried to stay safe —or we were led to believe silence would keep us safe. Shame is also a natural reaction to sexual abuse, which initiates a spiral into low self-worth and unconsciously blaming one's own body for failing to prevent abuse (when, of course, the blame belongs to the perpetrator). For sexually abused children, the splitting of self between defense responses and efforts to get on with ordinary life can become complex and entrenched if the abuse was chronic. Unfortunately, after childhood sexual abuse, it typically takes several years to learn how to live peacefully and safely within one's mind, body, and relationships without shame.

Adult survivors of sexual violence are also at risk of becoming entrenched in traumatic defense responses exacerbated by feelings of shame. Even when a woman knows she is not to blame—and many doubt themselves—she can feel profoundly humiliated by sexual violence.

Most women, if not all, are aware of societal perceptions of women as irrevocably damaged by sexual violence. Even worse, in some countries, a woman's "failure" to resist rape can lead to her death. In countries where men are prosecuted for rape, age-old distinctions between *madonna* and *whore* initiated by patriarchal religions thousands of years ago continue to influence how women are perceived and treated in courts of law. Women who have been raped and sexually abused are regularly judged as at least partially at fault for their victimization. It's worth repeating: no wonder so many of us stay silent about sexual trauma.

The taboos that silence survivors of sexual violence also interfere with recovery. Although silence may feel as if it protects from further harm or judgment, it erodes mind, body, and spirit. Furthermore, when the survivor remains silent about the abuse, parts of herself she once cherished can also be buried deep within and feel unreachable.

To know ourselves and fully recover, we must story our lives and share our stories with others. We must pull together the unintegrated bits of memory and make ourselves and our stories whole again. However, storying trauma doesn't require telling every bit of the rape or sexual abuse, or even remembering everything that happened. The need to know everything beyond a fraction of doubt is the mindset of the courtroom, not the healing attitude of recovery. Instead, we need what psychiatrist Daniel Siegel called "feeling felt" by another, sharing what we feel and having our feelings validated. Without this experience, we fall further victim to our sense of selves as shameful.

But the taboo surrounding sexual violence is real, and telling others about sexual violence can be compromising, even dangerous for some women. Fortunately, there are anonymous resources such as the Rape, Abuse & Incest National Network

(RAINN). Eventually, though, most women need and deserve professional support and the company of other survivors.

Like Freedman, I started my recovery work with a therapist and then took part in a group dedicated to survivors. Eventually, I began helping others with their recoveries. In areas in the West where therapists and mental health services are accessible, this approach to treatment is common and, I believe, a good one. Specific modalities such as Eye Movement Desensitization and Reprocessing (EMDR), sensorimotor psychotherapy, and somatic experiencing are exceptional at treating traumatic reactions to sexual trauma. One primary goal of therapy is mindful awareness of how defense responses get triggered and learning how not to be overwhelmed by them. Recovery also involves ceasing to be afraid of memories of what happened.

Treatment is most successful when joined with personal efforts at creating safety and peace in daily life. For me, this has included yoga, Buddhism, art, journaling, self-defense classes, exercising regularly, and deep connections with people I love and trust, especially my husband. Everyone has unique ways of creating safety and peace, and we must make them priorities in our lives.

Recovery also involves feeling part of society without the fear of further violence or retribution for protecting oneself. Survivors share this aspect of recovery with all women. None of us really feel safe when rape and sexual abuse occur with regularity and impunity, as they do today. Can any women feel safe when nearly 20 percent of women in the US have experienced attempted or completed rape and one in five girls in the US are sexually abused before the age of 18? In many countries, the percentages are even higher.

Sometimes I go weeks without my fear being triggered, which I feel is quite an accomplishment since I live in a densely populated city. I tend to enjoy these periods; they're like extended vacations. I know eventually I will read or hear that a woman has been assaulted somewhere near where I live or I will be sexually harassed. My old fear will be rekindled, although it is muted these days. Still, I hold out for the possibility of full recovery and wait on society for the safe environment we all need and deserve.

WHY DO WOMEN HAVE
SEXUAL FANTASIES OF RAPE?

The United Nations describes violence against women as a "pandemic in diverse forms."[1] Thirty-five percent of women worldwide have experienced sexual and/or physical violence, often in intimate relationships. In some nations, an unimaginable 70 percent of women have suffered sexual and/or physical violence in intimate relationships.[2] In every country in the world, the threat of violence is one that women must adapt to rather than overcome.

The possibility of sexual violence alters all aspects of women's lives. It impacts how we navigate public spaces, with half of all women in the United States never using public transportation after dark due to fear of rape. Sexual violence also impacts how we navigate relationships, as many are haunted by memories of sexual or intimate partner violence.[3] The threat of sexual violence also impacts how we navigate our inner lives and sexual desires, including how we fantasize about sex.

In what follows, I hypothesize about the impact of sexual violence on women's sexuality. I consider two phenomena: 1) the large percentage of women who have sexual fantasies of rape, and 2) the fragmentation between physiologic arousal and subjective arousal thought to be common to the majority, if not all women. I hypothesize that sexual fantasies of rape are an outcome of living in societies in which sexual violence impacts a significant minority of women (and in some places, a majority) and has since at least the advent of civilization. I consider sexual violence against women to be what epigenetic researchers call a *legacy trauma*, a wide-scale trauma, such as the Holocaust, the effects of which continue to impact future generations physiologically, psychologically, and culturally. But since sexual violence against women continues, often in isolation, the effects of this legacy trauma may include unusual warnings to the danger. I believe sexual fantasies of rape may be such a warning and method for managing the fear caused by the ever-present threat of sexual violence.

Looking at Female Sexuality through a Trauma Lens

Sexual fantasies of rape are relatively common. One 2009 study of 355 female undergraduates that used a fantasy checklist based on criteria for the legal definition of rape in the United States discovered that 62 percent of study participants had sexual fantasies of rape.[4] Other studies of sexual fantasies discovered between 31 and 57 percent of the female participants had such fantasies.[5]

Another commonality in women, one that seems nearly universal, is the splitting of subjective arousal from physiologic arousal. Psychologist Meredith Chivers studied this by assessing genital responses to sexual imagery and then comparing this result to what women said aroused them.[6] By measuring genital blood flow when women looked at potentially arousing imagery, Chivers discovered little agreement between what women said aroused them and what their bodies registered as arousing.

Regardless of sexual orientation, or women's subjective statements about what they found arousing, women in Chivers' studies experienced genital arousal to almost every sexual image they were shown. Women registered physiologic arousal when looking at images of men with women, women with women, men with men, a woman exercising, and bonobo chimps mating. No fewer than 130 scientific studies have confirmed this separation between women's minds and bodies.[7]

Chivers theorized the prevalence of rape plays a central role in the divide between subjective and physiologic arousal in women. Women who experience physiologic arousal when sexually threatened produce genital lubrication and thus are less likely to be physically injured by aggressive penetration. She theorizes that arousal during sexual violence likely evolved:

> To reduce discomfort, and the possibility of injury, during vaginal penetration.... Ancestral women who did not show an automatic vaginal response to sexual cues may have been more likely to experience injuries during unwanted vaginal penetration that resulted in illness, infertility or even death, and thus would be less likely to have passed on this trait to their offspring.[8]

Indeed, sexual arousal, even orgasm, is not uncommon during rape. However, surviving the threat of sexual violence involves more than ensuring the body's integrity.

To understand the fragmentation between subjective and physiologic arousal, we need to understand how *both* mind and body attempt to survive the threat of sexual violence and the fragmentation it causes. In the case of the mind, fantasies can play a central role in surviving trauma. Like dreams and night-mares, fantasies are often repositories of experiences that seek integration, if not resolution. Like the body's lubrication, sexual fantasies of rape may serve to protect a mind that must inhabit a world in which sexual violence is a ubiquitous threat and denial or dissociation of this threat is necessary for keeping potentially debilitating fear at bay. This point is best under-stood by looking at women's sexuality through the lens of trauma.

Splitting between mind and body, sometimes called *disso-ciative splitting*, is a common response to traumatic experiences and chronically traumatic conditions. Through a complex chain of events triggered by overwhelming emotions and body sensations, the mind can escape what the body must endure. In extreme cases, this can involve feeling outside one's body.

During dissociation, the body releases endorphins, the body's natural opioid, which reduces pain.[9] This unconscious and automatic reaction increases survival but also the likeli-hood of dissociation occurring in future traumatic conditions or when triggered by reminders of past traumatic events. I want to suggest that, especially in women, the fragmentation between physiologic arousal and subjective arousal is related to dissociation. Furthermore, dissociation is thought to exist on a continuum from very mild occurrences, such as spacing out while driving, to out-of-body experiences during life-threat-ening circumstances, such as rape. On the lower end of the spectrum, the mind is also prone to fantasizing.

When the Best Defense is Submission

There are at least six basic defense responses: fighting, fleeing, freezing, submission, pleasing/appeasing the aggressor, and attachment crying or calling out for help. Theoretically, these defenses are available to all of us anytime we experience a threat. However, social conditioning, personal temperament, and personal history influence which defense responses are activated.

The most common defenses available to women faced with sexual assault are submission, pleasing/appeasing, and freezing. In part, this is due to being generally physically weaker than the assailant and/or dependent on him (e.g., in cases of intimate partner violence or childhood sexual abuse). Women also submit to gender-based violence because they have been inculcated to cultures of violence (and thus perceive violence as normal or inescapable) or fear alienation or abandonment if they resist or speak out.

Submission increases the likelihood of dissociation and the tendency to mentally escape overwhelming emotional and physiologic arousal that the body cannot escape.[10] However, submission, along with pleasing/appeasing and freezing, can be considered last-ditch efforts at defense, taken only when evading harm by fighting, fleeing, or seeking help are not perceived as options.[11] Although submission, pleasing/appeasing, and freezing may optimize survival in certain conditions, they are more likely activated when the other defense responses are not viable options or are truncated by the overwhelming nature of the threat.

Submission and dissociation may facilitate survival, but they also contribute to the likelihood of sexual fantasies of rape. In 1973, Nancy Friday published *My Secret Garden*, a collection of women's sexual fantasies.[12] One of her interviewees, Johanna, had been raped at knife point while living alone in Mexico City. After the assault, Johanna's sexual fantasies compulsively focused on the trauma. Johanna remarked, "You could say that my inner sexual life still revolves around the rape."

For women with histories of sexual violence, sexual fantasies stemming from an assault can become an inescapable aspect of their sexuality—sometimes triggered by physiological arousal, sometimes used to facilitate orgasm. For survivors of sexual violence, these fantasies can cause guilt and self-loathing. Sexual fantasies of a rape are a private validation of both the perpetrator's and societal attitudes that the victim "wanted it." Such fantasies can also inhibit sexual intimacy. This was the case for Johanna. "It's no good when I'm in bed with Charles [her partner], telling myself that I love him and that I hate that other strange man.... It just kills whatever erotic feelings I have."

When something traumatic happens, memories of what occurred are fragmented due to the overwhelming nature of the experience. These fragmented memories seek integration with non-traumatized aspects of the self. In fact, recovery from trauma, if not mental health in general, can be thought of as the capacity for integrating all aspects of experience plus the ability to emotionally regulate when distressed.[13] For women with sexual trauma, fantasies of the rape may be unconscious attempts to integrate memories of sexual violence into their larger narrative while also managing fear.

Epigenetic Transmission of Dissociation

Current research on the epigenetic transmission of traumatic stress has shown traumas like rape irrevocably change women, both psychologically and physiologically, even when they go on to recover. Since the 1970s, genetic researchers have known of the existence of methyl groups, organic elements that "tell" DNA which genes to transcribe as a result of environmental feedback. Referred to as *epigenetic tags,* the presence of methyl groups confirms to some degree Lamarckian evolutionary theory and the idea that changes an organism undergoes during its lifetime can be inherited by its offspring. Whereas DNA, the fundamental building blocks of life, remains unaltered across the lifespan, how genetic code is interpreted is changed by traumatic events and conditions, recalibrating basic physiologic systems in enduring ways.

Rachel Yehuda, director of the Traumatic Stress Studies Division at Mount Sinai School of Medicine, studied epigenetic change in children of Holocaust survivors.[14] These children often showed similar signs of traumatic stress as their parents, who had lived in concentration camps, despite the children's relative safety in the suburbs of Cleveland, Ohio. According to Dr. Yehuda's research, the children of Holocaust survivors generally showed difficulty with separation, higher levels of vulnerability, and a greater likelihood of developing posttraumatic stress disorder if exposed to a traumatic event. Thus, the children of Holocaust survivors "inherited" some of their parents' orientation toward survival in concentration camps, along with the effects of the traumas they suffered.

Epigenetics may also explain why defenses such as submission, pleasing/appeasing, and freezing become normative responses to sexual violence, as well as habitually dissociating in intimate encounters, thus increasing the likelihood over generations that physiologic and subjective arousal become fragmented. Although dissociation has not been studied from the perspective of epigenetics (as far as I know), research has shown that children whose caregivers use dissociation as a defense response are more likely to dissociate in response to overwhelming stimuli they experience in their lives.[15]

Do Sexual Fantasies of Rape Optimize Survival?

Dreams and fantasies seem a likely avenue for epigenetic transmission of defenses against traumas, especially so-called "legacy" traumas that impact an entire population. Dreams are evolutionarily adaptive. Much like the body's virtual reality, dreams are opportunities to rehearse behavioral strategies that optimize survival.

Irrespective of culture, people experience dreams in four general categories, all related to survival. These categories include feeding, fighting, fleeing, and fornication. As Jungian analyst Anthony Stevens put it, "[Dreams] enable the animal to respond appropriately to food, threat, attack, and sexual encounters even before the gustatory, threatening, erotic stimuli are encountered."[16] Dreams are one way we learn how to react to encounters that have been crucial to the survival of our species. Fantasies may also function like dreams, especially when common to a significant portion of the population.

Given the threat of gender-based violence to women and the stigma of survivors of rape and and other forms of sexual abuse, it is important to consider how fear of these pervasive threats has been managed over millennia, and what adaptations have resulted that increased the likelihood of survival. How do women learn ways to protect themselves and their children from sexual violence when there is little discussion of these topics? The answer may be found in our imaginations.

Carl Jung wrote that dreams, "...are the language used in the lifelong dialogue proceeding nightly between the ego and the unconscious: they are the means by which the individual becomes psychically related to the life cycle of the species."[17] For women, especially in the first decades of our lives, we must contend with the pervasive threat of rape and other forms of sexual abuse. Sexual fantasies of rape may be one way to come to terms with this threat while remaining a sexual being. This may be why sexual fantasies of rape are more common in women who are sexually active.

The taboo that for centuries has surrounded speaking about sexual violence has limited opportunities for creating strategies for self-protection. Instead, through sexual fantasies of rape, there is an opportunity to practice dissociating fear while remaining sexually aroused. For some women, these fantasies may feel empowering. Susie Bright who described using sexual fantasies to overcome an attempted assault, wrote, "You see the difference between your real life anxieties and limitations versus your potential to go to any extreme in fantasy. Now *that* is empowering."[18]

Collectively, women have had to adapt to societies in which sexual violence can happen to any woman at any time, even (or especially) in her most intimate relationships. This has consequences for all aspects of ourselves—our bodies, thoughts, emotions, and even our fantasies. Rather than a release of inhibitions as some researchers suggest, sexual fantasies of rape reduce the stress caused by societies in which violence against women is ubiquitous.

There are parallels between how dreams optimize survival and how the body attempts to overcome a traumatic event. Like dreams, the body orients toward optimizing best outcomes. During a traumatic event, the body registers the sensations and muscle movements of what the body wanted to do—the movements that might lead to fighting off the attacker, running away, or crying out for help. As mentioned earlier, Pierre Janet, a pioneer of trauma-focused treatment, called the movements and actions the body wanted to take *acts of triumph*—what would have led to a different history, one that involved facing down or escaping the threat. The acts of triumph that would have led to escape or defense are split from awareness, or dissociated, along with unintegrated thoughts, sensations, emotions, and images associated with the actual traumatic event.

As a trauma-focused psychotherapist, I helped women identify acts of triumph that would have led to their preferred outcome—such as fighting off rape, escaping childhood sexual abuse, and leaving a batterer. By integrating the split-off defense responses within a state of emotional regulation, they gained a sense of mastery over their fear and decreased dependency on dissociation. However, for some survivors of sexual violence, the inability to express the desired act of triumph correlates with an increased fantasy life and nightmares. The imaginal space becomes overrun, as it were, with memories, perceptions, and imagined scenarios seeking integration.

Sexual fantasies of rape are also efforts to optimize survival and manage dissociated fear. Like dreams, they suggest what helped our ancestors survive sexual violence. Most often, women and girls submit to sexual abuse because submission has likely led to the survival of more women across history than fighting, calling out for help, or even running from abusers. This is the nature of legacy traumas: having to endure the unimaginable.

Sexual fantasies of rape are in the woman's control. In her mind, she can determine the nature of the threat and decide who the perpetrator is and how she responds and feels—even replacing fear with desire. Perhaps this is how sexual fantasies of rape optimize survival of the subjective sense of self, setting the foundation for habituating the mind to threats the body cannot escape.

I don't think sexual fantasies of rape are empowering. More likely, they keep women inculcated in cultures of violence. Self-defense and cultures of equality are better solutions. As political philosopher Iris Young wrote, "We have to learn to feel entitled to occupy space, to defend ourselves."[19] I believe that when we habitually do so, in a world where gender-based violence is an aberration rather than a norm, women will experience the joy of individual and collective acts of triumph, and we'll see a lot fewer women aroused by sexual fantasies of rape.

INTERGENERATIONAL TRANSMISSION OF RECOVERY

Shakespeare's first tragedy, *Titus Andronicus* (c. 1590), tells a story of rape used as revenge. In the play, the Roman general Titus murders the son of Queen Tamora. In turn, Queen Tamora's two remaining sons avenge their brother's death by raping Titus's daughter, Lavinia, and then mutilating her, cutting off her tongue and hands to keep her from testifying against them.

In some parts of the world today, just as in Shakespeare's story, rape is less an injury to the woman than an indignity suffered by her husband, father, or brothers. In fact, *rape* derives from the Latin *raptus*, meaning *theft of property*.[1] In their examination of *Titus Andronicus*, researchers Kaitlyn Regehr and Cheryl Regehr noted in early productions, "Titus and not Lavinia is the victim of the crime, it is his suffering that is important."[2] Like many survivors of rape, Lavinia is silenced by both perpetrators and prevailing mores. Yet Regehr and Regehr also observed how modern discourse and trauma-based treatment of survivors of sexual violence radically altered perceptions of rape survivors in ways that would also change how the story of Lavinia's rape was told.

Regehr and Regehr contrasted Jane Howell's 1985 BBC

production of *Titus Andronicus*, which strayed little from Shake-speare's original text, with Julie Taymor's 1999 film, which adapted the play to a modern context. Regehr and Regehr iden-tified an important revision in the portrayal of Lavinia between these two films: she shifted from silent victim in Howell's production to active agent of her own recovery in Taymor's film. They also observed that the wider cultural discourse on rape radically shifted during this period.

Like Shakespeare's original *Titus Andronicus*, Howell's 1985 film silenced Lavinia and the horror surrounding her victimiza-tion. At the time of Howell's production, the mental health field and advocacy groups were beginning to create opportunities for survivors to address their traumas, but the larger public still ignored the ravaged lives of rape survivors. Fourteen years later —a speck of time given the many millennia survivors have been silenced—Taymor's *Titus Andronicus* highlighted Lavinia's inner terror and her efforts at recovery, mirroring the widening awareness of the tragic effects of rape and the courage displayed through efforts to heal.

In the 1980s, rape was categorized for the first time as a trau-matic experience, and reactions to rape were medicalized as symptoms of PTSD. Rather than being scorned or silenced, rape survivors were increasingly seen as profoundly injured and needing support. By the 1990s, PTSD gained wider recog-nition as a response to trauma requiring professional interven-tion. As Regehr and Regehr pointed out, Taymor's version of *Titus Andronicus* was distributed in 1999, seven years after Judith Herman's landmark *Trauma and Recovery*,[3] which not only unflinchingly examined the inequities in power that make traumas like rape possible but also outlined what it takes to recover.

Using non-pathologizing discourse, Herman generalized the consequences of trauma so that experiences as varying as rape, war, domestic violence, and childhood abuse were seen as having similar effects. *Trauma and Recovery* also outlined generalizable stages of trauma treatment, which today remain standard of care. Not only could rape be discussed, but it could be talked about in a language shared by other victims of atrocities, and with hope for recovery.

It can be difficult to acknowledge victimization when we don't know what to say or doubt anything can be done to alleviate suffering. The discourse of *Trauma and Recovery*, and the trauma model in general, gave a way to talk about the consequences of rape with hope that the "ending" might turn out differently for survivors than in past generations. It is still true most people don't want to hear stories of rape. Much like *Titus Andronicus*, which Victorian audiences found excessively gruesome, rape narratives can be deeply disturbing. However, when we believe in the possibility of recovery, a new and different story can be told, one focused on overcoming rather than victimhood.

In the recent focus on the intergenerational transmission of trauma, the enduring effects of recovery work are often overlooked. Instead, many of us have focused on epigenetic reactions to traumatic events that irrevocably change people on a physiological level. This supports what many people say about themselves after they have experienced a traumatic event: "I'm different now. I'm not the person I used to be." A similar, albeit more hopeful, change also emerges with recovery. People still say, "I've changed," but they also observe, "The trauma is behind me now." Unlike the traumatic event, which upends life in an instant, recovery takes time and commitment, but the effects are also enduring—for survivors, their families, their communities, and society.

The transition from Howell's to Taymor's version of *Titus Andronicus* might be thought of as part of an epigenetics of resilience in the making, one based on a willingness to witness the suffering of others, as well as examine our own traumatic wounds and seek their resolution. Perhaps more than time, it is the capacity to transform how we story trauma that heals individuals and generations.

SOCIETY AND TRAUMA

A SKETCH OF SOCIETAL-BASED OBSTACLES TO TRANSFORMATION AFTER TRAUMA

In the preface to his book *The Order of Things*, Michel Foucault shared the following excerpt from an ancient Chinese encyclopedia:

> Animals are divided into: (a) belonging to the Emperor, (b) embalmed, (c) tame, (d) sucking pigs, (e) sirens, (f) fabulous, (g) stray dogs, (h) included in the present classification, (i) frenzied, (j) innumerable, (k) drawn with a very fine camel hair brush, (l) *et cetera*, (m) having just broken the water pitcher, (n) that from a long way off look like flies.[1]

With this list, Foucault juxtaposed aspects of Western thought typically taken for granted. A modern Western lexicographer avoids referencing the subjective ("fabulous") and personal ("belonging to the Emperor"). Instead, every entry has the stamp of the scientific method: the capacity to be replicated by trained minds according to shared rules for experimentation and classification.

When Western taxonomy is contrasted with the ancient Chinese approach to ordering the world, it's easier to identify how the Western style of thinking diminishes the role of emotions and imagination for how we understand the nature of things. James Hillman argued the West lost its soul when it ignored the significance of the *imaginal* for human societies and psyches. As noted in a previous essay, according to Hillman, the soul is "the imaginative possibility in our natures, the experiencing through reflective speculation, dream, image, and *fantasy*"—what science, after the Enlightenment, came to depict as the wellspring of irrationality and madness.[2] Yet, if the nearly worldwide obsession with the internet, smartphones, online gaming, and pornography is any indication, it's the imaginal and other *non-rational* aspects of experience that preoccupy many of us, at times to the point of obsession, if not addiction.

Attention to the imaginal aspects of psyche and society is a needed corrective for the current emphasis on rationality at the root of unimaginative policies, bureaucracies, and institutions, which, despite their influence, have failed to curb the proliferation of risk, environmental degradation, and vast inequities in access to resources.

To support this point, I look briefly at two ruptures in human history: the Upper Paleolithic, around 40,000 years ago, when the first cultures began to flourish, and more recently when the Enlightenment radically changed societies, humanity's relationship to nature, and conceptions of personhood. The thread I see joining these two periods is *dissociation*, a basic physiological defense against the overwhelming effects of traumatic events. Dissociation appears to have coevolved with the human capacity for mythic imagination. I hope to convince you that the traumatic reactions we often attempt to deny, or escape, are the very sources of transformation that we desperately need when trying to envision new societies or ways to repair current conditions.

The Imaginal and Trauma

When trauma alters the course of development—whether an individual or collective trauma—the imagination and emotions are usually greater causal agents than thought or reason. This has to do with how the human body has evolved to deal with trauma. When the body mobilizes in response to a perceived threat, recollections of what happened may fail to consolidate into retrievable, long-term memories. Nevertheless, enough may be remembered to tell the story of what happened and discuss the trauma.

Still, fragments of unconscious body and emotion memories can lead to feeling as if the trauma is happening all over again when encountering stimuli associated with the original traumatic event(s). You *know* the trauma is in the past, but your body and emotions don't. These unconscious memories have not integrated with the larger narrative because areas of the brain necessary for consolidating them were not functioning effectively at the time of the trauma.

During a traumatizing experience, attention narrows to focus on the threat, and blood flow is directed to parts of the body necessary for survival—for instance, large muscle groups that might help with defense or escape. With less blood flow, parts of the brain that might interfere with responding rapidly to threat are attenuated, including two regions that contribute to self-awareness: the *hippocampus*, responsible for consolidating memories, including body and emotion memories, and regions of the *prefrontal cortex*, which contribute a sense of an observing "I" of memories and experiences.

When triggered by traumatic reminders, trauma survivors again enter the experience of *not* thinking—or more accurately, *lack of* intentional and reflective awareness. Fragments of memory that weren't consolidated during the trauma resurface. This is witnessed in intrusive imagery, fantasies, flashbacks, and nightmares. These imaginal states can be thought of as unconscious attempts at integration. They compensate for the lack of a coherent narrative of the traumatic event. When transformative, they act as a bridge to posttraumatic growth. However, posttraumatic growth may depend on grieving what has been lost, including the sense of security and worldview that dominated before the trauma.

Movement between so-called rational thought and the imaginal happens unconsciously and automatically. Carl G. Jung focused on the interrelationship between these two distinct yet intertwined ways of knowing, which he referred to as "direct" and "indirect" thinking and associated with consciousness and unconsciousness. He wrote:

We have...two kinds of thinking: direct thinking, and dreaming or fantasy-thinking.... The one produces innovations and adaptation, copies reality, and tries to act upon it; the other turns away from reality, sets free subjective tendencies, and, as regards adaptation, is unproductive.[3]

While fantasy-thinking is unproductive, it is a central and necessary part of human experience. Fantasy-thinking, or the imaginal, is the psyche's opportunity to retreat from the external world into a symbolically guided moment that is potentially self-soothing, where we confront unarticulated fears and desires and find creative ways to emerge into different environments by molding them or ourselves to fit our imaginations.

I hypothesize we stagnate, as individuals and collectives, when these two modes of awareness function as distinct spheres, thus failing to produce opportunities for meaningful transformation. This can happen when, after traumatizing experiences or conditions, a person is overwhelmed by the contents of the imaginal, such as flashbacks, and attempts to avoid engaging constructively with the imaginal. Alternatively, fantasies can become a means of escape, and the imaginal is sought for self-soothing rather than growth and meaning-making. Both avoiding and submerging in the imaginal may be common after trauma, for at least a while, and part of recuperation. However, when prolonged, escaping through the imaginal, or numbing to its contents, likely leads to becoming stuck in posttraumatic stress reactions and reduces the resilience necessary for transformation and meaningful change.

Dissociation and Society

The use of the imaginal to deal with trauma seems to be an evolved capacity that coincides with the evolution of dissociation. Understanding this connection requires looking at how power and the threat of social alienation impact psyche and society.

Dissociation is thought to have originated as a property of all mammals and likely evolved with other defense reactions, such as freezing in the face of threat and tonic immobility ("feigned death"), central defenses for surviving predatory attacks.[4] However, for social animals, alienation can feel as precarious as being attacked by a predator. As human dependency on the social group increased throughout our species' evolution, dissociation may have developed to protect against social-based threats, along with the anxiety that comes with the potential loss of social connection.

According to psychiatrist Horacio Fabrega, dissociation also evolved to include psychopathological states in response to increased social dependency. He speculated this occurred during the Upper Paleolithic Era over 40,000 years ago, when artistic expression, protolanguages, and protocultures began to flourish throughout the world. Why would this be the case? Why would the imaginal and dissociation coevolve, and to include psychopathological states, no less? To make sense of this connection, Fabrega looked at two cultural practices synonymous with the Western expression of dissociation: *trance* and *possession*.

According to Fabrega, trance and possession are ritualized forms of dissociation that *communicate* a person's social-related distress, including the threat of social alienation caused by inequities in power. Fabrega wrote:

> States of dissociation provided inner spaces or psychological arenas in which those stresses tied to psychopathology could be worked out by channeling psychological experience in a positive, conflict-alleviating direction and by producing scenarios of behavior that communicated the distress and played out in ways that were safe and culturally understandable, and capable of eliciting sympathy and support.[5]

Supporting Fabrega's ideas, psychologist Peter Levine observed that shamans in indigenous cultures often treat trance and possession where they also perceive "illness and trauma as a problem for the entire community."[6] Shamanism in many nature-based communities has been a vital method for reuniting members of the group when social conflicts threaten cohesiveness.[7]

Thus, dissociation is more than a physiological defense mechanism. It is also an opportunity for creating a new sense of self and adapting to social dynamics, if not challenging those dynamics. Enacting and creatively expressing dissociated contents of the imaginal potentially reduces feelings of overwhelm characteristic of traumatic stress. Expressing these imaginal aspects of the psyche in socially sanctioned ways may also communicate a need for "gentler" opportunities for reintegrating into society. Thus, dissociation can also be a plea to the social world for concessions and changes that increase adaptation for vulnerable members of society.

But what happens when evidence of trauma fails to mobilize support or contribute to transformation? I believe *learned helplessness* is a likely outcome, along with apathy and numbing, which can lead to retreat in fantasy worlds or avoidance of the imaginal all together, along with unhealthy and misdirected expression of emotions. Furthermore, when we can't heal from a traumatic event, we are more likely to live in fear of its recurrence or other forms of victimization. Thus, there is a need for communal support after trauma to feel safer and more resilient.

Furthermore, when traumatic reactions do not act as catalysts and instead become habituated responses, there is often a failure to grieve what has been lost due to the traumatic event, such as feelings of safety, a sense of innocence, or the mental, physical, or environmental conditions that preexisted the trauma. Lack of opportunities to grieve also contributes to seeking the imaginal as a method of escape or numbing, or, alternatively, complete avoidance of the imaginal.

Grief is a response to trauma seen in both individuals and societies. Jungian analyst Greg Mogenson observed, "The mourning of losses and the making of culture are synonymous activities."[8] I hypothesize that if a culture or society fails to create conditions in which individuals' traumas can be grieved and transformed within a community setting, the other option is to organize the culture or society in ways that ensure the propagation of traumatic defenses. This point brings me to another historical rupture, the Enlightenment, which seems to have dissociated the inevitability and centrality of grief—as well as the imaginal—for collective and individual growth following trauma.

The Enlightenment and Dependency on Dissociation

The Enlightenment promised knowledge of the inscrutable, predictions for the future, and a method for controlling nature, including human nature and the scourges caused by vast inequities in resources, power, and status. The Enlightenment also vowed to reduce suffering for those who lived rational lives. Such were some of the stated advantages of Enlightenment ideology.

However, the Enlightenment also initiated an epoch distinguished by it tolerance, if not manipulation, of traumatic stress. This shadow side of the Enlightenment was necessary for the Industrial Revolution, which caused loss of community and led to slavery and colonial oppression around the world. This was a period of upheaval and trauma, yet there was little space or time for grieving. As individuals and collectives, we are weakened by conditions that obstruct our need to mourn losses. When we are weak, we are easier to manipulate and more readily submit to deplorable conditions.

Furthermore, when we lack opportunities to mourn, we are at greater risk of developing *complicated grief*. Instead of mourning, we try to avoid the emotions of grief, such as sorrow, longing, and emptiness, which are partially expressed by fantasies, dreams, nightmares, memories, and reveries—that is, the imaginal aspects of psyche. When not dealt with, these emotions can begin to feel as if they would be too overwhelming to even acknowledge. The same is true of the associated reveries, fantasies, and other imaginal contents that can begin to feel intrusive, much like being triggered by traumatic reminders. Like trauma, with complicated grief, we respond to loss as if stuck in time. The deceased is "too dead." By avoiding the emotions of grief, we fail to integrate memories of the deceased with our new way of being in a world forever changed by their death.

Complicated grief seems to occur on the group level and may contribute to religious fanaticism, reactionary politics, and the inability to stop overconsumption. When we lack communities to support the grieving of losses, we are more susceptible to seeking collective ways to defend against being overwhelmed by grief-related emotions and imaginal contents of our minds. We are at risk of using ideologies to defend against the fear of being engulfed by grief.

An example of how the Industrial Revolution became organized around the propagation of traumatic defenses is found in historian Danial Lord Smail's book, *On Deep History and the Brain*. Smail argued capitalism exploits the body's survival responses (e.g., freezing, fighting, fleeing, and submission) by creating conditions of psychological domination *and* providing relief from feelings of powerlessness that capitalism and social hierarchies engender.[9] According to Smail, capitalism generates stress through its unpredictability and hierarchical power structures, but it also alleviates stress by producing an economy organized around the production and circulation of addictive substances and practices.

Smail noted that, from its inception in the 17th and 18th centuries, global capitalism has been organized around creating and feeding addictions. The first imports to Europe from Africa, the Arab World, and the Americas were coffee, sugar, chocolate, tobacco and "spirits"—all mood-altering substances. During this time, the term "addiction" gained its modern meaning as a self-inflicted behavior rather than the state of being indebted to another (serfdom), which previously distinguished the addict. With this shift in understanding of addiction also came a new way of responding to inequality and oppression—away from a focus on altering external forms of control to a focus on internal ways of responding to dominance by self-medicating.

Today the use of addictive substances and activities to regulate stress is so common it is difficult to demarcate between what counts as recreational use of substances and what constitutes lifestyle maintenance. Addictions are a widespread way of managing feelings of agitation and overwhelm, which, for many, are habitual responses to the pressures of depending on an unpredictable economy. Typically, when we anticipate danger, the body either becomes so activated that it enters a state of extreme agitation (*hyperarousal*) or moves toward a state of emotional shutdown (*hypoarousal*). Addictive substances and activities are now everyday methods for escaping such states— a role spirituality has also served, especially in the pre-industrial world.

By perpetuating traumatic defenses, there may also be greater likelihood that the imaginal is used as a state of escape. Thus, the significance of the imaginal for transformation after trauma and living an integrated life is ignored or, more likely, never learned.

Descartes's Fateful Night

I trace the overreliance on dissociation, traumatic defenses, and complicated grief back to René Descartes, noted architect of the Enlightenment and champion of the human capacity for reason.[10] Although much is made of that fateful night when he sat by a glowing fire and heard reason assert itself—*I think, therefore I am*—it was madness that set the stage for his obsession with rationality.

Descartes's famous *Discourse on the Method* emerged from several sleepless nights during which he resisted the unconscious pull of his nightmares, a time remembered as "near madness."[11] Descartes was a soldier at the time—a freelance fighter in the Duke of Bavaria's army during the Thirty Years War. Because of his unusual genius, he felt out of place among his fellow soldiers, perhaps even alienated.

War, as we know, is traumatic. Like all traumas, it leaves traces of its horrors in the imaginal, including flashbacks and nightmares. It was during a period of being overwhelmed by the imaginal, perhaps even while self-soothing the psychological wounds of war, that Descartes discovered the foundations of his method.

While experiencing a delusional state induced by fear and sleeplessness, Descartes had the dream that relieved him of his near madness. In this dream, Descartes claimed he was visited by "the Spirit of Truth, who presented him with books containing all the knowledge in the world."[12] Thus, Descartes's method, although meant to stage a break with a superstitious world, was initiated much the way self and cultural change have occurred after trauma for millennia: through dissociative retreat into the imaginal.

Descartes meant to create a psychotherapeutic method, yet the cure omitted the significance of the imaginal for self and cultural change and bypassed grief for a lost world. Descartes's method, along with the Enlightenment, initiated a split between the imaginal and rational thought and denied the significance of trauma and its resolution for the making of cultures. As a result, the imaginal and dissociation have also changed. Rather than catalysts for personal and collective growth, our imaginal worlds are often habitual reprieves from vacillating between feeling overwhelmed and emotionally shutting down. Granted, at least in dissociated, imaginal worlds, the possibility of escape from suffering exists. However, prolonged escapism is a serious threat to psychological integration and collective transformation.

Looking Forward

Perhaps all lasting changes in human history are marked by denial or sublimation of one way of being to make space for alternative societies and their corresponding beliefs and behaviors. This was certainly the case with the emergence of modernity. The elevation of rationality, equality, and basic human rights was an honorable goal in a world overrun with superstition and aristocratic power grabs. Nevertheless, in the rush to revolutionize the world, the significance of the imaginal for transformation after trauma was lost, along with the centrality of the collective for resolving grief through mourning.

It seems habitual these days, if not "natural," to depend on the imagination as a dissociated experience where one can escape reality. For some, this means using the imaginal to exist within conditions of oppression, dominance, or abuse (or other ongoing traumatic conditions) without outlets to safely address abuses such as trance and possession that are found in some non-Western cultures. Because conditions of abuse and oppression foster alienation, there is the added risk of losing one of the potentially transformative aspects of human groups: the opportunity to grieve and grow together.

To find our way back to more integrated selves and collectives, we must be willing to learn to grieve collectively again and rely on each other when overcoming loss and trauma. The imaginal plays a central role in this process, especially when expressed through art, music, dance, and storytelling. But rather than an endpoint, these creative expressions are the integrative bridge across the liminal in our psyches and the alienation in our communities, ways we begin to let go of what no longer buoys humanity and discover what actually uplifts us.

INTRODUCING THE COMMUNAL RESPONSE TO TRAUMA INDEX (CRTI)

The Great Recession and, more recently, the economic fallout caused by the Covid-19 pandemic, much like financial disasters before them, take their toll on bodies and psyches as much as they do on bank accounts and lifestyles. Suicides, family violence, stress-related diseases, and mental disorders increase in response to most economic crises. For many, the hardships continue long after markets settle.

Even during the best of times, financial inequality is stressful. For decades, researchers have documented the physical stress caused by status hierarchies.[1] Irrespective of how secure a person's circumstances, a subjective interpretation of oneself as having low social status contributes to stress-related diseases. A person's *perceived* socioeconomic status is a good predictor of cardiovascular disease, obesity, and the level of stress hormones circulating in the body. Consequently, a poor Appalachian miner in the affluent United States experiences more status-related stress than a relatively poorer member of a community in rural Africa, where the majority endure the same level of financial hardship. Furthermore, countries with the highest levels of economic inequality have the greatest number of people with stress-related diseases.

Capitalism's capricious economic cycles can also raise anxiety to the level of traumatic stress. The body responds to threats with agitated alertness, especially when coupled with the belief that taking action is necessary to avoid being hurt. In trauma lingo, we refer to this as a state of *hypervigilance*, or the need to continually scan the environment for the possibility that past threats will reemerge and again endanger one's survival. For many, living in a capitalistic and globalized economy requires hypervigilance, anticipating the possibility of job loss and decreasing funds, if not the decimation of entire market sectors and local economies.

For the most financially precarious (an ever-widening sector of the population), capitalism creates a state similar to the psychological domination that can occur when people are held in captivity. Psychological domination is more likely when 1) the threat is unpredictable and 2) there are periods of relative safety amid the chaos and abuse. Psychologist Judith Herman observed, "The ultimate effect of [psychological domination] is to convince the victim that the perpetrator is omnipotent, that resistance is futile, and that her life depends upon winning his indulgence through absolute compliance."[2] Certainly, the psychological impact of capitalism fails to reach the severity of a person whose basic right to freedom from harm is taken away. Rather, my argument is that capitalism is more precarious than reliable, creating conditions that are often inhumane and lead to traumatic stress. Therefore, we should question whether the gross domestic product (GDP) is a detrimental way to measure our country's well-being. But what should take its place?

For some time, the small Buddhist nation of Bhutan has preferred gross national happiness (GNH) as an indicator of progress—a reflection of the culture's preference for emotional well-being over the production of goods and services. In the US, the American Human Development Project identified several markers of well-being to create a new way of measuring our country's worth, which they call the Human Development Index (HDI). The HDI reveals dramatically different levels of well-being across the US, depending on such factors as region, gender, and cultural group. Furthermore, the study's authors, Sarah Burd-Sharps and Kristen Lewis, noted that measures of HDI were inseparable from the ability to survive crises: "The capabilities a person has going into a crisis—ranging from a financial downturn to a man-made or natural disaster— strongly determine how fast he or she can bounce back."[3] "Capabilities" include a person's health, education, and income. Yet, I believe, these resources are a measure of recovery because our society is more alienated than united, and disasters have become measures more of individual resilience than community cohesiveness.

I propose adding another measure of well-being: the *Communal Response to Trauma Index (CRTI)*, which would measure a community's response to disasters, crises, and other traumatic upheavals, such as sending young people to war. The CRTI would assess the resources communities commit to restoring hope and integrity of all its members after traumatic experiences. This could include evaluating:

- *Psychological openness to the impact of traumatic events.* As Herman observed, "Repression, dissociation and denial are phenomena of social as well as individual consciousness."[4] The CRTI would measure a community's commitment to facilitating open communication about traumatic events rather than silencing or ignoring their effects, which contributes to addiction, dissociation, projection, and shame.
- *Investment in storytelling, including writing, music, painting/drawing, and producing plays/movies that model communal responses to trauma.* The focus would also include countering how trauma often leaves us

without words or ways to story what happened, which, in turn, increases the likelihood of suffering in isolation.

- *The creation of public spaces devoted to healing trauma's effects.* These spaces would transcend cultural groups, age, gender, sexual orientation, income, education, and all other measures of difference. These spaces would support healing through dialogue, community activities, and self-expression, witnessing both trauma's effects as well as the healing capacity of the human spirit. Historically, places of worship and clinics have served this function. Yet, given the dramatic increase in crises and disasters, no longer can healing trauma be primarily a responsibility of one or two sectors of society.

The best measure of a country's worth may be its ability to protect citizens from being overwhelmed by stressful experiences. Indeed, the belief that uniting the colonies would provide such protection contributed to the creation of the United States of America. Given traumas such as environmental disasters, the impact of war on veterans and their families, the pervasiveness of social ills, such as domestic violence, rape, racism, and extreme poverty (to name just a few of our personal and collective traumas), only the most optimistic believe in the capacity of individuals to deal on their own with overwhelming stressful experiences. Instead, we should hope for a return to a sense that we are the *United* States of America. This may require an awareness of how traumatic our history has been—as well as our collective need to heal from trauma, which measures like the GDP ignore.

ALEXITHYMIA, EMOTIONAL NEGLECT, AND CAPITALISM: ARE THEY RELATED?

Alexithymia. Now that's quite the word. Derived from the ancient Greek, it means *without words for emotions,* thus difficulty recognizing and naming feelings. Since emotions are central to understanding oneself and others, not being able to discern what you feel can cause distress, agitation, and anxiety, along with rocky, unsatisfying relationships. Signs of alexithymia include:

- Difficulty identifying feelings.
- Difficulty finding the correct words to describe feelings.
- Difficulty distinguishing feelings from associated body sensations.
- Restricted imagination, including having few fantasies and very realistic dreams.
- A focus on the external world and information.
- Highly logical thinking.
- Low levels of empathy.

Although alexithymia is often considered a personality trait, it can reach the level of a disorder and become an obstacle to finalizing decisions and making commitments. Alexithymia can occur with Asperger's syndrome and has been identified as a precursor to posttraumatic stress disorder and affective disorders. It is also associated with traumatic events in childhood, such as physical and sexual abuse.

Research conducted by Sabine Aust and colleagues showed that alexithymia might also originate with early emotional neglect that is too mild to cause psychological disorders but strong enough to strain the flow and interpretation of feelings.[1] In their study, Aust and colleagues examined the role of early attachment and emotional regulation for developing alexithymia. Using questionnaires, they assessed early-life stress, emotional functioning, and alexithymia. They discovered the greatest impairment was present when emotional neglect had occurred in childhood. However, their research confirmed that people with alexithymia and histories of emotional neglect could also be psychologically and physically healthy. Finally, their study revealed that some people with alexithymia lack histories of emotional neglect. The latter finding could suggest genetic precursors to alexithymia. Yet, it is also possible there is another underlying cause, such as societal practices that interfere with emotional connection and expression.

At birth, the human brain is only 25 percent developed. The genes that program its developmental trajectory wait for cues from the outside world on how to proceed. Like the responsive dance partner sensing a subtle shift from heel to toe, neural networks and synaptic connections are laid down and pruned back in response to even the most muted nuances of culture, relationships, and sensory data. In a perfect world, genes and the environment find a rhythm that supports optimal adaptation and growth.

However, as neuroscientist David Linden pointed out in his book *The Accidental Mind*, "in the extreme case of environmental deprivation...the effects of the environment become much greater and largely overcome the effects of genes."[2] As an example, Linden relayed what happens when a patch covering an injured infant's eye is left on too long:

> If a baby has an eye closed with a bandage (to treat an infection, for example) and the bandage stays on for a long time, then that baby can be blinded in that eye for life.... The reason for the blindness is not that the eye has ceased to function...but rather that the information from that eye was not present to help retain the appropriate connections in the brain during the critical period for vision.[3]

A similar case could be made for the impact of emotionally neglectful caregivers and cultures: When emotional neglect occurs in childhood, emotional regulation and communication atrophy. Yet, as Aust and colleagues showed, emotional neglect is not the only cause for later difficulties with feelings. I wonder if more "low-level" disturbances in attachment could also lead to reduced emotional capacities.

One possible culprit is the Western style of child-rearing. Few things are as unnatural and engineered as child-rearing in Western cultures, where the need for highly individualistic people dictates what successfully raising a child looks like. To understand the impact of Western child-rearing practices on emotional development, it helps to look at how non-Western cultures raise children. Jean Liedloff conducted ethnographic work with the Yequana Indians of the Amazon Rainforest and wrote about their parenting practices in her book, *The Continuum Concept.*[4] Liedloff developed the continuum concept to describe "natural" ways of raising children that evolved over hundreds of thousands of years when humans primarily lived as hunter-gatherers. According to Liedloff, the Yequana's child-rearing practices respond to innate expectations for the kind of social environment humans evolved to inhabit.

Liedloff identified one of the Yequana parenting practice that differed significantly from child-rearing in the United States: Yequana caregivers continually hold their infants until they develop the need to roam freely. Liedloff believed the Yequana's habit of honoring their children's innate timeline for developing independence contributes to the general sense of well-being seen not only in children but also in adult members of the Yequana tribe. Liedloff argued the Western emphasis on children gaining independence at the earliest possible moment contradicts innate developmental needs, which for thousands, if not millions, of years, centered on fostering healthy attachment, not preternatural independence. Liedloff claimed the West's emphasis on independence leads to emotional suffering for both mother and infant:

> The violent tearing apart of the mother-child continuum, so strongly established during the phases that took place in the womb, may understandably result in depression for the mother, as well as agony for her infant.[5]

If reducing opportunities for physical closeness has such dire consequences, what is the impact of denying or ignoring emotional needs? According to Liedloff, "There are neuroses and insanities to protect the deprived from the brunt of unmeetable reality. There is a numbness that overtakes pain beyond bearing."[6] This numbness, like Linden's eye patch blocking the development of sight, may very well be part of the developmental trajectory toward alexithymia.

What happens when children must behave as individuals too early in their development? For one thing, concerned parents may speak harshly to the naturally curious child on the verge of being harmed, such as when reaching for a hot stove. Conversely, even a good parent risks being permissive to the point of neglect, letting the child do what she pleases if she stays out of trouble, like quietly watching television or streaming on a tablet. There's a double risk here, one obvious and the other imperceptible. The obvious risk is that, when left to their own explorations, children's interests do not necessarily lead to optimal development. When a caregiver continually holds her young child, the child has the advantage of sensing the rhythms of the type of life she will eventually lead, and her experiences will be meaningful and engaging since they relate directly to her future. She will also have the added benefit of associating her actions with feeling close to another person.

A more imperceptible outcome of early independence is the internalization of the critical voice of the well-meaning parent, which, although intended to protect and guide, is potentially pernicious in its invisible influence on the developing child. Depending on the child, the caregiver, and the nature of the criticism, the internalized voice can reduce self-empathy, which could limit internal emotional communication, thereby impacting the development of the *corpus callosum,* the "superhighway" connecting the right and left hemispheres of the brain. The corpus callosum transfers emotional information from the right hemisphere to the left, where associations between language and emotions occur. Reductions in the volume of the corpus callosum have been found in people who suffered severe childhood abuse. Studies also associate a smaller corpus callosum with alexithymia. Like an eye patch that inhibits a child's vision, limited opportunities for developing safe, internal emotional communication through supportive, external attachments might make the corpus callosum more of a goat path than a major thoroughfare.

Capitalism needs winners and losers to keep the system going. It's a fear-based system, one that promises great rewards for those who master the game and abject poverty for those who don't. Individualism is a key trait of capitalism's winners, in part because high levels of individuality seem to dampen the fear capitalism instills. According to psychologist Hazel Markus, in middle-class communities (the supposed winners), people are more likely to see the world as welcoming and seek opportunities to express their individualism, whereas working-class people more often perceive the world as uncertain and protect themselves by fitting in.[7] Markus also claimed that for members of the middle class, individual achievement is a prized experience, whereas being interdependent and part of the community is the greater goal for lower-class people.[8]

Capitalistic societies reward people whose brains and relationship styles adapt to their needs, but not without cost. Increasingly, burnout and the lost capacity for emotional engagement are prices of "success." For some, alexithymia might seem worth the consequences in exchange for financial reward or to ease the emotional toll of the capitalistic grind, but such an attitude ignores that one of the most debilitating consequences of alexithymia is increased anxiety since, without the ability to identify and name feelings, intense emotions can be overwhelming and indiscriminate. To protect themselves from the onslaught, people with alexithymia often build walls around their hearts, and in the process, they limit opportunities for emotional connection with others. There is profound suffering here, too.

Perhaps it's better to acknowledge that alleviating the symptoms of alexithymia is just as important as relieving the symptoms of capitalism, much as Liedloff discovered the cure for mental illness is found in cultures as much as brains. But how do we begin to "cure" capitalism? Perhaps the same way the pain of alexithymia is alleviated: opportunities for safe relationships that honor the complexities of human emotions.

I like to believe that in the well-armored heart of every

person with alexithymia—as well as every industrious, over-focused individualist—is a longing for tenderness and connection. The good news is our brains are forever growing and continually redefining "normal," not only changing us but potentially society as well.

ARE WE HARDWIRED FOR AVOIDANCE?

Humanity seems to have given up on millions of years of evolution, during which we became exquisitely adapted for face-to-face communication through body language, subtle facial expressions, and the prosody of speech. Now most of the world's population use smartphones to keep in touch and create community.

Some of us still long for communicating the old-fashioned way, such as Susan Maushart, who chronicled in *The Winter of Our Disconnect* her family's attempt to live without wireless connections after realizing "it was like real life was an appendage to what everyone was doing. We had stopped making eye contact. I was literally text-messaging them to come to dinner."[1] More than once, I've emailed or called my husband when he was in another room. In the beginning, it felt like the convenience of a walkie-talkie with an internet connection. But then, like Maushart, I began to notice the lack of eye contact not only in personal relationships but public spaces as well.

The seeds for our collective fascination with smartphones may have been planted over five million years ago when our hominin ancestors left diminishing jungles during their epoch of climate change and began living precariously on open savannas with only tall grasses to protect them. In the jungle canopies, they were accustomed to a solitary existence, but in the open grasslands, they were easy prey and had to learn to band together for survival. The sociologist Jonathan H. Turner claimed that modern humans retain these early hominins' propensity for solitary living, despite our species' evolution toward increased social connection and dependency. He wrote:

> At our ape core, we are individualists who chafe against organizational constraint, but we are also an animal that can use a highly attuned emotion system to create social bonds and to sustain tight-knit social structures.[2]

To support his argument, Turner looked to highly ritualized behaviors, which, he argued, dampen the varying degrees of anxiety present in most social interactions. Whether celebrating a holiday, attending a concert, visiting the doctor, going on a first date, or simply meeting a friend for coffee, we scan for social cues that suggest the most adaptive way to behave while also being mindful of who we are as individuals. Turner observed:

> Interaction is always double-edged: we recognize emotional cues that signal associative tendencies, but at the same time we generally seek to avoid interpersonal immersion and, thereby, attempt to sustain autonomy of self and a certain interpersonal distance.[3]

In some societies, the propensity for autonomy is greater than in others, although studies of close-knit indigenous cultures noted for their high levels of sociability also emphasize respecting personal freedom.[4]

It may be more than coincidence that smartphones became

ubiquitous when so many sources of ritualized interactions, such as extended family networks, places of worship, schools, and governments, are in decline or in full-fledged chaos. Rather than repairing and rethinking institutions that have been the bedrock of community, we increasingly depend on smartphones and other communication technologies to create virtual communities that require less commitment or personal risk. We are like our hominin ancestors when they left the jungle canopy, daunted by the task of needing to create close bonds and intimate relationships when our environments are receding—but instead of a lost jungle, we anticipate institutional collapse and the loss of spaces and practices that once guided anxiety-ridden attempts at connection.

Like our hominin ancestors, we, too, are uncertain about what the future may hold and often find ourselves depending on near-strangers for emotional survival. Yet we also seem to be evolving in a different direction. With the need to navigate near-constant social and institutional upheaval, intimacy risks becoming a liability. Sociologist Zygmunt Bauman observed:

> The main identity-bound anxiety of modern times was the worry about durability; it is the concern with commitment-avoidance today. Modernity built in steel and concrete; postmodernity, in bio-degradable plastic.[5]

Bauman's observations resonate with Temple Grandin's description of living with autism in a postmodern world.[6] Autism is a spectrum of disorders marked by high levels of anxiety that occur in response to a person's limited capacity for emotionally comprehending the meaning of social cues. In the 1950s, when Grandin was a child, there was far more adherence to social norms. She could memorize expected behaviors and fit in with peers at school and in after-school clubs. Her keen intelligence allowed her to identify repetitive patterns in structured social environments that she could mimic and thus avoid the overwhelming anxiety of not understanding the subtle, intuitive nature of emotional communication. However, with the unraveling of modernism, Grandin found the increased social flux disorienting and unnerving. She's not alone, nor is her reaction limited to those disposed to feeling anxious in social situations.

Given the social and environmental degradation caused by modernity, the restructuring, if not dismantling, of some institutions is likely necessary to create truly humane and sustainable societies. Nevertheless, a cultural "autism" seems to have emerged in which the avoidance of social anxiety, or at the very least, *soothing* such anxiety, has become as important as creating meaningful and intimate connections. Our wired world may have, in part, evolved as it has because of the need to keep anxiety at bay while also staying socially connected.

Another contributor to the ubiquity of smartphones comes from a different type of "autism," or emotional misalignment, due to a significant portion of the world's population having histories of *adverse childhood experiences*. According to a study conducted by the Center for Disease Control and Kaiser Permanente, adverse childhood experiences include:

- Recurrent physical abuse
- Recurrent emotional abuse
- Sexual abuse
- Emotional or physical neglect
- Alcohol and/or substance abuse in the household
- An incarcerated household member
- Someone in the household who is chronically depressed, mentally ill, institutionalized, or suicidal
- Domestic violence
- One or no parents

Up to two-thirds of the 17,000 participants in the initial study had at least one of the above experiences in childhood. The size of this study, and the reproduction of its results in various settings around the planet, support the conclusion that a significant portion of people had experiences as children that can negatively impact their emotional development.

One of the primary consequences of adverse childhood experiences is unintentional emotional neglect and, in the case of abuse, purposeful invalidation of emotions. According to psychologist Marsha Linehan, "An invalidating family responds to private experiences [e.g., beliefs, thoughts, feelings, sensations] with either nonresponsiveness or more extreme consequences than more sensitive, validating social environments." A major consequence is "an intensification of the differences between a child's private experience and the experience the social environment actually supports and responds to."[7]

Emotionally invalidating environments impede a child's development because humans naturally anticipate emotional responses to certain conditions. Through our first relationships, we learn the nature of our feelings when they are mirrored back to us through body language, facial expressions, and the tone of voice of our caregivers. We learn to identify a smile with happiness, a grimace with disgust, and a startled look with fear. However, if we learned as children that it's not safe to openly express emotions, or if we feel we must show one emotion (or no emotion) when we are feeling something else (e.g., anger or fear), the foundation is set for increased anxiety when we later find ourselves in social spaces or more intimate encounters. Beneath our conscious awareness, an unconscious, habitual search for the resurgence of emotional betrayal or neglect can develop.

Turner identified challenges to face-to-face communication that can emerge for those with a history of adverse childhood experiences, which also may contribute to a preference for connection at a distance via smartphones:

- Uncertainty about how to "read" which social cues are important and which are irrelevant
- Uncertainty about what is considered normal
- Uncertainty about what is being exchanged in the encounter
- Uncertainty about whether one's subjective experience matches the subjective experience of the other person
- Doubts about the inherent significance of the interaction
- Lack of confidence about the outcome of the interaction
- Lessened trust

Granted, these challenges can also occur without smartphones, yet for the socially adverse, connection at a distance may feel a bit like a social-enhancement drug. When on a smartphone, we can cut the connection more easily if anxiety threatens to overwhelm us.

Having human connections, whatever form they may take, may seem ideally better than having none at all, but evidence suggests reliance on smartphones and social media for connection increases feelings of alienation and depression. As exciting as the new frontier in artificial intelligence may sound, and the even greater dependency on wired connectivity it will bring, we seem to be going in the direction of *de-evolution*, back to our solitary ancestor in the jungle canopies. What started as a postmodern revolution increasingly looks like the modernist mistake of fabricating ideal worlds befitting only a small part of the population while the rest of the world suffers the environmental and social devastation on which that "perfect" world depends. This latest evolution in world-building may be even worse since now the mind is the focus of colonization. To save ourselves, we may need to come down from our virtual social worlds and once again meet in the open to foster those precarious human connections on which our species' survival depends.

GLOBALIZATION: THE AGE OF PSYCHOLOGICAL NEOTONY

The term *neoteny* refers to when traits typically associated with juvenile stages of development are carried into adulthood. An example is the Mexican salamander *axolotl*. At full maturity, the axolotl looks like a tadpole, which is supposedly more adaptive to its environment than the typical adult salamander body. As the axolotl demonstrates, sometimes immaturity gleans the greatest advantages.

Biologist Stephen J. Gould believed neoteny contributed to the evolution of humans, distinguishing us from our hominin ancestors, who, at full maturity, were significantly hairier and thicker-boned than modern *Homo sapiens sapiens*. Supposedly, our analytical minds compensate for the loss of physical resilience.

One could argue neoteny continues to evolve in present-day humans, although it is our psychology, not our physiology, that increasingly remains immature. If key indicators of psychological age include how people spend their time and the content of their fantasies, psychological immaturity is at risk of becoming so pronounced that our era may best be described as the *Age of Psychological Neoteny*.

Mere science fiction, you might say, or just another hypothetical dystopia? Perhaps. However, the novelist Michael Crichton, in his techno-thriller *Next*, didn't need science fiction to underscore his suspicions. He quoted the very real Dr. Bruce Charlton:

> According to Dr. Bruce Charlton, evolutionary psychiatrist at Newcastle upon Tyne, human beings now take longer to reach mental maturity—and many never do so at all...
>
> He notes that "academics, teachers, scientists and many other professionals are often strikingly immature." He calls them "unpredictable, unbalanced in priorities, and tending to overreact." ...
>
> Charlton thinks this may be adaptive. "A child-like flexibility of attitudes, behaviors and knowledge" may be useful in navigating the increased instability of the modern world, he says, where people are more likely to change jobs, learn new skills, move to new places. But this comes at the cost of "short attention span, frenetic novelty-seeking, ever shorter cycles of arbitrary fashion, and...a pervasive emotional and spiritual shallowness." He added that modern people "lack a profundity of character which seemed commoner in the past."[1]

In another nonfictional commentary on the emotional state of the American male, *The Demise of Guys: Why Boys are Struggling and What We Can Do About It*, Philip Zimbardo and Nikita Duncan wrote:

> The excessive use of video games and online porn in pursuit of the next thing is creating a generation of risk-averse guys who are unable (and unwilling) to navigate the complexities and risks inherent to real-life relationships, school, and employment.[2]

It seems, in the Age of Psychological Neoteny, men are the

only juvenile adults. Yet psychological neoteny, if it is occurring, certainly impacts both sexes.

Some men's predilection for online escapism may not be psychologically different from some women's obsessive pursuit of youthful beauty found in magazines, movies, and online media. When women seek Botox, collagen injections, and other youth-enhancing procedures, they may also resist growing up while also avoiding appearing old. Perhaps female neoteny is less interesting. It's socially acceptable for women to pursue eternal youth, especially if it means we are more seductive and financially or emotionally dependent because of our efforts.

Psychological immaturity does seem rampant these days, and Charlton's description of neoteny as causing "a pervasive emotional and spiritual shallowness" seems all too real. But is psychological neoteny in the 21st century limited to wayward men who have moved back home and whittle away time playing video games and watching porn or young women obsessed with beauty and fashion? I don't think so. Rather, I believe these men's and women's actions exist on a continuum with many other strategies for dealing with the psychological overwhelm that is a common response to life with the internet.

With the expansion of the internet around the planet, we have become aware of the lives of many people we will never have contact with, though we know intimate details from their lives. This includes a global obsession with the rich and famous and the desire to imitate their lavish lifestyles. However, the internet fosters fantasies that ignore an unsurmountable problem: The profoundly unequal distribution of wealth means only a few will actually attain lives of luxury, let alone a Western, middle-class way of life.

Granted, before the internet, extreme differences in wealth existed. What perhaps makes the current moment different is how our fantasies and imaginations are being exploited in ways that assure inequality continues, if not increases. Despite rumblings about the death of the American dream, the current round of globalization succeeds in large part because people can easily use the internet as fodder for fantasizing about being the exception to the rule. However, when we fill our minds with fantasies of a perfect self and ideal life, we are also more likely to chisel away at Earth's precious resources as well as our own limited financial capital in pursuit of dreams we cannot afford and may never be able to achieve.

The coveted self-image or lifestyle is also about acquiring emotional states, such as a sense of superiority, or avoiding painful emotions, such as envy. Superiority and envy are two emotions commonly stirred by extreme inequality, along with feelings of shame for not attaining greater status or success.

When I think of young men in the prime of their lives, getting lost in imaginal worlds, I wonder if they feel they have no chance at the American dream, that they are exhausted by the quest to create a real-world identity and have discovered they can get just as much emotional satisfaction out of their imaginal escapes—at least until reality comes breaking through.

The preference for fantasy over reality is a relatively common defense against chronically traumatizing conditions. Research has also shown that exposure to extreme wealth disparities causes chronic stress.[3] Less research, however, has revealed why we not only tolerate economic systems that propagate disparities in wealth and power but also become dependent on such disparities to fuel fantasy worlds that rarely come to fruition and often cause longing, dissatisfaction, and hopelessness.

Globalization Requires Our Psychological Immaturity

While many factors have contributed to the expansion of the internet, I am most interested in the role of globalization and how it creates conditions of emotional dependency that have us wasting so much time in fantasy worlds driven by products and experiences found through the online marketplace. At the inception of globalization, which included colonization and the enslavement of people of color, not only were indigenous peoples often physically beaten into submission, but their polytheistic beliefs systems were also attacked, including the myths and rituals that contributed to social cohesion and guided growth over the lifespan. Without their spiritual beliefs, indigenous peoples were more susceptible to psychological and spiritual dependency on their colonizers.

It was common for colonizers to assert that polytheistic, nature-based belief systems were evidence of the psychological immaturity of the "natives" and a reason to convert them to monotheistic belief systems, such as Catholicism. I imagine the "natives" in turn discerned that Western spiritual beliefs were treated as separate and distinct from the rules and conditions guiding the marketplace. Separation of church and state, though intended to provide greater spiritual freedom, also allows for the splitting of spirituality from the materialistic conditions that contribute to survival. Thus, the marketplace can become as ruthless as necessary to attain its goals, while organized religions can pursue their spiritual commitments without seriously challenging the immoral conditions of the globalized marketplace, which has included slavery since its inception.

Spirituality is heavily influenced by the imaginal aspects of psyche, if not synonymous with them. The division between the marketplace and spiritual life allows for the use of the imaginal as an escape from the conditions of our secular lives rather than as the driver of spiritual transformation. For indigenous populations, this division replaced belief systems that acknowledged the interdependency of the spiritual and natural world, which supported healthy interrelatedness and environmental sustainability rather than globalization's exploitation of resources and the need for excessive dependency from its members.

In the United States, which was founded partly on the opportunity for religious freedom and the separation of church and state, emotional immaturity appeared early in its history. In his visit to America in 1831, the French political thinker Alexis de Tocqueville noted the emotional immaturity plaguing Americans. He wrote in *Democracy in America*:

> Above this race of men stands an immense and tutelary power, which takes upon itself alone to secure their gratifications and to watch over their fate. The power is absolute, minute, regular, provident, and mild. It would be like the authority of a parent if, like that authority, its object was to prepare men for manhood; but it seeks, on the contrary, to keep them in perpetual childhood.... For their happiness such a government willingly labors...provides for their security... facilitates their pleasures, manages their principle concerns... what remains, but to spare them all the care of thinking and all the trouble of living?[4]

The Central Role Myth and Ritual Play in Human Development

From the perspective of psychology, the pursuit of eternal youth is typically considered a neurotic defense stemming from maladaptive conditions in the family. In pop psychology, it's called the *Peter Pan complex*, which describes men who are resistant to growing up and taking on responsibilities typically associated with being an adult male. Peter Pans perceive adulthood as drudgery, if not the death of the soul.

Jungian psychologists use the Latin terms *puer aeternus*, the eternal boy, and *puella aeterna*, the eternal girl, to describe the pursuit of eternal youth. However, Jungian psychology sees both positive and negative aspects of *puer/puella*. Whereas one aspect is the refusal to grow up, more positive qualities include novelty and an infectious hopefulness necessary for optimal change and growth.

As an archetypal force rather than just a neurotic defense, we can see *puer* and *puella* as part of all of us. We are all capable of regressing to our childish selves (and some of us use the weekends as a form of structured indulgence). When circumstances support or encourage regression, people who easily activate their internal *puers* and *puellas* are often perceived as innovative, life-affirming, and fun to be around. They are the creative geniuses and thought leaders who dauntlessly take us into uncharted territory.

Western models of human development that focus on attaining a unitary self as the hallmark of maturity tend to depict childhood as something we outgrow. In contrast, Jungian psychology depicts development more as expanding possibilities, including having multiple aspects of the self to inhabit in response to different social and environmental demands. From this perspective, we don't necessarily get rid of our child selves; rather, other archetypal possibilities (e.g., hero/heroine, partner, parent, elder, healer, etc.) develop as we inhabit different situations and roles across the lifespan.

Jungian analyst Anthony Stevens described development as a process of fulfilling *archetypal intent*. When a society or environment fails to provide the conditions that activate archetypes, the result can be emotional and psychological immaturity, if not neurosis. In his book, *The Two-Million-Year-Old Self*, Stevens wrote:

> Mental health depends upon the provision of physical and social environments capable of meeting the archetypal needs of the developing individual. Psychopathology can result

when these needs are frustrated. This formulation gives rise to two fundamental questions: (1) What are the archetypal needs of the developing individual? (2) What environments, physical and social, are capable of guaranteeing their fulfillment?[5]

Myths and rituals have been carriers of the wisdom and experiences necessary for activating archetypal intent, thus fostering full maturity and psychological integration. Through myths and rituals, members of some indigenous communities learn which role they are expected to play in their social group and when they are expected to play that role. They are also supported through the inevitable grief that comes with letting go of one way of life, along with the anxiety common to entering a new stage of life or role.

This is not to say that myths and rituals are paths to utopia. Rather, I'm pointing out that when we meet the challenges life presents us head on, and with support that helps contain potentially overwhelming emotions, we tend to fare a lot better and with a lot less neurosis and mental illness.

Perhaps living in fantasy worlds such as those created by video games, online porn, and fashion are misguided efforts at directing archetypal energies toward development. The pursuit of fantasy can be a psychological defense that emerges during periods of uncertainty and anxiety—a kind of psychological hyperbaric chamber that preserves psychological energies until the conditions necessary for fulfilling archetypal intent are present.

In many regards, the current global economy is in constant flux due to its acute sensitivity to diasporas, civil unrest, pandemics, global warming, dwindling resources, and environmental degradation. Despite these currents of change, there is also rigidity, largely due to the unequal distribution of resources. Many people today feel impotent in the face of the financial disparities that threaten their ideals and attempts to create a life worth living, which, for most, includes having family, friends, a home, meaningful work, and supportive community.

When an absurdly small percentage of the world's population holds the majority of the world's wealth, and hence, power, it impacts the development of youths expected to gain economic independence as evidence of maturity. The marketplace has its own markers for the attainment of adulthood—an education, a job, material wealth, status—yet these milestones may not be enough to activate the transcendence of youth that in some indigenous communities contributed to both spiritual growth and social cohesion. Furthermore, the imaginal aspects of the psyche enlivened by myth and ritual are exploited by the marketplace, which needs consumers to redirect their imaginal energies toward the pursuit of success promoted through media rather than through gratifying relationships and spiritual enlightenment. The latter likely require ignoring, if not rejecting, the push to purchase the identities and lifestyles that continually bombard us through media.

When so few young people can ever hope to live the lives of our society's heroes—the movie stars, athletes, and billionaires—but can, at a lesser cost and with limited effort through the internet (and a credit card), manipulate themselves and their imaginations so that, for at least some of the time, they feel as if they have transcended their current selves, is it any surprise that many escape in video games and the pursuit of beauty? And the corporations that financially benefit from these emotional "fixes" are more than happy to comply.

ALL THOSE LINGERING LUSTY IMAGES

There's something untoward about a married woman my age writing about lust, let alone feeling it. I should be spending time managing my hormones rather than having hot flashes of an entirely different sort. But I am here to disclose that, yes, lust continues well into middle age. And here lies the problem: *lust continues well into middle age*. Even if I want to stroll quietly into my elder years, tending my senility alongside the geraniums, sexy advertisements block my path. I can barely open a webpage without some scintillating image reminding me the seduction game is always afoot. And then there's porn, just a free click away.

Despite the seemingly worldwide sex obsession, sex isn't what sells. *Lust* sells. Lust, like sex, physically stirs, but lust is a longing that exists separate from fulfillment. Lust draws us to the object of desire—or as on the web, to an *image* of what we desire.

Social life depends on separating lust from sex. Whereas lust can innocuously stir our bodies and minds, acting on lust without another's consent breaches personal liberties. Sexy advertisements and porn exploit the division between lust and sex, doing everything possible to stimulate lust while pretending what they sell is sex. Implicitly, they suggest that the pitched product or experience can lead to an escape from social prohibitions and personal limitations. They flirt with taboos and encourage fantasies about experiences that are often off-limits.

In a less rapacious world, caution for lust's penchant to rasp at Pandora's box is enough to contain the shadow parts of ourselves stirred by lust. But caution has been thrown to the wind. In the virtual world, a feeding frenzy of lust is underway.

Sex is a central way we feel enlivened and why so many just can't stop thinking about it. Sex matters a lot. How else to explain the evolution of eight thousand nerve endings on the clitoris, making it the most sensitive part of the female anatomy? Granted, the penis has about half the number of nerve endings, but that certainly doesn't mean men can't feel something equally extraordinary. Yet all this sensitivity can go to waste when tied to a habit of gorging on lusty images.

Sex is one of the most intimate and vulnerable connections people can have. However, having a mental storehouse of lusty images can reduce the power of sex for mind-bending intimacy to the banal practice of being a consumer. Granted, there's the possibility of mentally flipping through fantasies to find the one that drives the encounter to an explosive finale, but such mental preoccupation can lead to the desire to control sexual encounters rather than foster mutual gratification and intimacy.

Objectification of lovers is also a possible outcome, along with a preference for the internal mental landscape over the real deal, both of which are becoming such common outcomes of habitual porn consumption that mentioning this feels obvious. Nevertheless, the point is an important one. As one man remarked:

It can be a kind of problem to think about porn as much as I do, especially when with my girlfriend. It means I am not really present with her, my head is somewhere else.[1]

For youths reaching sexual maturity with pornography readily available on the internet, their first exposure to sex is likely formulaic and faked. Such impressions can impede sex's power to deeply stir the senses and soul. Porn also contributes to viewing one's body as an object, which is deeply depersonalizing. In contrast to experiencing oneself in an authentic and embodied way, viewing oneself as an object to be manipulated can make sex feel like a performance and fuel obsessions with appearances at the expense of pleasure.

Dana Crowley Jack associated this "over eye" view of the self with women's experiences of depression, but when it comes to porn, men can similarly suffer.[2] (How many men, without chemical enhancements, can match the stamina of porn stars? But how many men who regularly watch porn think they should?) As one man remarked:

Porn taught me all I know about sex. My parents never mentioned the word sex at home, and sex ed in school was a f**king joke. I had this image of how great sex would be, both of us going at it for hours. So it was kind of a shock the way the real thing turned out...she didn't [have an orgasm] and I came really quickly.

Some try to control sexual encounters in their quest to reproduce what they witness in online porn, often with complete disregard for their partner's satisfaction or safety. All this need for control in the current free-for-all oddly makes intimacy seem like the greatest threat to sexual satisfaction.

The web is a social experiment. Ignore what software updates tell you; we're still in beta version. We have no idea what the long-term impact will be of continual exposure to lust-provoking images, but some parallels seem to exist with what we know about the lingering impact of early-life sexual trauma.

When there's a history of early-life sexual abuse and memories of the abuse are triggered, it is not uncommon for sexual arousal to occur. This may seem strange, but from a survival perspective it makes sense. As mentioned in a previous essay, if the body is already aroused before sex, there is less likelihood of physical injury due to forced penetration. Furthermore, the level of physical arousal associated with sex can be too much for a young body and mind to tolerate. Even if sex was coerced rather than forced, there can be a compulsive need to master feelings of overwhelm experienced with molestation, which can contribute to compulsive sexual behaviors, including compulsive porn consumption. Furthermore, orgasm may become associated with the end of the sexual encounter and, therefore, the end of the abuse. This can contribute to more concern with sexual release than intimate connection and mutual pleasure.

For many people with histories of early-life sexual abuse, the abuser was an attachment figure. However, the sex of abuse is not about attachment or intimacy but dominance, exploitation, and control. Along with traumatic stress, feelings of betrayal can lead to high levels of dissociation during molestation and hence not being emotionally engaged with what's happening. One consequence is that intimacy is not experienced as part of sex. The need to emotionally check out results in sex more likely becoming an obstacle to intimacy than an avenue.

Similar to early-life sexual abuse, compulsively viewing porn contributes to emotional shutdown, intrusive imagery, intrusive body sensations, and the experience of sex as an obstacle to intimacy. Perhaps the trauma of compulsively viewing porn is what trauma specialists refer to as a little "t" trauma that impacts attachment, such as intimacy between lovers. It could be called "it," or *image trauma*, for the lost capacity to experience sexuality without lusty images intruding at least some of the time in ways that threaten to depersonalize the encounter. If there is such a trauma, perhaps it's happening to just about everyone who regularly views porn on the web.

On that Orwellian note, a cautionary quote by C. L. Rawlins is in order: "Mass culture draws collective power from blocking individual development." None of us can develop on our own. We need each other in intimate, embodied, safe, and authentic ways.

THE LONG SHADOW OF MASS MURDER

On the eve of World War I, Carl Jung had a vision:

> I saw a blood-red glow, like the flicker of the sea seen from
> afar, stretched from East to West across the northern horizon.
> And at that time someone asked me what I thought about
> world events in the near future. I said that I had no thoughts,
> but saw blood, rivers of blood.[1]

Jung was not alone in this vision; around this time, apocalyptic images were common in the works of artists and writers.
Many creatives intuited the troubled times before they
ruptured into awareness and before the machinations of war
marched irreversibly into history.

I thought of Jung's dream in the wake of the murder of 20
children and six staff members at Sandy Hook Elementary
School in Newtown, Connecticut. Jung's vision resonates with
the darkness that spread collectively over minds and hearts
after this brutal and senseless act. There have been so many
mass shootings in the United States, and like natural disasters,
their numbers threaten only to increase. Nowhere seems safe
from random, senseless acts of violence. Again and again, we

find ourselves tragically united in grief, fear, and images of an aftermath otherwise too horrific to imagine.

The Newtown shootings pierced deep into the shadows of the collective unconscious of our era. What kind of person, many wondered, could kill a classroom of children? The question itself borders on the incomprehensible. The assumption that the killer was mentally ill is a natural one to make. *Only an insane person would commit such a heinous act,* many want to believe. Yet most people diagnosed with a mental disorder could never imagine such profound disregard for life.

Placing blame on one person also fails to satisfy our collective moral outrage and despair. We sense there must be something greater afoot and rightfully demand enforced gun control and the availability of affordable and effective mental healthcare. Yet the violence still seems to have deeper roots and suggests a change in the very fabric of our society.

Jung wrote in his autobiography:

> A collective problem, if not recognized as such, always appears as a personal problem, and in individual cases may give the impression that something is out of order in the realm of the personal psyche. The personal sphere is indeed disturbed, but such disturbances need not be primary; they may well be secondary, the consequence of an unsupportable change in the social atmosphere. The cause of disturbance is, therefore, not to be sought in the personal surroundings, but rather in the collective situation.[2]

It's difficult not to wonder what lurks in the collective psyche of a country that fears siege by some of its younger citizens, especially given that nearly half of the perpetrators of mass murder are under 30 years old.[3] Like Jung before us, we too are at risk of apocalyptic visions, although the enemy may well be within us—not as a deep-seated evil that threatens our human nature but something more banal—an oversight, really, in the failure to adequately support and protect the complicated and delicate task of raising vulnerable young minds.

In an article published in *Newsweek*, "The Kids Aren't Alright," Lee Siegel addressed Facebook's plan to allow kids under 13 to use their social media site. Siegel shared important concerns about the impressionable developing mind that seem relevant to understanding mass murders, especially given that a significant number are committed by individuals whose mental development arguably deserves scrutiny.

Siegel stressed that when kids are constantly interacting with the internet, they fail to develop inner resources that contribute to resilience and perseverance in the face of setbacks, disappointments, and stress:

> The process of maturing is a movement from a rich yet defensive inner space to the outer reality of pleasure postponement, setback, and perseverance. But the Internet offers one recessive chamber after another of inwardness; it is a place where distraction and immediate gratification become cognitive tools in themselves.[4]

Siegel also quoted Harvard psychologist Howard Gardner, who claimed, "It's often the case that today's youth don't know whether they're online or not."

Such observations may seem a bit nebulous. Certainly, one might argue the internet is incapable of having an impact great enough to lead to mass murder—except, of course, in someone already mentally unstable for more tangible reasons, such as the conditions in their household or being bullied at school—or so the argument might go.

However, such reasoning may reverse the order of things. Instead, perhaps, we should first ask, What in our individual psyches and collective unconscious led to the rapid acceptance and proliferation of the internet? What is so appealing about a technology that deliberately blurs the distinction between conscious reality and virtual awareness? Is this not the nature of dissociation, one of our more evolved traumatic defenses? Psychologist Peter Levine described dissociation as "the escape when there is no escape," available to all of us when we experience something psychologically overwhelming without a way to flee or fight the danger.[5] When we dissociate, we also defend against our own emotions, and emotions are how we connect to each other.

In a world overwhelmed by stress and frequent reminders of both personal and collective traumas, regularly checking out by activating dissociative states is a reasonable survival strategy —that is, until checking out, as Gardner suggested, is no longer discernible from being checked in. For some people, the ability to distinguish between reality and fantasy becomes a risk. At such times, there may be limited opportunities to test reality and gauge the potential impact of actions.

If we create societies in which the young fail to develop inner resources needed for navigating difficult times and instead the most reliable psychological defense is dissociation —and to make matters worse, images of violence are so prevalent that, according to the American Academy of Pediatrics, a child watching three to four hours of non-educational TV a day will witness 8,000 murders by the end of grade school—why would we expect a rigorous distinction between fantasy and reality, especially during times of acute stress?[6] In societies like the United States, with laissez-faire approaches to technologies and the marketplace, the focus isn't on creating mature, empathic, and resilient youths but on market share. This has led to the exploitation of the all-too-human need to escape overwhelming emotions, sometimes tragically, to the point where we have been brought to the brink of our collective destruction.

Yet it's not just youths who are increasingly dependent on dissociation, lost in fantasy, and overrun with violent imagery. We are all lost at sea to a certain extent, our imaginations sinking from too many harrowing images of the four horsemen of the apocalypse. In our era of 24/7 news coverage, repeatedly viewing catastrophes can leave us hypervigilant, emotionally numb, or paranoid as we worry we might be similarly victimized. Alternatively, we can feel too overwhelmed to entertain the possibility of catastrophe, and only by dissociating our fear do we stay afloat.

The period beginning with World War II and extending to the present has been depicted as an era of violence. Initiated by events such as Auschwitz, Dresden, and Hiroshima, and the technologies that made such destruction possible, this period is also distinguished from past eras by how communication technologies have made the passive witnessing of others' suffering commonplace.

Being inundated by images of violence has changed our relationship with violence. These images can fail to jar us as they once might have or how we expect they should. Writing about the period after 1954, historian and literary critic Lewis Mumford observed, "In thirty brief years, violence and slaughter had increased at geometric ratio, while the human reaction to it had altered inversely." Novelist Milan Kundera made the following observation about this new relationship with violence:

> The bloody massacre in Bangladesh quickly covered the memory of the Russian invasion of Czechoslovakia, the assassination of Allende drowned out the groans of Bangladesh, the war in the Sinai desert made people forget Allende, the Cambodian massacre made people forget Sinai, and so on and so forth until ultimately everyone lets everything be forgotten.

Many of the conditions of our late modern world are harrowing and deeply unsettling, but only if we allow ourselves to sit long enough with the emotional overwhelm and sense of helplessness that passively viewing violence can cause. Often we don't. Or won't. Or can't. We move on. We keep busy, sometimes out of the need for survival but often because staying active confines awareness to the events at hand. It's not that we are apathetic. Nor is it that we resist finding solutions. Instead, I believe we often cannot tolerate witnessing the suffering of others while confronting our own fragile existences. *How did we get here?* Are we really that different from past eras, or is there something unique about our times—about *us*—that makes emotional withdrawal a necessary survival skill in the 21st-century United States and throughout much of the world?

Though violence is a pervasive problem, our understanding of its impact is often quite circumscribed. As a society, we are well schooled in witnessing violent acts—we shell out money for the latest Bond picture that gets the adrenaline flowing and mirrors our collective habit (*need?*) of forgetting the effects of violence. But we are not so good at taking care of victims of violence, let alone witnessing the long shadow of suffering that violence causes.

The United States has fashioned itself as a nation of heroes, but we should wonder what images of heroism those who commit violent acts are emulating, especially if they are young, as their naturally outsized imaginations can overly influence their behavior. America's dominant notion of heroism is inseparable from our long history of war, and hence, violence. The United States has also preferred to play the hero to other nations' violence and oppression—protecting Koreans and Vietnamese from communism and, more recently, Middle Easterners from rogue dictators—while ignoring how the near continual involvement in foreign conflicts is inseparable from the violence in our streets and high levels of family and intimate-partner violence in our homes.

Our nation's habit of projecting victimhood to other countries may also play a central role in our dissociation from violence on our own soil. This near habitual "externalization" of the devastation caused by conflict perhaps makes it easier to avoid contemplating the consequences of violence in the lives of our fellow Americans. *Victimhood is someone else's problem.* This is especially true if we are not in relationships with victims of violence and instead learn about violent acts through media. When violence and its consequences are relayed through the news or other media, they can be encountered with a measure of emotional distance and, to some extent, felt as if "foreign" to one's lived experiences.

Although not a panacea to mass murder, a shift is needed from witnessing violence to witnessing overcoming the consequences of violence and the joys of peaceful living. We don't need images of violence. Instead, we need stories that cause us to grieve—stories about how violence alters the arc of a life and what it takes to regain a sense of safety, if not personhood, after violence. These are the images we need to overwhelm us. This is also where we will witness the greatest acts of heroism, if not also rekindle our connection to the preciousness of life, which we all need to foster in these troubling times and pass on to the children.

DREAMING OF A SAFE
AMERICA

In *Dreaming up America,* historical novelist Russell Banks identified three dreams at the heart of America's unconscious conflicts, dreams that originally drew people to the colonies:

> There was El Dorado, the City of Gold that Cortez and Pizarro dreamed of finding. And then there was Ponce de Leon's dream of the Fountain of Youth, where you could start life over again, and the New England Puritan dream of God's Protestant utopian City on a Hill, the New Jerusalem.... We can think of there being three braided strands, or perhaps three mutually reinforcing dreams: one is of a place where a sinner can become virtuous, free from the decadence of the secular cosmopolitanism of Old Europe; another is of a place where a poor man can become wealthy; and a third is of a place where a person can be born again.[1]

The three conflicting impulses of these dreams—renewal, materialism, and spirituality—shape the nation, its institutions and social life, and Americans' psyches. They influence the fantasies that grab our imaginations, the ideals we hold, and our expectations for the future. These dreams also have a

shadow side. They contain unresolved traumas of past generations and thus perpetuate fear, shame, addictions, and
disavowed needs. Without healing the shadow side of these
dreams, the United States has no other option than to play out
conflicting impulses in unhealthy and destructive ways.

These disparate dreams of wealth, rebirth, and redemption
have been with the American people since the country's inception, although according to Banks, they became a source of
internal tension after the Civil War. The United States emerged
from this conflict as a nation, which implied, at least in principle, the resolution of internal conflicts to create an integrated
and interdependent group of citizens. However, as we know all
too well, this was not the case. After the Civil War, the United
States was incapable of true integration. For one thing, the Civil
War was particularly gruesome. Over 620,000 people died—far
more Americans than in any other US-involved conflict.
Furthermore, although the Civil War ended slavery, it did not
end racism or inequality and thus failed to uphold the ideal of
universal, inalienable rights laid out in the Constitution, the
doctrine intended to unite us as equals.

Thus, after the Civil War, there was a false sense of integration. To use psychological parlance, we could say the US
created a *false self*. The creation of a false self is common to
trauma survivors. It hides the split-off aspects of experience
and identity that the survivor is unaware of or fears retribution
for if others knew about the traumatized parts and the memories they hold. Americans have suffered many traumas—
including numerous wars, slavery, economic oppression,
racism, sexism, homophobia, and family violence—and all
reveal the failure to create a country of safe and equal citizens.

In this essay, I try to understand how unconscious dreams
and unresolved traumas influence American's defensive reactions to threat, much like the child that suffers chronic traumatization is altered by conditions of abuse and neglect. I believe

we are at a time in our nation's history when we must examine the disparity between what we have dreamed of becoming and the reality of what we are: stressed, even traumatized, increasingly fragmented, yet also passionate, resourceful, and capable of honest evaluation.

When caught in a habitual cycle of denying or dissociating parts of ourselves, even the faintest reminders are susceptible to unconscious projection on others. When traumatic memories are particularly offensive and contain overwhelming feelings of shame or helplessness, the need to rid oneself of the offending and unacceptable beliefs and emotions can lead to a search for a scapegoat—someone or something that can contain the overwhelming feelings that otherwise might shatter the fragile persona keeping them at bay.

Indeed, the United States often functions much like a trauma survivor who projects wounded parts of itself on scapegoats rather than risk the uncertainty of facing a traumatized past. Scapegoating occurs in relation to other countries and peoples when we demonize them. It also happens in our own country when people are devalued or brutalized due to their ethnic origins, gender or sexual orientation, region of the country they live in, or lack of resources. Those victimized are also at risk of later seeking scapegoats.

Identifying with the Aggressor

Early in the twentieth century, the psychoanalyst Sándor Ferenczi explained why traumatized and victimized people might, in turn, victimize others. Ferenczi worked with people chronically abused in childhood, including people with histories of childhood sexual abuse. He identified in his patients a psychological defense he called "identifying with the aggressor."[2] Despite the horror of abuse, many children do not initially respond with rejection, hatred, or even disgust when the perpetrator is a caregiver or someone they know. Rather, overwhelming shame, moral helplessness, and paralyzing fear likely occur. Instead of defending against the aggressor, they survive by fusing with the perpetrator's identity, unconsciously assuming they somehow deserve the abuse.

Young children lack a separate and integrated identity. They naturally rely on caregivers to help them make sense of events, especially an experience as disturbing as sexual abuse. Thus, they are susceptible to looking to the aggressor to determine how to feel about themselves. This can lead to blaming themselves for the abuse and taking on the guilt and shame the aggressor refuses to feel for their destructive acts. Mirroring their aggressor, the abused child tries to dissociate these emotions, setting in motion the process of splitting off parts of the self. Dissociation also keeps awareness of the abuse and associated painful memories and emotions out of conscious awareness.

Lloyd de Mause, in his book *The Emotional Life of Nations*, explored how these disowned emotions and beliefs are later projected on others, including entire populations, in an effort to discharge the shame of childhood abuse. De Mause called them *social alters*:

> The social alter is the inheritor of earlier dissociated persecu-
> tory feelings and has as one of its roles the setting up of group
> punishments that are object lessons to us all.[3]

For example, psychotherapist Alice Miller argued high levels of corporal punishment of German children in the early decades of the twentieth century contributed to large numbers becoming Nazi youths.[4] According to Miller, Jews, the mentally ill, and homosexuals became social alters responsible for holding the projections of moral indignation that Nazi youths once felt as victims of childhood abuse. Today such split-off moral outrage is associated with *betrayal trauma*.[5]

Missed Acts of Triumph and the Emergence of Structural Dissociation

Pierre Janet, a contemporary of Sándor Ferenczi, developed his own theories about how trauma leads to psychological splitting. According to Janet, traumatic memories are not only the result of actual efforts to defend against threats. As discussed earlier, co-occurring with memories of a traumatic event are the imagined movements and actions the body wanted to take —so-called *acts of triumph* that would have led to a different history, one involving facing down or escaping the threat.

He wrote, "The patients affected by traumatic memory have not been able to perform any of the actions characteristic of the stage of triumph."[6] The actions that would have led to escape or defense are split from awareness, or dissociated, along with the memories, thoughts, sensations, emotions, and images associated with the actual traumatic event. As Bessel van der Kolk more recently claimed, "For human beings the best predictor of something becoming traumatic seems to be a situation in which they no longer can imagine a way out."[7]

Often defense responses are avoided when the source of threat is a caregiver on which the child depends for attachment and care. According to the model of structural dissociation developed by Onno van der Hart, Ellert R. S. Nijenhuis, and Kathy Steele (and discussed in the essay on moral injury), when a child is exposed to chronic traumatization, the personality can become fragmented as defense responses are chronically activated but not carried through, much as Janet described with his notion of incomplete acts of triumph.[8] Over time, these split-off defenses become aspects of the personality that are not

183

fully integrated; the person doesn't feel entirely in control of them, especially when triggered by reminders of past traumas.

For instance, there might be a "fight" part of the personality activated by a felt need for protection that results in impulsive reactions to benign situations as well as a general sense of mistrust. A chronically suppressed instinct to flee threatening conditions may later develop into a chronic sense of ambivalence or addictive behavior. When terror has habitually been split off, panic attacks and phobias might later develop. Furthermore, chronically submitting to abuse can lead to profound shame, a desire to please, and a near constant sense of helplessness.

National Defenses

In some regards, the United States' "false self" as a place where Enlightenment ideals of equality, safety, and justice are spoken about more than they are embodied parallels structural dissociation's model of the traumatized psyche, in which part of the self tries to live a good life but is continually triggered by traumatic reminders, thus activating the traumatized aspects of the self that perceive the world as dangerous and threatening.

Like all trauma survivors, the United States prefers certain defenses, while others are deemed inferior and even as signs of weakness. For instance, America began as a patriarchal country driven by the myth of the hero, witnessed in ideas like Manifest Destiny and the inalienable right of the unbridled pursuit of wealth. Aggression (the fight response), often masked as assertiveness, has been admired and encouraged when cast as a means to advancement or attainment of a goal.

However, many of the first immigrants to the United States suffered persecution and poverty before they were able to flee their home countries. Many experienced poverty and oppression when they reached the United States, sometimes for generations. Others were forced to come to America as slaves and lived through the most horrific abuses, while Native Americans were subjected to the terrors of genocide. Through epigenetics and attachment styles, many of the defenses our ancestors utilized or suppressed in their attempts to survive traumatizing conditions continue to influence present generations. It's not unreasonable to assume a truncated flight defense was "inherited" by some from their ancestors, along with a deep ambivalence about their connection to the United States.

Four other defenses—freeze, submit, attach, and appease— seem to cause the patriarchal vision of the United States the greatest problem. Historically, they have been portrayed as signs of weakness and associated in particular with minorities, women, and LGTBQ+, who like De Mause's social alters have been treated as culpable in their victimization.

Fantasizing and the Fountain of Youth

Ironically, the American idea of heroism, which denies attachment needs that might interfere with fulfillment of individualistic pursuits, is likely the source of the country's preoccupation with youth and fantasy. According to Banks, of the three American dreams, the Fountain of Youth is the most powerful:

> The dream of the Fountain of Youth may yet prove to be the strongest of the three, since it carries within it the sense of the new, the dream of starting over, of having a New Life. It's essentially the dream of being a child again, and it's the dream that persists more strongly than the other two and is today perhaps most vivid of the three.[9]

I have seen the influence of the Fountain of Youth in psychotherapeutic theories in which the first years of life are perceived as the most significant and innocence must somehow be redeemed for wholeness and healing to occur. I have also witnessed this dream when working as a trauma-focused psychotherapist with people who have fragmented in the face of chronic traumatization. I have seen this, too, in my response to my own early-life trauma. Along with truncated defenses, we can feel as if we harbor an isolated and innocent part of ourselves we unconsciously try to protect from further abuse, including the suffering caused by the unfulfilled need for a safe and supportive society.

Protection of an underdeveloped part of the self may be an instinctive response to early-life trauma. Part of early-life development occurs in what psychologist Donald Winnicott called "transitional spaces." These are psychological spaces of play, where children learn to engage with symbolic material and challenge distinctions between reality and fantasy. According to Winnicott, these transitional spaces are often disrupted when abuse happens to the very young. Rather than being the source of creative imagination, transitional spaces instead become places of retreat from reality in which fantasizing dominates. According to Jungian analyst Donald Kalsched:

> Fantasizing is a dissociated state, which is neither imagination nor living in external reality, but a kind of melancholic self-soothing compromise which goes on forever—a defensive use of the imagination in the service of anxiety and avoidance.[10]

I believe America's failure to deal with past traumas, especially those resulting from wars, racism, economic oppression, and family violence, has led to overreliance on dissociation, fantasy worlds, and unfulfilling dreams. Like the child of abuse, we unconsciously wait for a safe and supportive community that can make us feel renewed and whole. Perhaps this is why the world's greatest fantasy producers—Hollywood, Disneyland, and Las Vegas—took root on our soil. Democracy is a promise unfulfilled, and yet one of the most admirable aspects of the American spirit is our continued commitment to the dream.

The Power of Dissociation

In the latest round of globalization, the buying of fantasies has replaced the hard work of community building. Though often with good intentions, too many of us try to fulfill unrealistic fantasies in attempts to address split-off, unconscious needs and desires. Yet the transitional space of the imagination from which fantasies emerge is not necessarily pernicious. Fantasy and other imaginal aspects of the psyche are not themselves problematic, for they are also the source of acts of triumph and overcoming past traumas. Rather, it is the normalization of dissociated states of consciousness, along with conditions that lead to the continual activation of defenses, that is the problem. Fantasizing is potentially adaptive when it becomes the source of creative solutions that might have gone unidentified while attending to the realities of traumatizing conditions. The benefit of psychological escapism is the opportunity to self-soothe the wounds of trauma, and thus the possibility of keeping hope alive, especially when real world solutions aren't available.

As noted in an earlier essay, in non-Western indigenous cultures that utilize ritual as a way to foster social cohesion, dissociation can take the form of trance or possession in which members who experience social inequalities or victimhood, such as intimate partner violence, safely give voice to their suffering. Rather than a psychopathology, dissociation and its disorders signal the need to reunite with group members and reveal hidden wounds, especially when alienation, scapegoating, and conflict threaten social bonds. In America, however, dissociation has become paradoxically both a normative state and a sign of psychopathology, depending on how disconnected from "reality" a person appears to be. It has completely lost its potential as a sign of the need for greater social cohesion and integration. Yet I believe we can retrieve the power of dissociation through awareness of the outsized role it now plays in keeping America unsafe.

Dreaming in the Present Moment

Historically, America has relied on notions of psychopathology to identify those who might threaten the creation of a democracy in which justice, equality, and protection from harm can prevail. This approach has failed miserably. For millennia, civilizations have been engineering the conditions of human captivity. As a species, we are cut off from the natural world and our adapted existence within it. Everything about us is tainted with the "abnormal."

Instead of focusing on psychopathology, it's time to look at the conditions of our captivity and what options we have made available to ourselves. Then we might notice that the manipulation of our capacity to fragment in the face of overwhelming, and sometimes threatening, conditions has led to a largely emotionally alienating country, despite that dissociation also makes possible living solitary existences while feeling somewhat satisfied by the distracted pursuit of fantasies. But we are smarter than our captive conditions might suggest—mainly due to all those split-off parts.

Researchers have more reliable evidence about the human condition than when the American experiment to create a democratic and free nation began centuries ago. We now understand the necessity of healthy attachment during the first years of life for later healthy relationships and, by extrapolation, healthy societies. We now understand the nature of the body's defense system and what happens when we live in chronic stress conditions. We have identified circumstances, such as adverse childhood experiences, that lead to excessive arousal of the defense system, thus contributing not only to disease but also the intergenerational transmission of traumatic stress and, hence, more abuse, violence, and wars. We also have a model of what a healthy psyche looks like, and it involves neurobiological integration within an individual who is also integrated within a safe and supportive community.

The Dalai Lama believed Buddhist psychology should be subjected to the rigor of modern neuroscience, which he believed was a reasonable arbiter of the truth of human nature. I believe American democracy needs a similar relationship with research on the neurobiology of trauma so we can learn to live as a collective without chronic stress and heightened defenses. Such an appropriation of this research to the institutions and relationships that undergird American society would not necessarily lead to the end of all conflict and a state of enduring peace, but it might get us as close to such a state as humans can create. We will always have to deal with the biological legacy of past generations' traumas. Consequently, we likely won't ever create Shangri-La, but trauma-focused research could help us become more discerning and less reactive in the face of threats, more self-aware, and less driven by the need to project our disavowed parts on others or escape from the world through fantasies and addictions.

We will never be able to stop others from feeling hostile toward America, yet we can create a sense of safety within ourselves, families, communities, states, and the nation. We don't have to wait for conditions to be "right" or for our imagined "social alters" to change before we choose peace within our own bodies and intimate relationships. Meaningful change can start as a ripple effect. We can begin by committing to the present moment with full awareness of all that we are.

"Right here, right now" is sometimes said to mindfully bring oneself back to the present moment, where there is the choice to slow down and, with gentle curiosity, listen to habitual patterns of fear, anger, shame, and distress, accepting them as emotions meant to protect or connect us, and then nonjudgmentally letting go of beliefs that suggest something is fundamentally wrong with oneself. Often this can be very difficult to do. When defenses are activated, each second can become a choice to make peace with oneself and one's surroundings that must be continually renegotiated. However, with practice and time, a greater sense of inner safety emerges, along with dreams of a safer future—the kind that can lead to a safe and equal America, if not world.

NEED HELP LOVING HUMANITY? HOW TO EVOLVE BEYOND US-VERSUS-THEM THINKING

One of the greatest threats to humankind is our tendency to create what sociologists call *in-groups* and *out-groups*. Whereas such distinctions potentially contribute to group solidarity, increased safety, and a personal sense of belonging, they can also lead to the us-versus-them thinking that underlies humans' greatest acts of cruelty. The following examples precipitate from us-versus-them thinking and the failure to witness the humanity of the "other":

- *Stigma.* The term *borderline* is a common pejorative used in the mental health field that devalues women with early life histories of abuse. Distinctions between *schizophrenics* and *normal people* can also imply a person experiencing psychosis has less worth, or is even less human, than a nonpsychotic person.
- *Inequities in care.* A study of pain treatment in emergency departments revealed "black children were significantly less likely to receive pain medications when compared to their white counterparts."[1]

- *Gender-based violence.* Harassment, "slut shaming," sexual assault, and rape are tools of intimidation meant to degrade women and girls.
- *Genocide.* Dehumanizing a group and identifying them as a threat to the survival of the in-group paves the way for possibly the worst form of human cruelty.

Scientific research suggests humans naturally create in-groups and out-groups. In one study of in-group affiliation, American soldiers were less likely to remember Afghan soldiers' justifications for war-related atrocities (the out-group) than fellow American soldiers' justifications for committing similar atrocities (the in-group).[2] The researchers concluded soldiers' selective forgetting allowed them to morally condone in-group members' actions while distancing themselves from members of the out-group—a process that seemed to occur without intention on the part of the study's participants.

The seemingly natural propensity to form in-groups and out-groups presently threatens our collective ability to thrive as a species. Regardless of the role in-group and out-group distinctions have played in human evolution, or our natural tendency to create them, the time has come to explore how we might evolve *differently.* There are simply too many humans on the planet, too many weapons and other methods of destruction and dehumanization, not to search for a more interdependent approach to human relations.

The question is, *How do we evolve differently?* Personally, grand gestures that attempt to fix nature, like seeding clouds to produce rain or genetically engineering crops, make me anxious. Similarly, the explosion of antidepressants and anti-anxiety medications seems to be as much about social engineering as treating mental disorders. I prefer the power of modest ideas, which can start with minimal shifts in orientation yet nevertheless lead to lasting and meaningful change.

What follows includes suggestions for loosening the grip of us-versus-them thinking. But first, let's take a deeper look at why we likely evolved to create in-groups and out-groups.

The Evolutionary Origins of the Tribe

My understanding of why humans naturally construct us-versus-them distinctions relies on anthropologist and evolutionary psychologist Robin Dunbar's *Social Brain Hypothesis*. Dunbar hypothesized that the expansion of the neocortex region of the brain, the area most often associated with humans' enhanced capacity to process and remember information, was an adaptation to increasingly complex social dynamics. Thus, rather than evolving primarily for more advanced tool use, humans gained bigger brains to master the complexities that come with group living. There also appears to be an upper limit on the number of people in an in-group that humans can psychologically accommodate. According to Dunbar:

> The social brain hypothesis implies that constraints on group size arise from the information-processing capacity of the primate brain, and that the neocortex plays a major role in this. However, even this proposal is open to several interpretations as to how the relationship is mediated. At least five possibilities can be usefully considered. The constraint on group size could be a result of the ability to recognize and interpret visual signals for identifying either individuals or their behavior; limitations on memory for faces; the ability to remember who has a relationship with whom...; the ability to manipulate information about a set of relationships; and the capacity to process emotional information, particularly with

respect to recognizing and acting on cues to other animals' emotional states. These are not all necessarily mutually exclusive, but they do identify different points in the cognitive mechanism that might be the crucial information processing bottleneck.[3]

From his extensive research, Dunbar reached the following conclusion about the number of people we comfortably bond with: "Humans are said to be able to attach names to around 2,000 faces but have a cognitive group size of only about 150."[4]

Given the natural limits placed on human bonding, I find the number of relationships made possible through social media and online networking concerning. The amount of connections and group memberships available through the internet go well beyond the upper limits Dunbar found common to our hominin ancestors for whom face-to-face communication was the norm. Through the internet, many regularly project in-group status to complete strangers and rapidly gain membership in communities of supposedly like-minded people they often don't know. Furthermore, while social media use increased over the past decade, so did evidence of rapid us-versus-them thinking, wreaking havoc on elections around the world. On the internet, it is easy to dismiss or ridicule another person or group based on a few traits, beliefs, or iconic images. The internet even has a built-in method for punctuating out-group designations: moving to another website with the click of a mouse or tap of a button.

Part of what makes the internet so enticing is its potential to create emotional reactions we find soothing, exhilarating, stimulating—really, whatever we are looking for. However, when searching on the internet to fulfill needs and desires, we also come up against things that offend and repel us. At these moments, we are most likely to revert to us-versus-them thinking.

It's not that we necessarily think, *My group and I disagree with that*, but there is a felt sense of coming in contact with the "other" that seems to trip some hard-wired need to distance oneself to preserve real-world or virtual group affiliations. It's as if even listening to "them" or perusing their websites is tantamount to endorsing their attitudes and beliefs. We don't need members of our virtual or real-world in-groups standing over our shoulders, tracking us as we surf the web, since we are typically quite good at monitoring ourselves when it comes to in-group affiliations. Maintaining membership in groups, no matter how freely we join them, inherently involves a significant amount of self-discipline with regard to group norms.

Furthermore, because of the potential for blurring the line between the real and the imagined, it's relatively easy for the attitudes and beliefs we use to parse people on the internet to leak into our face-to-face interactions—especially when feeling strong emotions backed by a sense of being part of in-groups that share similar beliefs and goals. Anthropologist Arjun Appadurai warned, "The imagination, especially when collective, can become the fuel for action."[5] Unfortunately, the way social media is constructed, particularly the capacity for quick scrolling, enforces the habit of rapid conclusions about the "other" without equal opportunities for learning how to de-escalate face-to-face confrontations with people we perceive as threats.

The world we live in is profoundly different from our hominin ancestors' world. Neither the environments we inhabit today nor the relationships we keep are "natural" according to the conditions in which the human body, psyche, and social groups first evolved. Through the internet, we have the potential to witness and interact with the imaginations and realities of billions of people—galaxies more than Dunbar's 150. The more we live partially virtual existences, mentally revolving between us-versus-them thinking as we navigate a crowded internet and planet, the more we become entrenched in mental practices adapted to a world we no longer inhabit. And we have no idea what the consequences will be.

The Need for *Us-Us* Thinking

Our expanded *neocortex*, which facilitates complex group dynamics, can also be thought of as a system that interacts with other brain systems, including the *reptilian brain system* that governs basic body functions like respiration, and the *limbic system*, which houses a lot of our emotional architecture. The limbic system includes the amygdala, which activates fear-based defense responses. However, the limbic system is also influenced by its connection to the *anterior insula cortex* that is critical for emotional awareness, including provoking feelings of empathy.

Memories stimulated by the neocortex connect with emotions kindled in the limbic system, which the reptilian part of the brain pairs with body reactions. Distinctions between *us* and *them* likely rely on the interactions of these systems to provoke action tendencies that constrict consciousness, allowing for quick decisions about whether to orient toward attachment ("us") or defense ("them")—that is, rapidly concluding whether someone is friend or foe. Given the climate-related crises predicted to occur over the next few decades that will limit resources and increase mass migrations into ever-smaller regions of the planet, we collectively will have to resist the action tendency toward defense and "them" thinking if we will have any chance of living together peace-fully. Instead, we might imagine activating the anterior insula-tion cortex's emotional awareness, if not empathy, when we feel the grip of judgment and defensiveness.

The simplest way to avoid the action tendency of defense is to orient toward the opposite action tendency, which promotes empathy, attachment, and love. Such a shift isn't always easy. I know from personal experience, as well as working with people with horrific trauma histories, that sometimes this must be an intentional choice made every day, sometimes every hour, and on tough days, every moment.

Redirecting the action tendency of defense involves continually reorienting toward feelings of empathy or actively trying to imagine ways you might be like the "other." However, when frightened or angry, it can feel nearly impossible to access empathy. At such times, acknowledging you are having a natural, hard-wired defense reaction can help. Let go of trying to feel empathy for the "other" and instead witness your body's reactions while holding empathy for yourself. Mindfully witnessing slows down the defense response that might otherwise intensify painful emotions or lead to shutdown, which interferes with clear thinking and empathic engagement with others.

If neither of these strategies works, it might help to think about the added stress caused by frequently scanning for the "other" and the potential impact on your physical health and mental well-being. Remember, healthy self-love often translates into more compassion for others. (I have also found the Buddhist meditation practice Tonglen yields wonderful results.[6])

As we practice reorienting from defensive self-preservation to empathic engagement, we can also begin to change our thoughts, engineering in ourselves a new norm of *us-us* thinking, which rests on two seemingly contradictory beliefs:

1. We are all unique.
2. We are all alike.

This may well be the sweet spot of our collective survival.

WHAT TO CALL "TERROR"?

When I first saw the headlines announcing the bombings at the 2013 Boston Marathon, I quickly closed my browser, an impulsive defense against the horrific imagery I suspected would follow. I worried where in myself I might hold this senseless tragedy when already overwhelmed by thoughts and images of violence. At the time, I was writing a paper about the phenomenology of violence and reading the accounts by Tutsi and Hutu about the 1994 Rwandan genocide. On the days when I wasn't grappling with the inconceivable brutality that haunted the Great Lakes Region of Central Africa, I worked as a psychotherapist with people coming to grips with their own histories of violence.

Before the identities of the perpetrators of the bombings were known, debate in the media focused on whether to call them terrorists if they lacked a connection to a political agenda, which, supposedly, would have given a certain logic to the event. No doubt, the bombers' intentions included terror, but I feel that discussions like this that focus on concepts, although an attempt to create meaning out of an incomprehensible situation, also unintentionally block opportunities to prevent violence in the future and heal the wounds that can lead to violence.

Jean Hatzfeld's *The Antelope's Strategy: Living in Rwanda after the Genocide* shares interviews with both survivors and perpetrators of the genocide.[1] Reading remembrances of the killings and thinking about how the Hutu and Tutsi now manage to live side by side—former predator and prey, knowing who killed who—brings to mind the potential in all of us to split off parts of the self that hold silenced memories of hurt and betrayal. Such thoughts, of course, can fuel terror if one imagines people hiding cold and dangerous hearts. Even worse, in our internet-driven world, what is perceived through media can take hold of our imaginations and feel more real than reality and fuel hatred and revenge.

In his book, *Modernity at Large: Cultural Dimensions of Globalization,* Arjun Appadurai explained how violence against one's neighbor is more likely in our media-saturated world, in which we can know the intimate details of a celebrity's life yet very little about the person next door. Appadurai suggested betrayal may be a natural reaction to feeling a contradiction between how we imagine someone to be and how we experience them:

> At heart, this sense of betrayal is about mistaken identity in a world where the stakes associated with these identities have become enormously high. The rage that such betrayal seems to inspire can of course be extended to masses of persons who may not have been intimates, and thus it can and does become increasingly mechanical and impersonal, but I would propose that it remains animated by a perceived violation of the sense of knowing who the Other was and of rage about who they really turn out to be. This sense of treachery, of betrayal, and thus of violated trust, rage, and hatred has everything to do with a world in which large-scale identities

forcibly enter the local imagination and become dominant voice-overs in the traffic of ordinary life.[2]

Some of these feelings of betrayal can be understood in terms of neurobiology. All humans share the propensity to treat the contents of their imagination as real. The unconscious aspects of the brain from which images, emotions, and body sensations arise cannot distinguish between what is real and what is imagined. When caught in strong emotions triggered by fear or a sense of unfairness, the tendency is to believe what our preconceived notions tell us is true rather than be open to experiencing someone as different from what we imagined. A mediated life also persuades us to trust in images and concepts as the final arbiters of truth instead of trusting the ambiguity that inevitably arises when we choose to grapple with the contradictions between what we imagined a person to be and how they actually are when we risk engagement and connection.

In *The Antelope's Strategy*, Hatzfeld shared an interview with Joseph-Désiré Bitero, who planned and led the coordinated killings of Tutsi in the district of Nyamata. For Bitero, the idea of "Tutsi"—itself a category amplified by colonial Belgians in an attempt to mirror Western social hierarchy in the Congo—represented memories and historical accounts of oppression and marginalization:

> We believed that the *inkotanyi* [the Tutsi-led Rwandan Patri-otic Army], once installed on the throne, would be especially oppressive—that the Hutus would be pushed back into their fields and robbed of their words. We told ourselves we didn't want to be demeaned anymore, made to wash the Tutsi ministers' air-conditioned cars, for example, the way we used to carry the kings in hammocks. I was raised in fear of the return of Tutsi privileges, of obeisance and unpaid

forced labor, and then that fear began its bloodthirsty march.

These fears—and the images, memories, and ideas that fueled them—erased bonds between neighbors, pastor and clergy, teacher and pupil, doctor and patient, and led to the brutal deaths of nearly a million people in an attempt to exterminate an entire "ethnic group"—itself, in part, an imagined portrayal of the Tutsi.

The following passage is also from *The Antelope's Strategy*. In it, Innocent Rwililiza talks about the crucial issue of who can speak for the dead. His words address the limits of generalizations. Implicitly, Rwililiza reclaims the uniqueness of every human being denied by acts of genocide and all acts of violence:

> There are facts and feelings we can manage to describe, and others, no; only the dead could report them if they were here, and we must not describe these things in their name. Why? Because they alone here fully experienced the genocide, so to say. It's not possible to speak in place of the departed, because everyone has a personal way of telling that story. Marie-Louise has her own way, Berthe hers, Jean-Baptist his. The dead have theirs, which would be even more different, since they would be telling their story while holding death by the hand.

Concepts and ideas can be revolutionary and lead to justice, but they can also dehumanize and lead to crimes against humanity. Of course, concepts *per se* don't lead to violence. Rather, opportunities to dissociate from lived experience, which representations of reality afford us, reside on a dangerous slope to denying the uniqueness and humanity of another.

Recovering from violence requires staying grounded in our bodies and letting our embodied realities be the crucibles for resolving old hurts and betrayals, real or imagined. In our fast-paced world, deluged as we are with images and ideas that mostly go unconfirmed, we must invent new ways of existing as social beings, like adding a small seed of doubt to everything we imagine or believe, and risk vulnerability as we open ourselves with curiosity to what we otherwise might resent or fear. Images and concepts are important, but we might learn the importance of putting them aside when they distance us from ourselves and each other.

WHAT I LEARNED ABOUT THE IMPORTANCE OF "TEND AND BEFRIEND" WHILE SURROUNDED BY A SWAT TEAM

The pretty South African woman sitting next to me said our flight from Johannesburg to Port Elizabeth was taking longer than expected, though I hadn't noticed. I had arrived in South Africa only a few hours before. Jet lagged, I was wrestling with the cellophane wrapper guarding the plastic cutlery that came with my in-flight meal.

She told me she was flying to "PE" (what the locals call Port Elizabeth) to attend a luncheon with Bill Clinton, who had flown there earlier that day. As she smoothed her cocktail dress and pushed a loose hair behind her ear, she asked if she could squeeze past me for a quick exit once the plane touched down.

Having learned Clinton was in town, I wasn't surprised when we landed to see emergency vehicles, their lights flashing, parked near the terminal. Cynically, I thought of the money and resources spent in the spirit of *good deeds*, something I, too, was guilty of as I had flown from the US to South Africa for a conference on violence in the Congo. As if there wasn't plenty of violence in America I could be addressing.

I had come to think of violence as commonplace. The previous two years spent as a trauma-focused psychotherapist had largely involved supporting people as they worked to create lives without violence or its lingering effects. That's what being *trauma-informed* often means: being *violence*-informed. It wasn't easy work. I was suffering a bad case of vicarious traumatization from supporting too many people who had been senselessly hurt and were still hurting, often decades after being victimized. Some were still enmeshed in violent relationships. My heart was weary from trying to halt the intergenerational transmission of trauma. Those emergency vehicles were much like the state of my mind: constantly on alert.

It wasn't until the SWAT team, clad in all black—black fatigues, black boots, black bulletproof vests, black helmets, black goggles, and black machine guns—surrounded our plane that I began to think this might not be about Clinton. My jet lag began to evaporate, replaced by a sense of shock.

I blinked several times and leaned toward the window, trying to clear the incomprehensible sight from my eyes as soldiers surrounded our plane. Right outside our window, one dropped to his belly on the grass lining the tarmac, his legs spread apart behind him. He rested on his elbows and pointed his machine gun directly at our plane. I thought of the plastic toy soldiers my brother would use to threaten to kill my Barbie.

"What's this?" I asked the woman sitting beside me, hoping this was customary treatment for flights following on the heels of luminaries.

"It probably has to do with Clinton," she replied. There wasn't any nervousness in her voice.

"I don't think so," I said as my shock morphed into fear.

The tall, slender man sitting by the window agreed with me. His face looked like mine felt: big-eyed and expressionless.

The three of us surveyed the plane. Other people did the same. There wasn't a flight attendant in sight. Fear took an icy path across my body, settling in my stomach with a hollow thud. People around me started fumbling for cell phones. I scanned for signs, something that might explain what was happening. After what felt like an eternity, the pilot's voice descended from the speakers above our heads.

"You probably can see the officers outside your windows. It's very important that everyone stays calm. Please don't use your cell phones. In a moment, they will be coming on the plane. Please stay in your seats. Do not do anything that might make them suspicious. Please do not use your cell phones."

He sounded like he had discovered a cobra in the corner of his cockpit and was gingerly walking backward, trying to get everyone's attention without provoking the snake. But who or what was *our* snake?

In my already crisis-driven mindset, it didn't take much for me to imagine the worst. *So, this is it. This is how I am going to die. To hell with the pilot, I'm calling my husband. I'm not going to die without telling him I love him. Will calling him really get me killed? Is there a bomb on the plane? Is one of us a terrorist? What does it feel like to be blown up? Shot? Burned to death? God, I hate it when people scream.*

If not for the woman next to me, I would have continued to spiral in my apocalyptic internal rant.

"This is crap," she said. "Now I'm going to miss the entire luncheon. Clinton's probably already arrived and left by now." Pointing to the officer outside our window, she added, "Look at him. He gets to lie down on the job. Where can I get a job like that?"

The man by the window this time laughed and nodded. I could only sense the tightness in my throat. I told myself to feel my feet on the ground and *breathe*.

"You don't sound too nervous about this," I said, trying not to squeak as I spoke.

"No. This kind of stuff happens all the time."

She was texting rapidly, visibly annoyed by the inconvenience of law enforcement. I was curious about what she meant by "this kind of stuff" but was more worried a trigger-happy cop would shoot her as she texted her kid's sitter.

I asked if she could turn off her phone anyway, "just in case." She complied, but as she did, I caught a glimpse of her home screen. It was a photo of her grinning baby boy. My heart sank. What if this wasn't the usual terrorist hoax? Just three days before, the US had issued a global terror warning for travelers. They had intercepted an Al Qaeda communication that suggested an increased likelihood of attacks in Northern Africa. What if our would-be terrorists were geographically challenged?

I found myself beginning to psychologically unravel in response to the threat of violence. As a trauma therapist, I knew all the signs of an impending trauma-based reaction. I was frightened and on the verge of feeling overwhelmed. I could feel myself starting to dissociate as my mind got ready for a quick psychological escape. But something also felt *non*-traumatic. I didn't feel alone.

I have had trials with violence and the threat of violence, and for me, facing it and dealing with the aftereffects alone caused the most suffering. Though I was scared on the plane and uncertain about the future, there was a cabin full of people, including the friendly people in my aisle, going through this craziness with me. For me, this was deeply healing.

I felt drawn to them, these two strangers, like I would be drawn to a buoy if I were drowning. I dropped my usual trauma defense—stoicism in the face of threats—and instead reached out. "I'm from America (as if they didn't already know). I'm here for a conference at Rhodes University. On violence. Violence in the Congo. Ironic to be greeted by machine guns on my arrival. I also practice trauma therapy. Boy, am I having a few trauma-related responses right now! What about you?"

They laughed at my feeble attempt at cross-cultural

exchange in a potential terrorist situation. And then, as if a gift to my rattled nerves, they shared, too—their feelings, their reactions to threats of violence, and what it was like to be young and black in South Africa. We also talked about what we didn't like about America—mostly capitalistic greed and hypocrisy as the US propagated violence abroad while claiming the role of peacekeeper—yet they also shared how they were inspired by the civil rights movement. They believed they could learn from the American people about race relations and entrepreneurship.

As we spoke, I kept my eye on the officer stationed outside our window and anxiously awaited more news from the pilot. I felt like two people, each with her own purpose though both vital for living through uncertainty. This felt different from the splitting that often happens when violence is endured alone. It was more like multitasking—staying alive while remaining connected to what mattered. People. Ideas. My body and sense of self.

About the time I was settling into my fate as a potential hostage, the doors opened, and we were free to go without the fanfare of a SWAT team swarming among our seats. The woman went ahead of me as planned, and the man by the window and I left each other with a handshake and genuine appreciation.

As I walked down the stairs at the plane's exit door, I caught wind of a burning smell—likely flares—and saw the men in black huddled below the belly of the plane. I thought maybe a bomb had been defused, probably because I have seen too many action thrillers. The next day, my husband could only find a short article about the "incident"—a prank call to air traffic control.

While taking the shuttle from PE to Grahamstown, the home of Rhodes University, I tracked my body for signs of trauma-related dysregulation. As I began to get a dull headache, I knew my parasympathetic stress response had settled in and my body was leaving the freeze state I had entered when I first saw the SWAT team surround the plane. Though my body showed signs of traumatic stress, *I* felt okay— the *I* who feels free to openly express myself without judgment or threat.

I believe this was largely because two people were willing to cross the divides created by countries, continents, cultures, and skin color to talk meaningfully and honestly with me. I didn't get lost in crazy thoughts or the panicky feeling in my body. Instead, I was left with a deeper appreciation of that often-used adage, "What doesn't kill you makes you stronger." Those young South Africans sitting beside me had that spirit, likely modeled by the struggles of their parents, grandparents, kin, and community. They also helped me see this adage is especially true when you have people willing to go through rough patches with you.

In remembrance of Nelson Mandela, 1918–2013

A MEDITATION ON VIOLENCE AGAINST WOMEN AND NATURE

He says that woman speaks with nature. That she hears voices from under the earth. That wind blows in her ears and trees whisper to her. That the dead sing through her mouth and the cries of infants are clear to her. But for him this dialogue is over. He says he is not part of this world, that he was set on this world as a stranger. He sets himself apart from woman and nature.

— Susan Griffin, *Woman and Nature*[1]

When Earth is Feminine and a Mother

The Great Lakes region of central Africa is mineral rich, yet many people live in extreme poverty and suffer chronic malnourishment. From the beginning of colonialism—and Belgian King Leopold's quest for fortune and fame by harvesting rubber—to more recent conflicts in eastern Congo, the Great Lakes region has also been the site of brutal violence. Economic exploitation and sexual violence, in particular, go hand in hand in the region, whether rape of slaves by colonizers or, more recently, rape by armed rebels, soldiers, and foreigners, breaking women's bodies and spirits along with social bonds that traditionally hold communities together—communities that might otherwise subsist on their land rather than lose their homes to the frenzied quest for natural resources that plagues the area.

Presently, there is a proposal to construct the largest dam in world history on the Congo River. According to its promoters, the so-called Inga 3 Dam could create electricity for half of Africa. However, in a more critical analysis, journalist Peter Bosshard claimed the dam, "would primarily generate electricity for the mining companies and middle-class consumers of Southern Africa," not the rural poor that make up much of the Congolese population.[2]

This mega-dam project ignores copious scientific evidence that large-scale dams destroy ecosystems, cause species extinction, and displace communities. Furthermore, wind and solar energy are now practical and effective approaches to creating electrical power and better serve rural villages. Yet the World Bank, the project's organizer, appears to have taken a step back in time, preferring centralized projects rather than distributed, small-scale investments adapted to the needs and conditions of local populations. Commenting on the absurdity of the project, Bosshard wrote:

Is the World Bank blinded by an outdated ideology? More likely, its return to mega-dams is driven by institutional self-interest. A strategy paper leaked from the bank in 2011 recognised that the increase in project size "may seem somewhat at odds with the goal of scaling up activities in areas where many potential projects—such as solar, wind and micro-hydropower...tend to be small." Yet, the paper argued, the "ratio of preparation and supervision costs to total project size" is bigger for small projects than large, centralised schemes, and so bank managers are "disincentivised" from undertaking small projects.[3]

Inga 3 reveals a long-standing ideology portrayed in civilization's relationship to nature that also mirrors dynamics between men and women in patriarchal societies. The preference for efficiency and centralized power over local communities and adaptation to the natural world dates back to the first cities and what mythologist Joseph Campbell called the *hieratic city state,* such as the Sumerian civilizations that emerged around 3500 BCE. Distinctions between a masculine sky god and feminine earth goddess were widespread, organizing both spirituality and city life. A similar dualism is reproduced today in projects like Inga 3 and the violence perpetrated against women in the Congo. Yet before I can support this claim, I must go further back in time.

Archaeological evidence suggests it wasn't until the emergence of agriculture-based cities and the organization of daily life around specialized work and roles that distinctions between *masculine* and *feminine* became rigid and polarized. Prior to the widespread emergence of agriculture-based city states in the Fertile Crescent, egalitarian foraging communities were the predominant form of social organization. In foraging, or hunter-gatherer, communities, each member generally masters all the technologies of their social group by the age of 12 or so years and thus can be relatively autonomous with regard to their survival. Psychoanalyst and anthropologist Géza Róheim observed:

> The outstanding characteristic...is the absence of a true differentiation of labor. An incipient or rudimentary division of labor may exist along sexual or age lines, and there may be some incipient and part-time specialization in matters of

ritual and magic. But true specialization is lacking. This means that every individual is technically a master of the whole culture or, where certain modest qualifications are necessary, of almost the whole culture. In other words, each individual is really self-reliant and grown up.[4]

Societies organized around large-scale agricultural production increased reliance on specialization, which eventually upended the conditions that supported autonomy and mastery, causing instead an infantile dependency not only on agriculture but also on fellow humans. Relationships once based on relatedness were replaced with connections based more on dependency. This shift from relatedness to dependency found an analogy in the child's relationship with his mother: The earth began to look a lot like a maternal figure. When crops were abundant, Mother Nature was giving and kind. When the yield was poor or nonexistent, Mother Nature was stingy and cruel. This shift in relationship with the natural world would emotionally stunt humankind and foster the devaluation and degradation of real women and girls.

Whereas hunter-gatherers created a relatedness with nature that depended on reading the natural world for signs of how best to survive, thus existing in relationship with the natural world, the lives of early city dwellers engendered a drive to control nature rather than relate to "her" ever-changing ecosystems. About this ensuing relationship, Paul Shepard asked:

What are the results of a lifelong subordination to mother? Among them are resentment and masked retaliations, displaced acts of violence, and the consequent guilt—all of which can be exploited to intensify the maternal dependence. Here I wish only to raise the question whether lifelong subordination to a vast Earth Mother might not affect men in similar ways.[5]

Metaphorically, the relationship with the natural world has also been sexualized, especially in discourses originating with the Enlightenment, in which knowledge was obtained by lifting nature's "veil" to "penetrate" her dark and hidden secrets. Likewise, nature was perceived as needing a domineering partner capable of taming her wildness through technological achievements, like Inga 3 or the 19th-century construction of America's transcontinental railroad. Immigrant, author, and statesman Stoyan Christowe described the national railroad as adorning the "bosom of American earth" like a gift from a controlling lover:

> Upon the white bosom of American earth we engraved a necklace of steel—set in tie plates, clasped with bolts and angle bars, brocaded with spikes. And there it lay secured to the earth, immovable.[6]

The Enlightenment preference for scientific objectivity also initiated the rejection of myths and rituals as part of a superstitious ordering of the world. For thousands of years, myths and rituals guided the transformation from childish dependency to mature sensibilities. According to Joseph Campbell:

> [Through myths and rituals] the infantile system of responses is erased and the energies carried forward, away from childhood, away from the attitude of dependency that the long infancy characteristic of our species tends to enforce—on to adulthood, engagement in the local tasks of man- and woman- hood, to an attitude of adult responsibility and a sense of integration with the local group.[7]

Today the scientific method quantifies the intuitive and transcendent aspects of human growth once guided by myth and ritual. Research studies, books, and manuals on child development at times overwhelm parents, teachers, and child psychologists with their multitude of models and evidence for how best to raise a child. The child's developing mind is treated much like the natural world—a feminine space in need of mastery and control. What once was a mystery known obliquely, guided by myths and activated through rituals, would eventually become tangible matter—*the brain*—which through proper conditioning is supported to its full maturation. Despite reams of materials written about the ideal conditions for a developing child and brain, the critical moral and emotional transformation from childhood to adulthood regularly escapes many.

More than mere stories and cultural artifacts, myths and rituals model human behavior while integrating psyches and communities. Myths and rituals locate growth in culture and individual bodies where they attend to the inevitable tensions that emerge between feelings of emotional dependency and the will to power. Through their repetition, myths and rituals distill an emotional and embodied integrity necessary for collaborating in communities that might otherwise be threatened by envy, betrayal, and jockeying for power. Without myths and rituals to repeatedly bring people together and remind them of their responsibilities to one another, the risk of childish self-absorption increases. This, Shepard argued, characterizes the modern world. "The West," he wrote, "is a vast testimony to childhood botched to serve its own purposes, where history, masquerading as myth, authorizes men of action and men of thought to alter the world to match their regressive moods of omnipotence and insecurity."[8]

The Making of Narcissistic Wounds

Many of the materials extracted from the Congo serve as little more than status symbols—fancy jewels and the latest smartphone or computer that depends on coltan for its lightning-quick functioning. But what, exactly, is the quest for wealth and status? If it were just about the attainment of shiny baubles, there likely wouldn't be *extremely* wealthy people, since once the bounty was secured, there would be a tendency to enjoy the spoils. Instead, the pursuit of wealth and the accumulation of things is often its own reward, which points to a deeper gratification than enjoying nice things.

In his book, *Status Anxiety,* Alain de Botton spoke of two types of love, one that arises from intimacy and the other from the crowd:

> Every adult life could be said to be defined by two great love stories. The first—the story of our quest for sexual love—is well known and well charted, its vagaries form the staple of music and literature, it is socially accepted and celebrated. The second—the story of our quest for love from the world— is a more secret and shameful tale. If mentioned, it tends to be in caustic, mocking term, as something of interest chiefly to envious or deficient souls, or else the drive for status is interpreted in an economic sense alone. And yet this second love story is no less intense than the first, it is no less complicated, important or universal, and its setbacks are no less painful. There is heartbreak here too.[9]

I believe de Botton is correct and the quest for status is a universal phenomenon. Yet how this quest is emotionally experienced and how status is gained are contextually and culturally dependent. Perhaps the most influential context is our first experience with love as children when we learn how to get our dependency needs met. When love is not forthcoming in the first years of life or is intermittent or unreliable, the quest for status is at risk of becoming the more gratifying form of love. In psychology, this is often described as a *narcissistic wounding*, which, at its root, is a deep sense of shame for feeling unworthy of the more intimate type of love. If we can't trust love in relationships, we are more likely to seek gratification from the image the world projects on us. But status is a poor substitute for intimacy and quite destructive when it becomes an individual's or culture's preference.

The search for love is complicated for a developing boy who feels he must shift from being dependent on women to being distinct from them. This shift involves moving from having a nonsexual relationship with women to potentially having sexual relationships with them (assuming heterosexuality). If the mother is experienced as unfeeling and cold, or alternatively, smothering, then the passage to manhood may be experienced as a need to reject her, which challenges the capacity for a sense of relatedness to women and feminine aspects of the self present in all human beings regardless of sex or gender. Furthermore, if domestic violence is present in the home and the mother is perceived as weak due to subjugation by her husband, then distinguishing himself from the feminine may feel akin to separating himself from the possibility of victimhood.[10]

If boys need ways to distinguish themselves from women as part of their development into men, and there are no rituals or myths to guide this deeply transformative process, they may nevertheless create ways to symbolically represent this transition. However, where once an inner transformation, including spiritual development witnessed in shifts in character, was the central focus of transition to manhood, we moderns are at risk of relying solely on visual "evidence" of change—what depth psychologists refer to as *literalization,* or the acting out of inner psychic processes—which rituals can do in symbolic ways that don't necessarily involve deleterious consequences to women or the natural world.

King Leopold's Narcissistic Wounds and the Legacy of Colonization

This depth psychological analysis of the violence in the Congo requires a brief look at the childhood of King Leopold and the men who first colonized the people of the Great Lakes region of Africa.

To describe King Leopold's childhood as emotionally cold would be an understatement. His parent's marriage was politically motivated and loveless. His mother barely contained her disdain for her son, who likely took the brunt of resentment she couldn't show his father. Her tone with Leopold was cold and judgmental. In a letter to him about his academic performance, she wrote:

> I was very disturbed to see in the Colonel's report that you had again been so lazy and that your exercises had been so bad and careless. This was not what you promised me, and I hope you will make some effort to do your homework better. Your father was as disturbed as I by this last report.[11]

Whereas his mother was cold, his father was emotionally and physically unavailable. According to Adam Hochschild in his remarkable account of the history of colonization of the Congo, *King Leopold's Ghost:*

> If Leopold wanted to see his father, he had to apply for an audience. When the father had something to tell the son, he communicated it through one of his secretaries. It was in this

cold atmosphere, as a teenager in his father's court, that Leopold first learned to assemble a network of people who hoped to win his favor.[12]

Rather than learning to establish relationships of trust, Leopold learned how to manipulate power. Where love might have been, a quest for high esteem grew forth. Having not been treated as a person with feelings, it was easy for him to disregard the pain of others. I imagine that for Leopold, the feminine was a devouring, life-destroying force that required domination (which is probably why he sought relationships with teenage prostitutes). When faced with the possibility of unbridled power and riches, there was no sense of relatedness, or even humanity, to stand in his way.

It would be easy to blame Leopold's mother for his sociopathic pursuit of power and status, but his relationship with his father may have been the more deciding factor, which is likely also the case for men perpetrating violence against women in the Congo today. If de Botton is correct in his formulation of two types of love, they are also characteristically gendered in patriarchal societies. Romantic love is often feminized, whereas the pursuit of status has historically been associated with the masculine heroic quest.

Since the Industrial Revolution, a dominant model of masculine success has been a man who goes out in the world to work while his wife stays home to tend hearth and progeny. Generations of children have been raised without their fathers around much of the time and thus with the sense of the masculine as a distant presence experienced for brief hours at the end of the workday or on weekends. Manhood has been equated with leaving home and the supposed world of women and childish emotional needs. Rather than as a shift in ways of relating during the transition from childhood, manhood became characterized as a rejection of emotional needs that became signs of infantile dependency.

How different is this model of manhood from the role taken by the World Bank proposing Inga 3 for the Congo? Does not the World Bank act much like a distant father dictating the realities of daily life despite minimal observation of what actually occurs in the lives of Congolese people?

Ideally, we all have both around, men *and* women, who model for us how to modulate emotions and express the desire for achievement, and these models are men and women who have had the benefit themselves of witnessing the embodiment of both masculine and feminine aspects of the self regardless of sex or gender. In patriarchal societies, however, where gendering the sexes divides personhood into unequal parts and makes one dominant over the other, men can find themselves in the difficult position of not only needing to separate from so-called feminine traits but even feeling obligated to dominate, if not denigrate, the feminine in their quest for manhood. Such a dynamic between masculine and feminine gets expressed in men's relationship with their internal sense of the feminine (including the capacity to experience feelings of dependency and vulnerability) in relation to actual women (whether perceived as equals or beings to be controlled) and the natural world (whether a sense of relatedness or domination ensues).

When King Leopold's cronies entered the Congo, they brought their understanding of the relationship between the masculine and feminine, their experiences as children of a patriarchal culture, and their sense that masculinity equated with status and power. They saw the people of this region as developmentally inferior (much how they perceived their own feelings of emotional vulnerability) and treated a feminized earth as something to master, if not exploit—justified by their perceptions of the Congo as dark, mysterious, and withholding.

Hence, violence in the Great Lakes region, and many acts of

colonization, may be seen as an unconscious acting out of a culture-bound understanding of masculinity in which becoming a man required denigrating females and perceived feminine traits. At its extreme, patriarchal masculinity rewards sexual violence and the exploitation and domination of natural resources as evidence of virility, status, and power.

Trauma Sinks Deep in the Congo

During King Leopold's reign, roughly ten million Congolese people died due to colonization and exploitation of the region. In the early 2000s, around 38,000 people died each month in the Eastern Congo due to war-related causes. Yet if the killings in Rwanda and Burundi are included, between 1994 and 2010, approximately 5.5 million people died from conflict-related causes in the region. It is hard to imagine that anyone living in the Great Lakes region today has not been personally traumatized by violence or is not the daughter or son of someone who has endured violence.

In the Congo, where the abduction and/or recruitment of young males by the army and rebel groups regularly occurs, violence has become a central aspect of the quest for manhood. Furthermore, the most lucrative avenue to status in the region is the country's mineral wealth, which is largely an unregulated industry motivating the ongoing conflicts occurring there. Yet relatively few Congolese profit from the mineral trade, and it seems the quest for status is more often played out on women's bodies.

The rapes of females in the region—acts typically characterized as weapons of war—often mirror the destruction of land in the search for mineral wealth. Victims are often violated with butts of guns or sticks, like pickaxes are taken to the earth in search of precious stones and metals. These brutal assaults are about men's relationship to other men—and thus about status and how other men perceive them—as much as they are about the denigration of women and destruction of communal and family bonds. Indeed, most rapes in the Congo are gang rapes in which men witness each other attack defenseless women, girls, boys, and even overpowered men.

It is easy to label such acts as savagery. They are. The people of the Congo need and deserve protection from such madness. But this madness has been ongoing since the initiation of colonization and is a continuation of the psychological trauma haunting its survivors. When the passage to manhood becomes dependent in part on successfully reproducing acts of the most aggressive, violence is at greater risk of becoming a cultural norm. The brutality committed against women in the Congo is no different from how women were once raped by colonizers, who, rather than butts of guns, stuffed cement in their victims' vaginas when they failed to meet their rubber quotas. No doubt, some of their children witnessed their subjugation.

When Westerners went into the Great Lakes region, they brought not only guns and chains to subjugate bodies but also beliefs and behaviors that put minds in captivity. Especially for the Congo, there was a projected sense of lawlessness that attracted particularly pernicious men—many were soldiers on "extended leave" from duty—not only lacking compassion but also relishing the opportunity to inflict cruelty. I suspect that if we examined how these men were raised, we would find profound discrepancies in power between their fathers and mothers and a devaluation of, if not disdain for, women in general and the "feminine" (and vulnerable) aspects of themselves.

Because of the brutality of colonization, especially in this region of the world, the people of the Great Lakes region were not only traumatized by their captors but many lost connection to their cultures' sense of the masculine and the feminine, their myths and rituals, their ways for becoming mature and interdependent men and women. Now they have the added burden of needing to rediscover a sense of themselves separate from the traumas inflicted on them throughout the history of colonization and globalization.

The sexualized abuse of women, as we all know, is not limited to the Congo. Many countries are increasingly concerned with the prevalence of *rape culture*. In the UK, former Prime Minister David Cameron successfully championed a ban on rape pornography, largely due to concerns that unsupervised children could access it on the internet and might normalize such acts. One obvious difference between youths in the West and in the Congo is that Congolese children are at great risk of witnessing the rape of their mothers, aunts, grandmothers, and sisters, while Western children are more likely exposed to images of rape. Yet in both the Great Lakes region and the West, children see the feminine portrayed and treated as vulnerable, objectified, and victimized. Not only will they potentially project such attitudes on females, but they may also become fearful of emotions associated with the feminine, such as vulnerability and receptivity, when witnessed in themselves.

Looking Forward

I am overwhelmed by the amount of trauma in the Congo, though I am hopeful about therapies developed specifically for trauma treatment. The situation is more complex than just healing the wounds of trauma. A profound shift in attitudes toward the feminine is needed in which the feminine is not identified as *other*, not equated with the state of being a victim, and not used in the quest for status by men.

For such a shift, we need men who are comfortable with all aspects of themselves, are emotionally receptive to gender equality, and committed to the constrained and respectful use of power. We also need more women like this, too, but we especially need men who can show boys a different path to manhood—in the Congo as well as other places around the world where violence against women and the exploitation of the natural world are evidence of the attainment of manhood.

SHOPPING OUR WAY TO EXTINCTION

Humans have been destroying environments and eradicating species throughout our history. When our ancestors arrived in the Americas over ten thousand years ago, they wiped out at least 70 genera of large mammals and millions of animals—including ground sloths, camels, wild pigs, and several species of horses.[1] Not much seems to have changed since then. According to the Global Footprint Network, today "humans use as much ecological resources as if we lived on 1.7 Earths."[2] In the Anthropocene, we are literally shopping ourselves to extinction.

We are a migratory species. Early in our evolutionary history, our ancestors left Africa in search of new theaters for survival. The strait of Bab el Mandeb at the southern tip of the Red Sea was a launching point for journeys into Asia and eventually Europe, Australia, and the Americas. Some say drastically changing environments necessitated our wanderings, including the eruption of Toba, a volcano in Sumatra. Others point to competition for resources, which naturally occurs when an environment is stretched beyond its supportive limits. Whatever the reason for our itinerant beginnings, we have thrived as a species through our capacity for altering environments to fit our needs, often without concern for the viability of the natural world that sustains us. Like fickle lovers (or spoiled children), we have a habit of taking from Earth what we want and then walking away when our needs are no longer met, confident there will always be greener pastures.

What compels us? Do our genes push us along? Could the driving force be more banal, like all the bacteria inhabiting our bodies? More than five hundred different species of "good" bacteria hitch a ride on the average person, filling over one hundred trillion cells—much more space than the "natural" components that make up a human body. Most of these critters aren't harmful, and most are quite communal, sharing responsibilities with the host body to keep it healthy and functioning.

Bacteria also act like a migratory species. Even when a bacterium is in an environment that meets all its needs—just the right temperature, plenty of food—it will still make excursions outside its little paradise to ensure there isn't a sweeter deal somewhere else. *Are we led unknowingly in the direction of the needs of the bacteria in our body?* I don't think so, but I do believe bacteria have a lesson to teach us.

Constantly checking for better environments is a great strategy if, in your species' evolution, there were frequent and relatively rapid environmental collapses. In these conditions, the propensity for migrating and having the capacity to exploit a variety of environments would be highly adaptive survival skills. Yet tying human evolution to surviving catastrophes implies, at least in part, we have evolved to survive traumatizing circumstances.

Given our unrestrained devouring of our planet, I imagine an unconscious drive at work, although I hesitate to propose the source is genetic (or bacterial), thereby suggesting the drive is outside our control and one we will inevitably follow, possibly to our collective demise. Rather, more akin to bacteria, I imagine a *repetition compulsion* catalyzing our consumption of

Earth. *Repetition compulsion* is the unconscious tendency of putting oneself in circumstances reminiscent of an earlier unpleasant, or even traumatic, experience.

Sigmund Freud originally described the repetition compulsion in his book *Beyond the Pleasure Principle*.[3] Freud became interested in repetition compulsion because it seemed to defy his ideas about the pursuit of pleasure. He hypothesized that repeating behaviors associated with unpleasant or even threatening events creates opportunities for integrating those experiences, perhaps even reaching a preferred outcome.

Freud's focus on repetition compulsion was originally framed by his reflections on relational dynamics between a caregiver and child that become unconscious blueprints for the child's later relationships. Yet the notion also applies to the tendency to unconsciously recreate circumstances associated with a past traumatic event to "master" the original trauma. Then repetition compulsion is an attempt to integrate memories dissociated when the body and psyche become overwhelmed by trauma.

One way to end the repetition compulsion is to finally reach, or discover, the missing *act of triumph*.[4] When people are provided a safe environment that supports reflective awareness, such as psychotherapy, they can begin to identify actions they might have used to defend themselves, like blocking a strike or pushing away an attacker—those so-called *acts of triumph*. Through mindfully witnessing what our bodies wanted to do in the face of threat, we can reintegrate natural defense responses and potentially end unconscious, compulsive actions.

The reason for our collective inability to stop devouring Earth may be that we have failed to identify the cultural equivalent of acts of triumph. Instead, we behave as if our survival depends upon compulsive consumption. Humans inhabit cultures very much as we do our bodies. Like bacteria, we have learned the advantage of repetitively searching for better environments, yet how we search (and destroy) has lost its adaptive benefits and seems more the result of the intergenerational transmission of trauma than a biologically determined behavior.

We don't have to look deep into our past to understand the traumatic impact of forced migrations on humans. In 2021, there were over 86 million displaced persons worldwide, often living in deplorable conditions. The uncertainty, fear, and deep sense of injustice they experience will be transmitted to future generations, especially through their emotions.

Children are primarily emotional beings. They breathe in their caregivers' emotions as naturally as they take in air. We adults do not need to express our fears and desires to children for them to sense our feelings. Even when our emotions are split from our conscious awareness because of overwhelming trauma—especially situations we are afraid to reexperience—children will feel the effects of the ghosts that continue to haunt us. What we cannot consciously express, we evoke in others, enact in our relationships, and embody. These evocations, enactments, and embodiments are often dissociated from our awareness, but they are still transmitted, especially to emotionally dependent children learning how to orient to their world.

The needed act of triumph for our increasingly aimless consumption may be a collective mourning for a lost sense of place that could securely ground us in the world and ourselves. Perhaps we unconsciously continue to evoke the dream of the Garden of Eden, a Mother Earth that always provides for us—a dream we unconsciously try to fulfill through compulsive consumption of her resources. As Paul Shepard observed, "We suffer for the want of that vanished world, a deep grief we learn to misconstrue."[5]

Our destructive entitlement with respect to Earth's resources is a repetition compulsion that bears witness to a felt sense of loss, but it fails to create the security longed for. The trauma of lost security preoccupies us as a need to right a felt sense of being wronged—even if the wrongdoers are simply Earth's natural shifts—her grief and her efforts to birth something new in the natural cycle of life and death.

"Good" bacteria, with their repetitive checks for better environments, act on their need for safety, yet they also balance their searches with respect for the needs of their current host, keeping the body alive, even caretaking in a symbiotic quest for survival. Indeed, we identify bacteria as pathological and as diseases when they fail to respect the principle of symbiosis. Like "good" bacteria, we could learn to be curious about the conditions of nearby niches while practicing sustainability in our own backyards. However, to live in such a state of balance and healthy survival may require identifying the acts of triumph that will release us from our compulsive need to consume.

In *The Red Book*, Carl Jung chronicled his healing journey and reconnection with his lost parts. He wrote, "Turn your anger against yourself, since only you stop yourself from looking and living."[6] This turning toward ourselves to learn the nature of our unconscious drives seems an important first step. However, rather than turning anger "against yourself," it is often much better to just witness how the emotions we cannot let ourselves feel are enacted, evoked, and embodied. By witnessing without acting, we can instead begin to grieve lost parts of ourselves, including the losses we have inherited from our ancestors.

Jung also distinguished between *being* and *becoming*. This distinction is central to a shift away from compulsive consumption, tied to a desire to *become* someone other than who one is —often in conditions other than the reality in which one lives. There is peace in acceptance. As Jung remarked, "Everything is riddlesome to one who is becoming, but not to one who is."

There is no shame in committing to one's survival or improving one's life. However, without awareness of what compels our compulsive consumption, we are not surviving or improving. Rather, *we are being consumed by haunting fears*, specters of past traumas we try to ignore by blindly shopping our way to extinction.

REFORMING MENTAL
HEALTH SERVICES

WANT TO REDUCE MENTAL ILLNESS? ADDRESS TRAUMA. WANT TO SAVE THE WORLD? ADDRESS TRAUMA

Some claim the large number of people diagnosed with mental disorders results from ever-expanding diagnostic criteria that risk medicalizing normal emotional reactions. Others argue the increase results from pharmaceutical companies financially courting the medical establishment and using advertisements to attract potential users for their drugs. While both arguments seem correct, they fail to address that an increasing number of people regularly experience despair and struggle to stay psychologically, socially, and financially afloat in an increasingly uncertain and unstable world.

I would like to suggest an additional explanation for the increase in mental disorders: The upsurge results from our collective failure to alleviate conditions that contribute to trauma-related stress. I also believe psychiatry's overreliance on diagnoses and medications has prevented people from overcoming mental disorders and returning to growth-centered lives. Models of mental illness as chronic, genetic-based disorders give the sense that we are reaching the origins of our suffering—that is to say, the genes we inherited—when, in actuality, we risk denying the traumatizing conditions in which many of us grew up or continue to live. Although diagnoses and medications may provide some relief, they may also cause people to avoid making the changes necessary for moving into emotionally sustainable futures.

Childhood abuse and other emotionally damaging experiences are so prevalent today that trauma-focused psychiatrist Bessel van der Kolk claimed the single most important health problem facing Americans is our exposure to what are increasingly referred to as *adverse childhood experiences*. These experiences have been rigorously correlated with chronic psychological and physical illnesses. As shared in an earlier essay, adverse childhood experiences include: recurrent physical abuse; recurrent emotional abuse; sexual abuse; emotional or physical neglect; alcohol and/or substance abuse in the household; an incarcerated household member; living with someone who is mentally ill; domestic violence; and one or no parents. (I would like to add to this already long list living in a violent community, the conditions of poverty, climate catastrophes, and the effects of racism, sexism, homophobia, and other forms of oppression.) Based on self-reports of over 17,000 adults, a study conducted by the Center for Disease Control (CDC) and Kaiser Permanente concluded that more than two-thirds of the participants had at least one adverse childhood experience and over two-fifths had at least two experiences.

A study at the University of Minnesota, Twin Cities, obtained results similar to the CDC-Kaiser study. Psychologist Patricia A. Frazier and colleagues administered the Traumatic Life Events questionnaire to 1,528 college students. The results showed 85 percent had at least one trauma in their relatively short lives, and on average, students reported a history of three traumas. The most common traumatic events included sudden bereavement (47 percent), the life-threatening illness of a family member or friend (30 percent), witnessing family violence (23 percent), receiving unwanted sexual attention (21 percent), and involvement in an accident in which either themselves or someone else was hurt (19 percent).[1] If "normal" correlates with the greatest number of people, then coming from a normal household in America means growing up in conditions that contribute to poor emotional and physical health in adulthood.

Historically, the denial of trauma's impact—or complete silence about its occurrence, such as the silence that often surrounds childhood abuse—has been a primary approach to dealing with the consequences of trauma. There are benefits, of course, to denying trauma. For example, trauma-focused psychiatrists Alexander McFarlane and Bessel van der Kolk pointed out, "Powerful social institutions such as insurance companies and the armed forces...benefit from downplaying the impact of trauma on people's lives."[2] By lessening or ignoring the impact of trauma, they relinquish themselves from responsibility for addressing its long-term consequences.

Medicine's reliance on clinical- and laboratory-based studies also allows its practitioners to ignore or play down the role of trauma in the development of mental disorders and physical diseases. Van der Kolk and McFarlane remarked:

> Hitherto, science has generally categorized people's problems as discrete psychological or biological disorders—diseases without context, largely independent of the personal histories of the patients, their temperaments, or their environments.[3]

One major consequence is that creating a sense of objectivity is prized more than emotionally taxing social work and psychotherapy. Conceptual rigor is preferred over the ambivalent yet more accurate outcomes that result when peoples' actual lives are the focus. This consequence has not gone unnoticed by those carrying out biomedical research on psychiatric disorders. Quoting Tom Insel, former director of the National Institute of Mental Health (NIMH):

I spent 13 years at NIMH really pushing on the neuroscience and genetics of mental disorders, and when I look back on that I realize that while I succeeded at getting lots of really cool papers published by cool scientists at fairly large costs—I think $20 billion—I don't think we moved the needle in reducing suicide, reducing hospitalizations, improving recovery for the tens of millions of people who have mental illness. I hold myself accountable for that.[4]

Yet the gravest consequence of the denial of trauma is likely how it unravels the social fabric of society. Again, quoting McFarlane and van der Kolk:

How are the memories of brutalization and cruelty stored at a societal level? How does this affect people's capacity for loyalty, personal and social commitments, beliefs in individual sacrifices for the common good, belief in justice, willingness to delegate decision making to elected representatives, and belief in the meaning of laws and rules?[5]

The United States is a country born from the traumas of colonization and displacement, and capitalism is a costly distraction from our deep, unhealed wounds. Furthermore, capitalism's ethos of progress and continual need for expansion and growth are not only diversions from our emotional wounds but can become like addictions, numbing traumatic remembrances of our individual and collective pasts as we chase more lucrative futures.

Medicine has gained prominence in our society as a method of denial likely because it successfully identifies in individuals' bodies the effects of social ills that as a society we have failed to alleviate. Instead, we often look to mental healthcare to "fix" individuals enough so they can function "responsibly" (often defined in terms of holding a job and paying the bills) in a society that habitually denies its responsibility to its members.

When we fail to grapple with the conditions that lead to suffering, and thus fail to address the root causes of mental disorders, we resign ourselves not only to repetition of the problem but also to a prevalent sense of "stuckness" that has us collectively doubting the possibility of meaningful social change.

It's time to rethink the nature of mental disorders and how, as a society, Americans can respond to conditions that contribute to adverse childhood experiences as well as other traumas, like rape and war. Doing so requires challenging the assumption that America's success is best measured by the marketplace and scientific advancement. During the past several decades, we have witnessed a shift from unprecedented —and largely unquestioned—growth in industry, science, and technology to the need to increasingly devote energies to managing the fallout and risks of the imprudent choices made in the name of financial and technological advancement. We have witnessed a similar arc in the mental health field concerning the marketing of a variety of medications that often fail to create sustained mental well-being while causing debilitating side effects and disease.

As we rethink our relationship with unmanageable growth in efforts to save our planet, we also need to reconsider our relationships with each other. How can we save the planet if we cannot even save ourselves?

SUBJECTIVITY AND BEING MENTALLY ILL

Mental healthcare is at crossroads. Again. This time, trauma-informed care challenges the biomedical model of mental illness. Some see this crossroads as potentially leading to a revolutionary shift in services. Others look for ways to join disparate ideas about the origins of mental illness into an amalgamated whole. Yet for anyone who has spent time in the field —as practitioner, service user, or both—the experience of continually returning to crossroads gets exhausting.

To avoid further restarts and regressions, I think it might help to look closely at some of the concepts that carry the most assumptions about human nature, like *responsibility*, *freedom*, *subjectivity*, *individualism*, and *community*. I had a professor claim these are the kinds of words you could "turn a truck around with," yet they rarely get addressed when we're at cross-roads trying to imagine a new future. Perhaps they're the culprit—all those words we think we agree upon but, on closer inspection, keep us tied to a past we have no interest in repeating.

In the following, I look at the concept of *subjectivity*. I reflect on the significance of subjectivity for treating mental disorders and share why I think we should pay attention to subjectivity, and what we think it means, when determining how well the field is serving both people and society.

Why Subjectivity?

Subjectivity is related to responsibility and the capacity for making rational choices. Thus, it is central to ideas about mental disorders. Through subjectivity, we witness our minds and internal experiences and use them in intentional ways. We also come to know ourselves as one mind among many.

Subjectivity is essential for success in an ever-changing world, which involves the capacity to manipulate mental states in pursuit of the imagined person one hopes to become and the avoidance of who one doesn't want to be. Personhood is a continual project, and subjectivity is a primary tool for staying the course and creating the desired self. Especially in rapidly changing and precarious economies, people feel confident when they can anticipate changes they need to make and then implement them. Subjectivity is central to this process of adaptation.

For the mental health field to stay relevant, it must also adapt—and to the very conditions its service users are adapting to. It must value the need for a fluid sense of self that most people find necessary for living adroitly in uncertain times. Diagnoses are typically not helpful in this regard. Although a diagnosis may seem like a steady mast in stormy waters, it also ties the diagnosed to a false sense of security when what is really needed is learning how to adapt to constantly changing seas.

Michel Foucault once described psychiatry as a discursive practice people use as a *technology of the self*.[1] By applying psychiatric discourses and practices to themselves, people learn if psychiatric knowledge is true of them and contributes to attaining the sense of self and life course desired. I believe this is the right way to think of mental health services—as technologies of the self to be tried on and tried out, relative truths that are valued for the comfort they provide and the possibilities they create for continually living in ways that feel true to the personhood imagined and desired.

The capacity for subjectivity has not always been granted to people experiencing mental illness. In the 18th century, when the mentally ill were locked in madhouses and suffered the most inhumane conditions, they were seen and treated as wild beasts in need of taming.[2] The introduction of psychiatry into the squalor of madhouses was a vast improvement and led to recognizing the capacity for subjectivity in people experiencing mental illness.

The Enlightenment's optimism for rational thought cast a spell on those early psychiatrists. For example, French physician Philippe Pinel's *moral treatment* worked on the premise that madness was a breakdown of rational function and, in the correct conditions, the mentally ill could become aware of their personal and collective responsibilities. That is, they could begin to exercise subjectivity.

Yet the subjectivity granted was never that of a full member of society but more like the subjectivity granted a child. Implicit in the earliest notions of subjectivity was that it was underdeveloped in the mentally ill person, and the role of the psychiatrist was to promote the development of self-awareness. This perceived underdevelopment has justified infantilizing the mentally ill and still influences how subjectivity is perceived in people diagnosed with mental disorders.

For instance, in her book, *Of Two Minds*, anthropologist T. M. Luhrmann described how biomedical psychiatrists in hospital settings listened for signs of underlying brain disorder in their patients' stories of suffering. How the patient perceived his suffering, as well as what he believed might provide relief, was largely ignored. Instead, the physician listened for symptoms of a brain disorder, identifying sleep patterns and mood states hidden in patient complaints. Furthermore, subjectivity was only granted when the patient willingly accepted the psychiatrist's biomedical explanation of his suffering:

> When that young man could say that he had been ill and begin to discuss the problem of being ill, his intentions and his reports on his state of mind began to be treated like responsible, reasonable assertions. That part of him moved into the adult category. He became a person with an illness, not an illness and a body. The unfortunate but accurate implication here is that if you wanted to leave the hospital, you were still sick, but if you agreed to stay, you were treated as if you are getting well.[3]

This account exemplifies how the patient is assigned the responsibility of abdicating his own subjectivity, including the truths he uses to construct his life, and replace them with his physician's medical model. Yet subjectivity, in its fullest expression, is about freedom of choice, including not only the choice of who one wants to become but the methods one uses to create oneself—that is to say, which technologies of the self will be employed. Furthermore, discursive practices are not always selected because they work, like a science experiment run according to cause and effect, but neither are they entirely random. Instead, they are often *ethical* choices that relate to the person's beliefs and feelings concerning the best way to live. In a world of ever-changing memes and scientific data, exercising one's choice about the discourses used to guide the construction of personhood may be the strongest evidence of subjective freedom.

How Do We Make Subjectivity Inalienable?

Until the mental health field consistently respects the subjectivity of service users—no exceptions, not even for psychosis—I think the field will continue to return to crossroads. To do otherwise is to leave open the possibility of harming the people it has committed to serve. Furthermore, the principle of *do no harm* that guides medicine may be inadequate for the mental health field and the sensitivity needed to truly avoid harming the very intimate experience of personhood. Instead, principles of nonviolence that respect the organicity of life are needed. Also, distinctions between the normal and pathological that play a central role in medicine can impede both the provider's and the service user's abilities to witness the value of all aspects of personhood that contribute to subjectivity.

The mental health field wrongly assigned itself the role of *developing* subjectivity instead of *witnessing* subjectivity. This is a subtle but profound shift. Witnessing subjectivity provides opportunities for respecting all parts of the service user, creates conditions for validating existing strengths and values, and avoids power dynamics that inevitably hamper progress. Witnessing subjectivity means actively looking for it and acknowledging the inevitable shifts in mental states that are a natural aspect of psychic life. These shifts are true of everyone. We are all at our best when our basic needs for sleep, food, shelter, safety, companionship, and stimulation are met. Failure to meet these basic needs can reduce anyone's capacity to act intentionally or responsibly.

It's questionable, however, if mental well-being has always been the primary concern of psychiatry. Granted, for over two centuries, the mental health field, and psychiatry in particular, has presented itself as a remedy for societal ills, although largely by adapting its philosophy and methods to the dominant social agenda. In 1793, when Dr. Pinel initiated reforms in the Salpêtriere and Bicêtre Hospitals in Paris, where the insane were often held in chains, the field cast itself as moral reformer and protector of human rights and thus mirrored the values promoted by the French Revolution and Enlightenment. When democratic societies needed ways to decide which of their citizens had free will and could act as autonomous subjects, the mental health field obliged with criteria for the insanity plea, protecting citizens from both dangerous minds as well as judicial systems unschooled in the limits of human reason. During darker moments in human history, the mental health field also complied, giving credence to the eugenics movement, forced sterilization, and even the "extermination" of the mentally ill during the reign of Nazism. For better and worse, where society has ventured, the mental health field has followed.

It's not a coincidence that psychologists have been criticized for their role in torture at Guantanamo Bay during the same time in history when prominent psychiatrists are accused of exchanging scientific principles for profits from pharmaceutical companies. Both situations rely on a two-hundred-year-old understanding of subjectivity as something that can be manipulated, if not dominated.

The long-held belief that people with mental illness somehow lack subjectivity has allowed a sense of urgency and fear to justify unethical solutions. I believe we keep coming back to crossroads because the mental health field has yet to fully embrace a principle of nonviolence that respects and protects the rights of the people it purportedly serves.

I also believe there is fear that respecting the subjectivity of people diagnosed with mental disorders or suffering chronically from the effects of trauma is equivalent to giving a gun to a child. Perhaps this is why a 19th-century conception of subjectivity continues to hold sway even today. Despite all that has been learned about the human psyche and the treatment of mental illness and trauma, a general association of mental illness with the lost capacity for subjectivity, and thus, an increased likelihood of violence, still exists.

Thinking this way has justified treating people with mental illness as if they have fewer rights than others, if not savagely, and leads to beliefs that the mentally ill should be feared rather than helped. If we start seeing subjectivity as an inalienable experience that is state dependent and acknowledge the necessity of freedom of choice for ethical living, we might also start seeing the tragedy that a lack of adequate mental health services imposes on people, especially at this particular moment in history, when to be human is nearly synonymous with the continual construction of personhood. I also believe that if we start seeing subjectivity as inalienable, there will be more of an expectation to change the conditions that contribute to mental illness and trauma.

What Does Inalienable Subjectivity Look Like in Practice?

Many providers already adhere to principles of nonviolence and consistently respect their clients' subjectivity and right to choice of treatment. These practitioners are not looking at service users for evidence that they have failed to develop or suffer from a pathology. Rather, they work with them to identify the strategies they have developed to survive, given their temperament, their body, the conditions in which they were raised, and the traumas they've experienced. Whatever modality is used, the goal is to help people develop new strategies or release old ones that interfere with growth and adaptation to current conditions in their lives.

These practitioners also increasingly focus on mindfulness and supporting service users in gaining greater awareness of present-moment experience. With practice, mindfulness increases subjective awareness and the capacity to witness what types of changes lead to desired outcomes. With increased awareness, the impact of change can be witnessed not only in thoughts but in feelings and body sensations, widening subjective awareness and increasing the ways to experience personhood.

Even with the use of developmental theories, such as attachment theory, treatment can focus on introducing new strategies rather than improving an underdeveloped mind. The different attachment styles—whether avoidant, disorganized, preoccupied, or secure—represent ways the developing child adapted to their caregivers. Even if attachment is disorganized and doesn't lead to satisfying relationships, adaptation did occur, and there is always the possibility of learning *different* strategies. With time and effort, a new way of being in the world can emerge. Treatment can also involve using subjectivity *differently*. For example, dialectical behavior theory helps service users establish nonjudgmental self-awareness rather than relying on a critical subjectivity that mimics the language and attitudes that often dominate in emotionally invalidating households.

I hope I have made the case that how we think about subjectivity is central to the success of the mental health field, which continues to rely on antiquated notions of subjectivity fashioned at a time when the mentally ill were seen as barely superior to untamed beasts. Fortunately, mental illness is increasingly seen as an experience and not a person, and there's more respect for the wisdom of the wildest among us— the truly wild and beautiful animals with which we share Earth.

Yet we've unwittingly left a loophole through which shoddy, if not unethical, treatment can still find its justification, and as long as the mentally ill or traumatized can be pathologized or perceived as underdeveloped, their rights, and the field, are at risk. However, by establishing and enforcing principles of nonviolence and respecting the organicity of life as it central tenets, the mental health field will more likely avoid the kinds of abuses that ignoring fundamental principles of nonviolence has caused.

SECRETS IN OUR SILENCES

I began reading *History Beyond Trauma* by Françoise Davoine and Jean-Max Gaudillière during a turbulent time in my life when deaths, losses, and uncertainties piled up.[1] Despite my best efforts to remain optimistic and push forward with life as planned, traumatic stress threatened to be more than a subject I researched or a condition I treated. At times, I felt I was only a narrow step beyond its grasp. I didn't speak of this at first, as if, by not voicing my fears, I would somehow outpace them.

During times when feelings of overwhelm constantly nip at our heels, folly is likely to enter our lives, and we take her hand willingly. I also sat aside *History Beyond Trauma,* which might have saved me a regrettable detour. Much later, I would learn the book sensitively looks at the intergenerational transmission of war-related traumas and critically analyzes the ways analysts and their analysands reenact not only their own unspoken traumas but also the silenced traumas of their parents, grand-parents, and other ancestors.

With folly by my side, I started analysis with a very control-ling man who was also my supervisor. In my state of duress, I ignored all I had learned in my training about the perils of dual relationships. More importantly, I ignored what I knew as a trauma survivor about the dangers of excessive power and control. Had I continued to read *History Beyond Trauma*, I would have come across Davoine and Gaudillière's discussion of Lacan's notion of the *Real*, which is concerned with the erasure of traumatic histories. In one passage, they wrote:

> What we are dealing with in that case is a normal craziness that bears witness to a normality that is crazy, trivialized, dehistoricized, and denied: 'What happened didn't happen.' From that time on, the place vanishes with the past: there is no place, no past. It has become impossible to trust one's own emotions and sensations.

Now, I am a middle-aged woman with four advanced degrees and years of hard-won street smarts. I am also blessed with a loving and supportive husband and good friends, all of whom repeatedly pointed to my folly, which I was too frightened to see. This is the power of the traumas that binds us to others and blinds us to reality—that "What happened didn't happen" stance toward life that Davoine and Gaudillière wrote about. We start ignoring what we know is real on an emotional and intuitive level, especially if we can't use our senses to access it in the tangible environment.

If I can deny what I know is real (or technically speaking, *dissociate* from it) and I am someone who *knows* better (at least on a rational level), how vulnerable are clients who are often isolated in their suffering, not to mention lack the years I have clocked studying psychotherapy and the mental health industry?

Most who practice psychotherapy are not by nature exploitive like my analyst/supervisor was, yet many have traumatic pasts. Sometimes we therapists like to pretend we have healed our personal traumas, or to a lesser degree, we pretend we can ignore the depth to which they inform so much of who we are and what we do. Yet it is the nature of trauma—just as it is the spiraling nature of recovery—that we must address our traumatic pasts over and again across the lifespan, though usually without the intense pain and distraction that can characterize early attempts to do so. (Hopefully, much of this early work is completed before working in the mental health field.)

Painful as such memories can be, we must consciously remember the traumas in our past because the problems that come with unconscious remembering are too risky. Davoine and Gaudillière wrote, "But whatever the measures chosen for erasing facts and people from memory, the erasures...only set in motion a memory that does not forget and that is seeking to be inscribed."[2] In effect, the "Real" we attempt to forget unconsciously pushes to become part of reality, which means clients are always vulnerable to therapists' failures to witness their own traumatic wounding.

I worry about the silences that shroud the practice of psychotherapy and therapists' stories of their own traumas— those silences that risk turning therapists into "blank screens." On the one hand, clients don't come to therapy to hear about us, and we wisely use the time to help them narrate their silences and dreams for whom they could become. On the other hand, if we pretend our own traumas are not at least, on an unconscious level, pushing for their own resolution, we increase the risk for folly to choose the direction the relationship will take.

According to Davoine and Gaudillière, telling stories of trauma and traumatizing relationships is central to healing. "The stories of deep connection and pain must be told." They also warned, "If for some reason, they cannot be spoken, they are told through an other," which is how the intergenerational transmission of trauma occurs.[3] The Real acts like a contagion passed from parent to child and, perhaps in a similar fashion, from psychotherapist to client. The transmission of the Real reminds me of Carl Jung's remark, "The greatest tragedy of the family is the unlived lives of the parents."

Yet the tragedy is not only their unfulfilled dreams and desires but also the Real silenced by their families and communities, who were unable or unwilling to acknowledge their own traumatic experiences. This goes on across generations. Stopping this cycle is the gift psychotherapy can potentially offer the world, but only if practitioners consistently acknowledge the Real in their own lives.

Speaking about trauma is not always enough to avoid its repetition and transmission. I was aware of some of my analyst/supervisor's traumas, just as he knew mine, but given how easy it is to deny the Real, the impacts of these past traumas on our current relationship were swept aside even as we spoke about them.

Unfortunately, our words cannot always protect us from what Janet identified as our unconscious pursuits of *acts of triumph* and what Freud identified through *repetition compulsion*. Trauma leaves too much unresolved and too much within us seeking resolution. Words are often a flimsy defense against profoundly visceral wounding, and so is *knowing* the right thing to do. This is largely why healing from traumatic experiences requires working with the body. We are all so much more than what we think, believe, and even feel is true about ourselves.

I quit working with my analyst/supervisor much earlier than planned. The ending was abrupt and ugly. I got out of that relationship as quickly as I did largely because of people who made the effort to pull me from folly's grasp and then support me as I finally grieved the losses that had piled up—including the added load of the analyst/supervisor I once trusted. It took a small village for me to actually see what was real and then act in accordance with it, regardless of what my analyst/supervisor wanted me to believe was true.

My relationship with my analyst/supervisor was the most defeating aspect of my training as a psychotherapist. I share it here because I don't think the mental health field is doing a good job monitoring its members with regard to their own trauma histories and how these histories potentially impact the people we hope to serve, let alone our relationships with each other. We use words like *countertransference* and *co-transference* to encapsulate when we unwittingly "leak" into the therapeutic relationship, which is an inevitable and natural aspect of the process. However, a systemic-level silence seems to permeate the profession around the topic of what it means to be a collective in which the majority of us have histories of adverse childhood experiences and other traumas. Where are the discussions about the inherent problems that arise within a community of wounded healers and their collective failures to deal with the Real?

There is something about the role of psychotherapist that encourages practitioners to act as if they aren't somehow wounded, or act as if they have moved so far beyond the experience of being wounded that they can ignore the traumatic experiences in their pasts—the very ones that often brought them to the profession in the first place. However, unlike other professions, where people can enjoy a cloak of professionalism that hides personal histories and idiosyncrasies, mental health workers need to be authentic and emotionally receptive while almost saintly in their handling of other human beings. At times, this leads to emotional ambivalence we attempt to push away by denying how our own traumas get activated, especially given the natural desire to feel we are doing a good job and are capable practitioners.

Psychotherapy is also a largely solitary profession, and psychotherapists lack opportunities for peers to observe their work. Supervision and consultation, although meant to be occasions for gaining objective insights and constructive criticism, cannot protect clients from what psychotherapists defend against seeing in themselves and their personal histories.

The situation is confounded by hierarchies impacting relationships between psychiatrists, psychologists, social workers, marriage and family therapists, and the like. Furthermore, many practitioners seem too easily caught in status-seeking (or playing out unresolved sibling rivalries) that traffics in feelings of shame, envy, and competitiveness. Such emotions make it difficult to access the more vulnerable aspects of ourselves, which we need to attend to as we deal with the multitude of feelings, memories, and body sensations invariably activated by our clients' traumatic experiences.

It is when we aren't supporting each other and safely identifying the potential follies within our midst that our clients are at greatest risk of falling victim to our traumas and our failures to witness the Real. Too easily we hide the past beneath the desire to be the "perfect" professionals we imagine our clients need us to be and who we often wish we were.

CAN DSM DIAGNOSES BE
OTHER THAN PEJORATIVE?

Name-calling. Cursing. Yelling when a calmer tone could deliver the same message. Who of us at times doesn't act outside the boundaries of civility and compassion?

The material world often gets the brunt of such outbursts. My previous work writing computer programs in Fortran left me with a childish wish to inflict pain on computers when they failed to do what I expected. If cursing didn't seem to work, I sometimes flipped off the power. *Yeah, I showed them who was boss.*

I know I am not the only one who so pointlessly loses their cool. How many of us let the expletives rip when house repairs turn toward the incomprehensible? Ever put together a propane grill or prefab bookcase whose screws seem stripped before they ever leave their sealed plastic pouches? Not a pretty sight.

Such object-focused rants seem like emotional outtakes, but they are also signs of a lack of curiosity about the world and a need for control. These verbal assaults would be fairly harmless if not for the sometimes-blurry line existing between how we anthropomorphize our possessions and objectify fellow human beings.

The *Diagnostic and Statistical Manual of Mental Disorders* (DSM) is a reliable resource if objectifying someone is the goal. "He's such a narcissist." "She's so borderline." "I can't talk to him; he's totally bipolar." Diagnoses are useful when there is a desire for distance and control, but perhaps more significantly, they protect oneself from feelings of vulnerability. No wonder many of us diagnose people close to us when relationships are precarious or we find ourselves in the wake of a breakup. Yet name-calling is a flimsy defense against heartbreak and the feelings that emerge when people disappoint or hurt us.

By virtue of how psychiatric diagnoses are increasingly used by both professionals and laypersons, they have become largely empty words that lack worth—what Jungian analyst Russell Lockhart called *words without souls*.[1] For a word to have soul, it must imply something about the nature of a person's being, although not of a general sort that applies to anyone who meets certain diagnostic criteria. Instead, words with soul speak to what is unique about somebody and in ways that draw us closer through a feeling tone, thus creating an emotional bond that validates uniqueness rather than effacing a person's individuality.

The DSM is the preeminent diagnostic tool for the mental health field, which, as you know, includes the practice of psychotherapy. The term *psychotherapy* is derived from two ancient Greek words, *psyche*, which means soul, and *therapia*, which means healing. Thus, psychotherapy is the practice of *healing the soul*, or tending the soul of someone in the process of returning to growth. To tend a soul involves caring about speech, listening to someone's distinctive story, hearing the worth of a word, and witnessing how a phrase or gesture carries individuality—that is to say, the act of *finding soul* in speech and soma. How odd it is that the DSM, a most impersonal tome, would be produced in a field that started with psychotherapy as such a personal relationship.

The DSM originated through a power struggle between two competing perspectives on the nature of mental illness, if not what it means to be human. The DSM codified a division in the mental health field between so-called *Axis I* and *Axis II* disorders, reflecting the split between biomedical psychiatry (Axis I) that originated with the work of Emil Kraepelin, and psychoanalysis (Axis II), which started with the work of Sigmund Freud. Along Axis I are mental disorders depicted as synonymous with chronic diseases of the body. In contrast, Axis II disorders emphasize the role of a person's character, temperament, and early-life conditioning. Disorders along both axes often carry the implicit belief that a diagnosis is likely a lifelong condition, which, through psychotherapy or drugs (or both), is altered but perhaps never completely escaped. Both risk producing calcified souls that are manageable and predictable and not enlivened and full of possibility, as real people are.

Perhaps a diagnosis can provide relief from the sense of alienation and shame that are often part of *feeling* mentally ill. As one woman emphatically stated, "I am not crazy, or bad, or lacking in faith or in discipline. I have a disease. It's called depression."[2] Often such an interpretation becomes a defense against the threat of emotional chaos, feelings of alienation, and intense self-doubt that are the subtext of most mental disorders. Yet the DSM also reduces opportunities for growth with its limiting beliefs about human nature and possibilities for change. Old problems have a way of resurfacing for all of us and growth is often a slow process, regardless if you have a diagnosis.

These names we call ourselves and others—diagnosing failures, anticipating compulsive repetitions—lack depth and are hollow places to hide our fears. And fear may be the reason psychiatric diagnoses have become part of our common vernacular. We use these diagnoses as slang because, through them, we distance another person—and potentially gain power over them and the feelings they evoke. These terms lack soul, and their nature is to *de*-soul, which is why they are so versatile when there is a desire to scapegoat someone, avoid the pain of a broken heart, or simply vent anger. With a diagnosis on the tip of the tongue, the speaker grows larger while his object of ridicule becomes stuck in the smallness of an ill-fitting label. Apathy or even revulsion replace fear.

Some may say sympathy is also a potential outcome, yet it is often mixed with pity that has a way of infantilizing persons diagnosed with mental disorders, diminishing their social standing if not personhood. With diagnoses, psychological banishment also becomes a very real possibility—a dehumanizing defense that may seem increasingly attractive on a crowded planet of nearly eight billion people.

Certainly, we need a language to understand how we suffer (and make others suffer) that can help us transcend old patterns of being and relating. But do we really need the DSM? And what, if anything, should replace it?

Reading Russell Lockart's *Words as Eggs* made me think that the DSM is a lot like Humpty Dumpty. As Lockart writes, when Alice (of Wonderland) met Humpty, he made a bold statement about his ability to control words: "When *I* use a word, it means just what I choose it mean—neither more nor less." Humpty Dumpty really liked adjectives because he had more control over them (like when we call someone a name). But Humpty wasn't so crazy about verbs: "They've a temper, some of them— particularly verbs: they're the proudest—adjectives you can do anything with, but not verbs."[3] Verbs, Lockart observed, "are words whose sole function it is to say that something exists, that it has being, that it lives, that it moves, that something has taken place."[4]

Reconfigured as verbs, diagnostic categories become strategies for living and not defenses against people (including oneself) when life is hurtful or uncontrollable. By becoming verbs, diagnoses become more soulful and open to growth and change, including outgrowing a mental disorder. Diagnoses would still point to how we hurt and repeatedly make the same mistakes and expose us to our blind spots, but they would also be a lot safer since they would tell us what we are doing rather than creating fixed references for who we are. As verbs, diagnoses might also contribute to growth and change in unimagined ways, which is how soulful people like to live—full of possibility.

I suggest doing away with diagnoses that cannot be verbs. Rid them from your vocabulary if they fail to make space for growth and uniqueness. All of us "narcissist" at times. Put any of us in a toxic work environment (or society), and we will definitely "schizophrenic" now and again. And granted, some people "borderline" more than others when the end of a relationship is on the horizon—that is, until they don't, and they do something else (such as house repairs), in which case, another verb can reveal their soul-filled efforts at growth, love, and self-discovery.

DOES GLOBALIZATION 3.0
NEED DSM 5?

The fifth edition of the *Diagnostic and Statistical Manual of Mental Disorders* (DSM) wobbles like jello. It has a hard time telling the difference between psychopathology, normal misery, and bad habits. When you know something is wrong and need help, it won't necessarily confirm your problem or suggest a solution. But the greatest obstacle to creating a relevant DSM may be that we can no longer rely on a 20th-century model of mental disorders in the 21st century.

The world has changed exponentially since the DSM first surfaced in the 1950s, and we have changed with it. Our psyches and lifestyles are even less reliable than the DSM. With the expansion of the internet and easy access to health-related information, many are diagnosing and re-diagnosing themselves with little regard for the DSM or the professionals that rely on it. Identities have also become one of our most prized possessions, and we are wisely cautious in our trust of others with their care, especially when the caregiver has a poor track record like the DSM.

In *The Geopolitics of Emotions*, Dominique Moïsi made a useful distinction between the 20th and 21st centuries, one that might benefit the architects of the DSM:

In the ideological atmosphere of the twentieth century, the world was defined by conflicting political models: socialism, fascism, and capitalism. In today's world, ideology has been replaced by the struggle for identity. In the age of globalization, when everything and everybody are connected, it is important to assert one's individuality.[1]

Moïsi's observation fits with Thomas Friedman's characterization of Globalization 3.0: "The dynamic force in Globalization 3.0—the thing that gives it its unique character—is the newfound power for individuals to collaborate and compete globally."[2] Psychiatrists and other mental health workers may be concerned about the validity of diagnostic categories, but for most service users, the value of a diagnosis is found in its promise to alleviate suffering and capacity to leverage a workable identity.

The shift from ideologies to identities parallels a shift of responsibility (and risk) from institutions to individual's shoulders. We are now the guardians of our own mental health and well-being. The DSM has become one more tool used by savvy consumers to access services and identify potential threats to the identities they work so hard to create.

Nevertheless, the DSM is largely unreliable because it attends to a new era's problems with an old era's ideology—one that barely passed muster even when ideologies ruled. Diagnoses in the DSM are typically seen as chronic disorders and lifelong conditions, and thus, according to the norms guiding medicine, require continual treatment, usually with medications. Research shows this approach in psychiatry has led to worse outcomes, more illness, and shorter lifespans.[3] That is enough reason to scrap the project and look for a replacement. Even if we only consider the DSM's usability as a resource for understanding the nature of psychological suffering, it doesn't serve people who need malleable identities to navigate a rapidly changing world. Using the distinction between the modern and postmodern, Simon Gottschalk made this observation:

> If we posit postmodern selfhood as a mutable, liminal, multiple, interdependent, and interactive process, then relying on DSM-IV [and -V] diagnoses will prevent us from understanding it, since DSM-type diagnoses rest on—and reproduce—the idea of a stable, self-contained, and isolated modern self. If the modern self is an obsolete construct...and if the DSM is the most authoritative tool which evaluates such a construct for its "deficiencies," then, logically, this tool is inappropriate to develop an understanding of postmodern selfhood.[4]

At best, the DSM serves psychiatry not only as a tool to seek financial reimbursement from insurance companies but also as part of the specialty's long history of seeking validation as a bona fide medical field. (Psychiatry has its own identity issues to contend with).

Along with identities in flux, the nature of emotions is changing. In a relatively slow-paced world, one with reliable institutions and the support of extended kinship systems—not to mention affordable housing, universal healthcare, nutritious food, access to nature, time for play, and soul-affirming work—we might enjoy a more "natural" flow of the cornucopia of emotions that are our birthright: love and grief, joy and fear, anger and hurt, envy and admiration, and so on, a mixture of feelings flavoring our days and spicing our relationships.

Instead, states of overwhelm and intensity are becoming new emotional norms. These states are often mixed with a sense of uncertainty and, at times, a wish to avoid feeling anything at all. According to Kathleen Woodward, author of *Statistical Panic: Cultural Politics and Poetics of the Emotions*, we are often caught bouncing between *statistical panic* and *statistical boredom*, which seem a lot like hyperarousal and hypoarousal, respectively:

> I understand statistical panic not as a psychological emotion (anger, jealousy, and grief are notable examples of psychological emotions), but rather as a sensation or intensity, one that is at base a charged anxiety. At the other pole of this structure of feeling is statistical boredom, a state characterized by lack of emotion—one *devoid* of sensation or intensity.[5]

Woodward associates statistical panic and statistical boredom with how we story our lives, especially around illness. Through chat rooms, blogs, social networks, and health information sites, we compare personal worries about our mental health to statistics, symptom lists, and stories of illness that we use not only to commiserate our misery but also to find ways to avoid the risks that contributed to others' suffering. Given all the information available, this is often a rapid search that lacks depth, skimming the surface over deep pools of hurt. What might start as an effort to self-soothe can become a state of exhaustion and emptiness. In the search for feeling better, we risk feeling nothing at all.

Should Woodward be correct about the 21st-century emotional landscape—flat emotions intermittently interrupted by quickly forgotten emotional intensity—then the DSM is worse than irrelevant; it stands in the way of creating depth in our emotions and our relationships just at those moments when awareness of their absence grabs our attention and we ask ourselves, "Is there something missing? Is there something the matter with me?"

THE RED BOOK: A PRIMER
FOR HEALING MADNESS IN A
MAD WORLD

Carl Jung spent 1913 to 1930 developing *active imagination*, a method for engaging creatively with the imagery and emotions he believed arose from the unconscious. A major outcome of Jung's efforts was his unfinished manuscript *The Red Book*, a mythical account of his journey out of madness.

The creation of *The Red Book* began during a period when Jung was flooded with disturbing imagery and dreams that threatened to mentally break him. At the time, the field of psychiatry was beginning to make a science of the study of madness. Practitioners still acknowledged the wisdom of artists, novelists, and poets to understand the nature of the human psyche. The soul was still in need of a cure, and hearts were broken as much as brains. Only about five diagnoses were in use—neuroses, hysteria, melancholia, dementia praecox, and mania. Mental illness was also a more fluid concept and existed on a continuum with sanity.[1] It was in this zeitgeist that *The Red Book* would challenge distinctions between reason and insanity on which today's conceptions of mental illness largely came to rest.

In the winter of 1913, Jung began writing down fantasies and dreams that would later become the focus of *The Red Book*. This was a challenging and painful time in his life. World events, misalignment between professional expectations and personal desires, failed relationships—especially his fallout with Sigmund Freud and the psychoanalytic community—and old emotional wounds all conspired to make madness not just something the distinguished psychiatrist would treat but also what he would have to address in himself. And isn't that the nature of madness? Inopportune, a perfect storm, a test of resilience, and sometimes a trial beyond measure, but also an opportunity to transform oneself, if not the world?

Confronting madness as a potentially transformative experience takes courage, and Jung's life was scarred by tragedy he often endured on his own, perhaps making him more courageous than he ever wanted to be. Early on, he survived loneliness, alienation, and betrayal. His mother was institutionalized for depression when he was a toddler. He was bullied as a boy for his preternatural intelligence. He had a difficult relationship with his father, a minister whose dogmatic religiosity contrasted with his son's imaginative spirituality. And an older man he deeply admired sexually exploited Jung as a teen.[2]

Despite these tragedies, Jung perceived his mind as both the source of suffering and its panacea. To help himself cope, as a child, Jung relied on what he saw as his two personalities, Personality No. 1 and Personality No. 2. In his autobiography, *Memory, Dreams, and Reflections*, Jung described his two personalities this way:

> Naturally I compensated my inner insecurity by an outward show of security, or—to put it better—the defect compensated itself without the intervention of my will. That is, I found myself being guilty and at the same time wishing to be innocent. Somewhere deep in the background I always knew

that I was two persons. One was the son of my parents who went to school and was less intelligent, attentive, hard-working, decent, and clean than many other boys. The other was grown up—old, in fact—skeptical, mistrustful, remote from the world of men, but close to nature, the earth, the sun, the moon, the weather, all living creatures, and above all close to the night, to dreams, and to whatever "God" worked directly in him.[3]

Personality No. 1, who grew out of the schoolboy, performed for the world according to its rules, while Personality No. 2 became Jung's private self. It preferred peace and solitude and was enchanted with the spiritual and mythical. Jung denied that these two personalities reflected a dissociated split typically associated with mental illness. He wrote in *Memories, Dreams, and Reflections*:

On the contrary, it is played out in every individual. In my life No. 2 has been of prime importance, and I have always tried to make room for anything that wanted to come from within. He is a typical figure, but he is perceived only by the very few. Most people's conscious understanding is not sufficient to realize that he is also what they are.[4]

For Jung, reviving Personality No. 2 and its fascination with numinous, mystical experiences marked the beginning of both madness and transformation. His attempts to validate No. 2's worldview became his window into a larger cultural split that he addressed in *The Red Book* and many later scholarly writings.

The fortitude required for creating *The Red Book*, a formidable artistic creation that grapples with overwhelming imagery, dreams, and scholarship from many disciplines, actually started early in life, when Jung first strove to balance the pull of the two parts of himself, each with different desires, drives, and needs. The child's natural sense of wonder and limited need for judgment kept him open to both parts, to seeing their inherent worth and limitations and accepting their contradictions. He brought this capacity for holding contradiction to the fledgling science of psychology and saw both the value and the meaning of so-called symptoms of mental illness while also acknowledging the great suffering they cause. Jung wrote, "If we feel our way into the human secrets of the sick person, the madness also reveals its system, and we recognize in the mental illness merely an exceptional reaction to emotional problems which are not strange to us."[5]

Jung's exceptional reactions included two visions he had in 1913 while traveling via train to and from a conference. In these visions, he saw Europe destroyed by a magnificent flood. Around that time, he was also feeling emotionally flooded, and he thought these visual representations of disaster were psychological signs of the "debris of his former relationships," including with Freud and a patient he had become romantically involved with, Sabrina Spielrein. About these visions, he wrote, "I thought to myself, 'If this means anything, it means I am hopelessly off.'"[6]

The outbreak of World War I confirmed for Jung that his visions were of an apocalyptic future. Similar visions and imagery were also found in the arts and literature leading up to the war. What made Jung's experience exceptional, perhaps, was his ability to bring together his awareness of the larger cultural currents with his personal stream of experience and continuously weave both into a synthesized understanding of the psyche and the times in which he lived. But it was a tenuous balancing act.

Pulling Away from the Fold

Eventually Jung would pull away from the outer world created through Personality No. 1. He would leave Freud's inner circle and the Burghölzli Hospital where he worked in Zürich and had a distinguished career. He would buy a house in the suburb of Küsnacht and start a private practice there, but he would also spend time studying mythology, folklore, and religion—the preoccupations of Personality No. 2. Here he began to inhabit both Personality No. 1 and No. 2, listening to both unconscious and conscious aspects of his psyche, exploring his inner imaginal world while also trying to stay socially engaged, see patients, and share his findings with a small yet receptive community.

Jung was looking for balance and integration of the different aspects of himself. He believed too much of either personality led to madness. In *The Red Book*, he gave a description of the "spirit of the times" that seemed much like the world of Personality No. 1—the modern world of science and achievement—that Jung believed had its own madness and which he escaped through the "spirit of the depths," or Personality No. 2. He wrote in *The Red Book*:

> If you do not know what divine madness is, suspend judgment and wait for the fruits. But know that there is a divine madness, which is nothing other than the overpowering of the spirit of this time through the spirit of the depths. Speak then of sick delusion when the spirit of the depths can no longer stay down and forces a man to speak in tongues instead of in human speech, and makes him believe that he himself is the spirit of the depths. But also speak of sick delusion when the spirit of this time does not leave a man and forces him to see only the surface, to deny the spirit of the depths and to take himself for the spirit of the times.[7]

At his home in Küsnacht, Jung immersed himself in the fantasies and dreams he once suppressed. Initially, the practice of exploring his fantasies and dreams was deeply unsettling to his psychic balance. When caught in the "spirit of the times" and his rational-minded Personality No. 1, he would react to such reveries as childish, describing them as "incestuous inter-course" unworthy of attention, if not degrading of the capacity for pure thought. Jung described the early time at Küsnacht this way:

> It seemed to me I was living in an insane asylum of my own making. I went about with all these fantastic figures: centaurs, nymphs, satyrs, gods and goddesses, as though they were patients and I was analyzing them.[8]

Eventually Jung began to make a method of his madness and searched for the myth he was living. He wrote:

> I was driven to ask myself in all seriousness: "What is the myth you are living?" I found no answer to the question, and had to admit that I was not living a myth, or even in a myth, but rather in an uncertain cloud of theoretical possibilities which I was beginning to regard with increasing distrust.... So in the most natural way, I took it upon myself to get to know "my" myth, and I regarded this as the task of tasks—for—so I told myself—how could I when treating my patients, make due allowance for the personal factor, for my personal equa-tion, which is yet so necessary for a knowledge of the other person if I was unconscious of it.[9]

The Birth of Jung's Analytical Psychology

Two robust theoretical ideas came from Jung's experiment of listening to madness. First, he identified two distinct yet intertwined ways of knowing, *imaginal* and *thought*, which he called "direct" and "indirect" thinking. As shared in an earlier essay, he wrote:

> We have...two kinds of thinking: direct thinking, and dreaming or fantasy-thinking.... The one produces innovations and adaptation, copies reality, and tries to act upon it; the other turns away from reality, sets free subjective tendencies, and, as regards adaptation, is unproductive.[10]

While fantasy-thinking is unproductive, it is nevertheless a central and necessary part of human experience. It is the psychic space where we can retreat from the spirit of the times—an imaginal experience that is potentially self-soothing—but also where we can confront unarticulated, often terrifying ideas, images, fantasies, and memories and find creative ways to make meaning of suffering and transcend it.

Second, Jung identified the compensatory, dialectic nature of the psyche in which the unconscious and conscious are not only complementary but need one another and naturally strive toward integration and wholeness. With Jung's model of the psyche, madness occurs when the conscious and unconscious become too separate, such as when a person lives either from the spirit of the times or the spirit of the depths and fails to heed and integrate the wisdom of both.

In a paper titled "The Importance of the Unconscious in Psychopathology," Jung described how madness is a response to living one-sided, either too much from consciousness, or rational awareness and directed thinking, or too much from the unconscious, or fantasy thinking.[11] However, throughout the history of Western psychiatry, one of the greatest fears has been of fantasy thinking and the power of the unconscious to override reason. For Jung, though, listening to the unconscious, even madness, was imperative for discovering the natural direction of growth.

Jung also found himself developing ideas antithetical to Freud and his followers, who looked reductively to childhood and repressed sexual desires as the origin of psychopathology. With Freud's psychoanalysis, unconscious material was brought into conscious awareness for the purpose of analytical reflection and resolution. However, through self-analysis, Jung identified the value of creatively exploring dreams and fantasies—the process he called *active imagination*—as a method for understanding psyche's desired direction of growth. According to Jung, the unconscious "only lives when we experience it in and through ourselves." From his perspective, the question to ask was, "How out of this present psyche, a bridge can be built into its own future?"[12]

Like Freud, Jung knew that events in childhood were significant contributors to later psychological problems, but rather than remembering the story of what happened, Jung believed it was more important to recover "the emotional tone of childhood," the part comfortable with symbolic play of the imaginal material of the psyche.[13] For Jung, unconscious fantasies and dreams were a bridge to reconnect himself to his lost parts, particularly Personality No. 2, which became central to the process of individuation and growth in the second half of Jung's life.

A Cultural Connection

Jung believed constraints on his psychological integration and individuation had much to do with the cultural fascination with *Logos*, or reason, and the neglect of *Eros*, or love. In *The Red Book,* he wrote:

The ancients called the saving word the Logos, an expression of divine reason. So much unreason was in man that he needed reason to be saved. If one waits long enough, one sees how the Gods all change into serpents and underworld dragons in the end. This is also the fate of the Logos: in the end it poisons us all.... We spread poison and paralysis around us in that we want to educate all the world around us into reason.[14]

Jung saw the loss of love (or more generally, *relatedness*) as the outcome of a world overrun by reason. He associated Eros with the unconscious, which he personified as Solomé in *The Red Book*. For Jung, Eros, and the unconscious, represented feminine aspects of the psyche.

In another book, *Answer to Job*, Jung connected Eros with Sophia, Yahweh's partner in the creation of Earth. Sophia was originally recognized as the fountainhead of wisdom. Her name is part of the etymology of the word *philosophy*. *Philosophia* translates to "the love of wisdom."[15]

In *Answer to Job*, Jung challenged the idea of God as perfect and entirely good. He wanted to show that the goal of perfection, witnessed in Yahweh's desire for perfect faith from Job, not only lacked insight but was also cruel. He stated:

The lack of Eros, or relationship to values, is painfully apparent in the Book of Job.... Yahweh has no Eros, no relationship to man, but only a purpose man must help him fulfill.... The faithfulness of his people becomes more important to him the more he forgets Wisdom [Sophia].... Against his own convictions Yahweh agrees without any hesitation to inflict the worst tortures on him [Job]. One misses Sophia's "love of mankind" more than ever. Even Job longs for the Wisdom which is nowhere to be found.[16]

According to Sonu Shamdasani, *The Red Book* and *Answer to Job* emerged from the same realization: the world's madness has to do with eradicating Eros, love, and the soul. The truth is a simple one—sanity is found in joining our hearts and minds —yet complex because even the most fundamental of human experiences can become contorted by social worlds that both sustain and hamper us with their limits and expectations. This is a maxim Jung discovered through his journey into madness and gifted the world through *The Red Book*.

LEAPS OF FAITH ON THE WAY
TO INDIVIDUATION

In many regards, *The Red Book* reads like a *healing journey*, the phrase often used to describe the process of reclaiming one's authentic self after trauma. This "journey" is often as unsettling as it is transformative. On the way to authentic living, it is often necessary to step away from the person one became in order to survive overwhelming traumatic experiences, especially when the trauma was ongoing, such as childhood abuse, intimate partner violence, or war. Usually, a part of the self has gone unacknowledged or been rejected and yearns to be reclaimed. Those confronted with this journey can experience a period of feeling as if "going crazy" on their way to establishing an integrated sense of self.

In *The Red Book,* Jung portrayed *individuation* as the integrating process of self-discovery. As he often remarked, individuation is an ongoing journey, not an endpoint. Jung also pointed to the need for continual leaps of faith: turning away from the larger world's expectations and toward oneself for guidance without knowing what the result will be. He wrote:

> Woe betide those who live by way of examples! Life is not with them. If you live according to an example, you thus live

the life of that example, but who should live your own life if not yourself? So live yourselves.

He also remarked:

The signposts have fallen, unblazed trails lie before us. Do not be greedy to gobble up the fruits of foreign fields. Do you not know that you yourselves are the fertile acre which bears everything that avails you?[1]

The Red Book chronicles how individuation is a blessed curse. Individuation opens the way to becoming one's authentic self, yet it also entails the risk of alienation. Trauma survivors devoted to recovery often know this conundrum intimately. Individuation can require a significant reorienting away from beliefs, feelings, fantasies, and relationships adapted to living in traumatizing conditions or silently holding within the wounds of trauma, which interfere with psychological integration and well-being.

Jung knew such a leap of faith was not easy. He wrote in *The Red Book*:

To live oneself means: to be one's own task. Never say that it is a pleasure to live oneself. It will be no joy but a long suffering since you must become your own creator.

But he offered helpful advice for the journey, particularly how to live if the world feels contrary to whom you are becoming. Then you must learn to be your own guide:

You change those things of the world that, not being useful in themselves, endanger your welfare. Proceed likewise with your thoughts. Nothing is complete, and much is in dispute.

The way of life is transformation, not exclusion. Well-being is a better judge than the law.

Johann Wolfgang von Goethe, whose work greatly influenced Jung, more simply wrote, "Just trust yourself, then you will know how to live." This gets to the purpose and the beauty of individuation: developing and fostering a profound trust in the nature of one's humanity that is both grounding and exhilarating. There is no better way to live.

DO WE STILL NEED THE "UNCONSCIOUS"?

The idea of the *unconscious*—that part of mental life driven by instinct and archetypal drives—was popularized by Sigmund Freud, who famously identified dreams and their symbolic imagery as the *royal road* to this untamed aspect of psyche. Carl Jung, Pierre Janet, Jean-Martin Charcot, and other theorists of the 19th and early 20th centuries similarly envisioned our symbolic, imaginal worlds as ways to glimpse the deeper layers of mental life. Whereas the unconscious is the wellspring of humanity's innate drives—the push to seek food, shelter, a mate—they knew life was more than simple survival. Every mammal plays and dreams, and all life is inherently creative in its adaptations to ever-changing environments. If humans differ from other mammals, it is in the desire to watch our own minds create meaning from experience.

In the 21st century, preference is for biological descriptions of the unconscious. Psyche's underbelly is generally envisioned as wet, gelatinous matter, a medium for electrical currents jumping across synaptic gaps and activating neural networks, resulting in cognitive schemas that predispose us to certain orientations, beliefs, and actions. Today the amygdala is often mentioned, along with how it is sometimes triggered by reminders of past traumas, mobilizing the body and mind for defense regardless of one's intentions or environmental conditions. Non-reflective *procedural learning* also gets attention, such as typing on a keyboard or any other activity, which, after enough repetitions, becomes like the proverbial bike you never forget how to ride. Yet if the unconscious is reduced solely to unintentional biological impulses, procedural learning, and other brain-based reactions, what is the value of dreams, fantasies, and other imaginal aspects of mental life?

Personally, I have never experienced my life as meaningful simply by executing a procedurally learned skill, and certainly not while in the throes of a traumatic stress response. I must put these experiences in the context of my mental life—tagged with images, dreams, fantasies, or memories—for them to gain meaning. And so, I type these words not because of an unconsciously driven desire to type (I am a very good typist, having mastered this procedure-driven skill) but because I desire to share an idea, and thus, create meaning.

Integration is at the heart of mental well-being and the focus of recovery from psychological trauma. The behaviors and attitudes that contribute to a well-integrated mind are usually interlaced with a sense of life as meaningful. The experience of meaningfulness typically involves a somatic/emotional aspect and an image, thought, metaphor, memory, or dream that "articulates" the emotions or body sensations at the root of *feeling as if* a moment, or life in general, is meaningful. This experience of meaningfulness is a primary reason for 19th-century psychiatrists' obsession with the unconscious, as if a bridge must be forged between psyche and soma for a fully realized, meaningful life.

Several experiences are so central to mental well-being that without their integration, we not only risk a sense of meaninglessness but are more likely to react rigidly or chaotically to circumstances in our lives (*rigidly* if prone to avoidance in the face of threat, *chaotically* if emotions tend toward overwhelm when scared). These experiences include:

- *Embodied awareness* and the capacity to mindfully feel sensations and movements in one's body.
- *A regulated mind*, where there is no need to obsessively grasp thoughts, images, feelings, and memories or push them away.
- *Empathic relating to self and others*, especially the capacity to witness others' similarities, differences, desires, and needs in relation to one's own.
- *The ability to tend to images, memories and fantasies* and use them to explore possibilities for greater awareness.

Most of the time, these ways of orienting seem to flow without awareness or intent. This is the job of the unconscious, and like an orchestra conductor, it ignites and directs the choices of the musicians—the actions we take in response to our inner drives and impulses. When we are virtuosos of our inner worlds, we trust the unconscious without reflection. We function *in concert*, much like the body's proprioception, which, without our awareness or intent, joins together bits of movement into fluid responses to the environment—such as coordinating the arm's reach for the door with the hand's turning of the knob.

Regardless of whether there is some material "thing" that constitutes the unconscious, the *idea* of the unconscious acknowledges the inner communication—*the music* within each of us. The idea of the unconscious is also an implicit acknowledgement of being aware of being alive. One of our greatest gifts—and at times, most painful reckonings—is to be aware of being alive and use this awareness to make life meaningful. When we describe the unconscious in biological and mechanistic terms, we exercise the peculiar human trait of reflecting on ourselves in our pursuit of meaningfulness.

Though I believe science is often correct and biology matters, I also believe we still need the "unconscious," if for no more than a nod to the maestro leading the musician. We are all so much more than any explanation we might ever create or believe.

FLYING SOLO

Psychotherapy has been described as the *hope manufacturing business*. Frankly, if my first meeting with a therapist left me feeling dejected, I'd likely think that person was lousy at their job. Psychotherapy is time-consuming and expensive. It shines a spotlight on the painful stuff we have difficulty getting over on our own. Most of us are pretty miserable before we seek help from a therapist, and most of us go to therapy because we believe, if we change, we'll feel better and maybe even become better people.

It takes courage to admit to a stranger how you are suffering and what you don't like about yourself. The entire enterprise goes against the status quo of maintaining appearances as a likable, fully functioning, if not envy-worthy person. Yet working with a talented therapist (or social worker or life coach) trained in helping people get unstuck and living growth-centered lives can be positively transformative.

Whether you are in therapy or just contemplating seeking help, I'd like to give two suggestions for how to get the most out of the experience. One piece of advice is about beginnings, and the other is about endings. Both are about taking leaps of faith, which are central to growth-centered living and thus apply to almost all beginnings and endings, but they are especially relevant if you have a history of trauma.

Beginnings

Whereas it's good to know what you hope to get out of therapy —or any significant effort at change—this isn't the real starting point. Instead, acceptance of yourself as you are—warts and all —is what gets the process going. I say this to save you time and money but also so you'll stop beating yourself up if you believe you need to be "fixed." Self-judgment is the death knell of happiness and deep, transformative change.

Nonjudgmental self-acceptance runs counter to the common habit of comparing oneself to others, which serves status-driven societies and the compulsive pursuit of more stuff and more achievements. Constant comparison is a zero-sum game. Think about it. If you judge yourself superior in the morning, by mid-afternoon, you often will identify someone you perceive as better than yourself. This is the golden rule of judgment: Eventually the overarching eye of comparison turns its critical gaze back at you.

When people seek therapy, they are often overwhelmed by self-judgment, warring with themselves if not also with others. They believe they *should* feel or act a certain way or want certain things. They may even be trying hard to be the person they *should* be, but something always seems to get in their way.

I say to this: *Welcome to humanity*. Internal conflict is common, especially in a society like the United States in which unspoken taboos restrain and dictate how we express ourselves, particularly around past traumas, like childhood abuse, or painful emotions, such as shame, sadness, and anger. We learn early in life to split off and ignore aspects of ourselves just to fit in and function.

Limiting self-expression is not necessarily repressive.

Privacy still has its merits, even in the era of social media. Furthermore, to create cohesion within a group or culture requires some limits on its members. Yet when people seek help from a therapist, often what has been silenced are the emotions, beliefs, and body sensations associated with big hurts, such as job loss, death, breakup, neglect, bullying, assault, rape, and other abuses that people are often reluctant to talk about because of fear of judgment, which might provoke feelings of shame, and they often already feel so much shame. Usually, there's also pain, fear, self-blame, and feelings of betrayal, which, understandably, most people want to avoid. When these are the reasons for seeking therapy, safely, and often slowly, bringing into awareness what has been avoided or denied *is* the work of therapy.

When we can acknowledge all of ourselves and what we feel without pushing anything away or clinging to anything, we tend to act in a more integrated fashion and not against ourselves or others. The habit of constant comparison also becomes a lot less interesting.

Being human is a fallible and messy enterprise, especially when traumatic stress is thrown in the mix. Critical self-judgment rarely helps, but curiosity does. It's better to approach therapy (or any effort to change, grow, or learn) with the attitude that you will accept first, then change. With the support of your therapist, give yourself time to observe how you organize experiences and approach relationships. Such nonjudgmental awareness will get the process going much more smoothly and quickly. (And if you can't accept yourself, accept that! Don't judge the judging.) Likely, you will see you make more sense than you think. Hopefully, you will also take a leap of faith and trust you are lovable and deserving of love, no matter what has happened to you or what you have done because you were overwhelmed by traumatic stress.

The goal of therapy should not be to avoid pain but to

change your relationship with pain and thus how you suffer. Bad times are going to happen. Count on it. Suffering is going to happen. Count on it. Perhaps the best any of us can do is witness the present with nonjudgmental curiosity and openness to all its possibilities.

Endings

Another valuable approach to therapy for both therapists and clients alike involves focusing in the beginning on the end of therapy. You don't need to articulate this inevitability every session, but it's good to keep in mind and revisit regularly. Regardless of how long therapy takes, it's wise to habitually envision how you hope to feel and think about yourself at the end, as well as give attention to how you want to experience relationships and community without the support of your therapist.

Because this is the thing—therapy, like any effort to get unstuck (whether stuck in grief, depression, anxiety, fear, addiction, or an abusive relationship), is ultimately about letting go and moving on. Yet as you do the work of letting go of self-defeating habits and old defenses and watch yourself grow stronger and more integrated, you may also grow fond of having someone there to help you and cheer you on. Your therapist will likely grow pretty fond of you, too.

The bond between therapist and client might be compared to the person learning to paraglide. When someone first learns to paraglide, they don't just walk to the edge of a cliff with a parachute attached to their back and jumps. *Absolutely not!* First, an experienced paraglider gets in the harness *with* the novice and teaches techniques for a good and safe flight and how to land safely.

A good therapist, like a good paraglide instructor, also keeps in mind that eventual solo flight. Yet too often, the dynamic between therapist and client loses focus on going solo. Rather than a guide, the therapist becomes like a parent to a perpetual child, continually activating unfulfilled attachment needs. In many regards, that's okay; it's part of the process. Therapy relies on the human capacity to revisit old hurts and unmet needs with openness and vulnerability, which can make us feel (and act) like children again. But like the student paraglider, these efforts need to be directed toward the eventual solo flight. And until you take that solo flight, you probably aren't really a paraglider. However, once you do, not only are you a paraglider, but you are also part of the tribe of paragliders. Similarly, isn't the goal of therapy to help a person feel part of the tribe, specifically the human tribe?

I like that the term *tribe* has been refashioned in the modern world to suggest relatedness, interdependency, and shared purpose. However, the interdependency that is central to membership in a group is not modeled by the therapeutic relationship—or at least, it shouldn't be.

Since psychotherapy often involves working with unmet attachment needs, it inevitably stimulates dependency. This is important to the work and even points to how a person gets stuck and what stands in the way of growth. Yet feelings of dependency can also cause a client to postpone the necessary leap of faith back into life without therapy. Therapy can also inadvertently contribute to treating relationships, and other people in general, as sources for meeting dependency needs rather than opportunities for *inter*dependency and relatedness.

Growing into ourselves invariably involves loss and breaking with the past. Perhaps the modern world's failure to provide meaningful rituals that demarcate the end of childhood from the beginning of adult life has hampered our personal and collective capacities for letting go and accepting irrevocable change. However, it is our ability (or inability) to deal with loss that often determines how we get stuck and for how long, as well as our courage to take leaps of faith when the time is right.

As we learn to take leaps of faith into our most authentic selves and fully commit to the people who share our dreams and our lives, we also release what is no longer part of who we are becoming, which can include letting go of a cherished and supportive therapist. At such times, it's good to remember that just because something is painful, it doesn't mean it's unnatural or should be avoided (which is probably why birthing metaphors have a way of popping up during transition points, like the end of therapy).

As much as what our dreams make of us, we are what our relationships make us. Effective therapy brings our attention to this reality and teaches us how to feel safe and thrive when alone and with others. Growth requires creative solitude and the willingness to risk individuation, including flying solo. When you risk loving yourself this much, you will soar and bring an equally freeing love to the world.

LEAVING THE LABYRINTH

DISMANTLING ALTARS

In a writing workshop at my alma mater Pacifica Graduate Institute, the focus was a "meditation" called *Dismantling the Altar*. According to the instructor, the purpose of an altar is to inspire us to be our best selves and buttress our confidence in the face of uncertainty. Although sometimes we create altars that galvanize us to reach our loftiest goals, other times our altars entrench us in beliefs, prejudices, and behaviors that inhibit *altering* ourselves in ways that fit the person we hope to become.

The instructor asked us to write about our personal altars, and I began imagining the pile of books stacked on my desk at home. Then a stronger impression and much larger altar took over my imagination—one made of marble pillars, darkened and chipped by time, but also strong and polished, with translucent streaks running throughout. These were my imagined Pillars of Modern Thought, and they were emblematic of the books I had left on my desk.

Well, dismantling those pillars would be near impossible. They're meant to stand the test of time, much like the approach to knowledge they represent, which espouses universality and rationality as eternal principles, along with indelible truths

capable of weathering dangerous ideologies and the dema-
gogues who espouse them. While this altar certainly has made
possible extraordinary things like justice, medicine, and civilization, it's also marginalized nature, emotions, and the art of
living a more accidental existence.

Since the task of the writing meditation was dismantling
altars, I thought about what it would take to demolish such a
large and enduring structure (my desk at home long forgotten).
I imagined that destroying such a stone edifice would take a
great act of violence. In my mind's eye, I saw sledgehammers,
explosions, and people being punctured by flying shards of
marble. This didn't appeal to me at all.

Then I thought: *What if instead of being dismantled or
destroyed, I accepted this altar as an unavoidable presence—a past
within our midst that we can neither escape nor completely ignore?*
This altar, and all it has stood for, could then become like the
ubiquitous exercise bikes and workout equipment littering
dens and bedrooms across the United States, parked there with
good intentions but so often repurposed as clothing racks and
room partitions when convenience or exigency took priority.

Now I think of what it takes to heal from traumas such as
childhood abuse, rape, and war and how it is impossible to
change the past, but how it is possible to find ways to grow
around what happened, not only making do but also making
well.

Still, sometimes it helps to imagine dismantling the past
and the altars that continually remind us of what has been.
Memories of past traumas often interfere with seeing possibilities and feeling the hope needed to imagine a better future. As
we try to imagine all we can become, we sometimes must first
imagine getting rid of the memories and fantasies that keep us
tied to the past. In the imagination and through art, memories
of past traumas and their altars can be safely changed no
matter how threatening they might be, like weapons melted

down and made into sculptures—perhaps like the faces of Easter Island, sometimes haunting in their silence yet just stone.

We may not be able to dismantle all the pernicious "altars" of modernity—the stockpiles of nuclear weapons, earthen scars of industrialization, or psychic wounds of colonization, slavery, and other forms of oppression. I fear the wounds are deep and entrenched and will take centuries of grieving to weather their hardened defenses.

And we are all so busy with the tangibles of life—the obligations, necessities, and urgencies. These days, I sometimes imagine walking away from a world built on permanence, though this leaves me feeling defenseless, as if I have somehow lost. I feel a need for defenses, not only from all the violence and chaos but from my anguish for being born during an era so focused on devouring in its habits and relations that we are destroying the very planet that sustains us, along with each other.

In *The Practice of Everyday Life*, Michel de Certeau shared a clever distinction between *strategies* and *tactics* that sometimes helps me when I feel small and defenseless in the face of seemingly unalterable altars:

I call a *strategy* the calculation (or manipulation) of power relationships that becomes possible as soon as a subject with will and power (a business, an army, a city, a scientific institution) can be isolated. It postulates a place that can be delimited as its *own* and serve as the base from which relations with an *exteriority* composed of targets or threats (customers or competitors, enemies, the country surrounding the city, objectives and objects of research, etc.) can be managed. As in management, every "strategic" rationalization seeks first of all to distinguish its "own" place, that is, the place of its own power and will, from an "environment." A Cartesian attitude, if you wish: it is an effort to delimit one's own place in a world bewitched by the invisible powers of the Other. It is also the typical attitude of modern science, politics, and military strategy.[1]

De Certeau contrasted *strategy*—what I think of when I imagine the pillars of Western thought—with *tactics*, for which he claimed:

> It [the tactical] takes advantage of "opportunities" and depends on them being without any base where it could stockpile its winnings, build up its own position, and plan raids. What it wins it cannot keep. This nowhere gives a tactic mobility, to be sure, but a mobility that must accept the chance offerings of the moment, and seize on the wing the possibilities that offer themselves at any given moment. It must vigilantly make use of the cracks that particular conjunctions open in the surveillance of the proprietary powers. It poaches in them. It creates surprises in them. It can be where it is least expected. It is a guileful ruse. In short, a tactic is an art of the weak.[2]

De Certeau emphasized the power of the strategic and the trickery of the tactical. As fate would have it, I have inherited the tactical way of the weak, although I try to avoid its trickery. The art of deception seems necessary only when under attack or when you set your intention on dismantling strategically placed altars. Yet having already chosen the path of the gentle trickster, I look to nature as a model for my tactics.

Take water, for instance. Water is tactical. It's also a bit of a trickster—both gentle and mighty, unpredictable and recurrent. It can be slow and repetitious, much like chores on Sunday, washing dirt from clothes, or watering the garden. After the chores are done, there's water again to quench the thirst of hard work. This is water working in repetitive and gentle ways. Yet in large quantities, or with enough time, water can erode mountains into pebbles and crumble marble into dust. These bits of past edifices we scatter on garden paths and roads, making use of all things great and small.

Water is often the slowest path of change, yet its effects are everywhere. When we take care of water and are mindful of its power, it has a way of taking care of us.

With water as my metaphor and model, I shift from an altar of permanence to one that upholds the principles of fluidity and inevitable change. I imagine the lives of the Tiebele or Ndebele women of Africa, who paint mosaics on the sides of their homes, attentive to detail and process, all while knowing that what is given loving attention in the dry season may wash away with the rains. And that's okay. There is peace in living according to the seasons and the wisdom that eventually everything begins anew, often with a familiar rhythm.

NOTES

How Chronic Traumatization Interferes with Goals and Completing Actions

1. Bubbers, S. A. "Encounters with the Body: Reflections on the Integration of Trauma Theory and Research into Short Term Therapy." Accessed October 27, 2021, https://www.keele.ac.uk/media/keeleuniversity/fac-natsci/schpsych/documents/counselling/conference/5thannual/Encoun-terswiththeBody.pdf (Lecture Notes).
2. Hart, Onno van der, Ellert R.S. Nijenhuis, and Kathy Steele. *The Haunted Self: Structural Dissociation and the Treatment of Chronic Traumatization.* New York: W. W. Norton & Company, 2006, 9.
3. Ogden, Pat, Kekuni Minton, and Clare Pain. *Trauma and the Body: A Sensorimotor Approach to Psychotherapy.* New York: W. W. Norton & Co, 2006.

We Can Do Better than Desensitization as the Goal of Trauma Treatment

1. Morris, David J. "After PTSD, More Trauma." *New York Times*, January 17, 2015, Opinionator Blogs. http://opinionator.blogs.nytimes.com/2015/01/17/after-ptsd-more-trauma/.
2. Kolk, Bessel van der. *The Body Keeps the Score: Brain, Mind, and Body in the Healing of Trauma.* New York: Viking, 2014, 222.
3. Ibid, 222–223.
4. Linden, David J. *The Accidental Mind: How Brain Evolution Has Given Us Love, Memory, Dreams, and God.* Cambridge, MA: The Belknap Press of Harvard University Press, 2007.
5. Van der Kolk, 73.
6. Ogden, Pat, Kekuni Minton, and Clare Pain. *Trauma and the Body: A Sensorimotor Approach to Psychotherapy.* New York: W. W. Norton & Co, 2006.
7. Ibid.

The Sensorimotor Approach to Storying Trauma

1. Written in a letter to Oskar Pollak dated January 27, 1904.
2. Olin Unferth, Deb. "Don't Tell It Like It Is." In *Rules of Thumb*, edited by Michael Martone and Susan Neville. Cincinnati, OH: Writers Digest Books, 2006.
3. Ogden, Pat, Kekuni Minton, and Clare Pain. *Trauma and the Body: A Sensorimotor Approach to Psychotherapy*. New York: W. W. Norton & Co, 2006, xiv.
4. Ibid., 40.
5. Ibid, 138.

Know Your Habitual Defense Responses and Live within Your Window of Tolerance

1. Herman, Judith. *Trauma and Recovery: The Aftermath of Violence—from Domestic Abuse to Political Terror.* New York: BasicBooks, 1997.
2. Siegel, Daniel J. *The Developing Mind: How Relationships and the Brain Interact to Shape Who We Are.* Second ed. New York: The Guilford Press, 2012.
3. Ogden, Pat. *Level I: Training in Affect Dysregulation, Survival Defenses, and Traumatic Memory.* Bolder, CO: Sensorimotor Psychotherapy Institute, 2012.

Searching for Nirvana

1. Collins, Steven. *Nirvana: Concept, Imagery, Narrative.* Cambridge, UK: Cambridge University Press., 2010.
2. Porges, Stephen. *The Polyvagal Theory: Neurophysiological Foundations of Emotions, Attachment, Communication, Self-Regulation.* New York: W.W. Norton & Co, 2011.

Responding to Moral Injury

1. Litz B. T., Stein N., Delaney E., Lebowitz L., Nash W.P., Silva C., and Maguen S. "Moral Injury and Moral Repair in War Veterans: A Preliminary Model." *Clinical Psychology Review* (2009). https://doi.org/10.1016/j.cpr.2009.07.003.
2. Nakashima Brock, Rita and Gabriella Lettini. *Soul Repair: Recovering from Moral Injury after War.* Boston, MA: Beacon Press, 2012, xviii.

3. Ibid, xiv
4. Ibid, 26.
5. Hillman, James. *Re-Visioning Psychology*. New York, Harper Perennial, 1975, xvi.
6. Litz et al.
7. Maguen, Shira, and Brett Litz. "Moral Injury in Veterans of War." *PTSD Research Quarterly* 23, no. 1 (2012): 1–6; Drescher, Kent D., David W. Foy, Caroline Kelly, Anna Leshner, Kerrie Schutz, and Brett Litz. "An Exploration of the Viability and Usefulness of the Construct of Moral Injury in War Veterans." *Traumatology* 17, no. 8 (2011). https://doi.org/10.1177/1534765610395615.
8. Sherman, Nancy. *Afterwar: Healing the Moral Wounds of Our Soldiers*. New York, Oxford University Press, 2015, 78.
9. Ibid, 79.
10. Nakashima Brock, and Lettini, 21.
11. Ibid, 29.
12. Ibid, 59–60.
13. Marlantes, Karl. *What Is It Like to Go to War*. New York, Grove Press, 2011, 18.
14. Kudo, Timothy. "I Killed People in Afghanistan. Was I Right or Wrong?" *The Washington Post*, 2013, Opinions. https://www.washingtonpost.com/opinions/i-killed-people-in-afghanistan-was-i-right-or-wrong/2013/01/25/cobod5a6-60ff-11e2-b05a605528f6b712_story.htmlutm_term=.d2dfcf51f40d.
15. Sherman, 7.
16. Nakashima Brock and Lettini, 18.
17. Ibid.
18. Ibid, xvii.
19. Ibid, 60.
20. Ibid, xvi.
21. Ibid, 82.
22. Bruner, Jerome. *Making Stories: Law, Literature, Life*. New York, Farar, Straus and Giroux, 2002, 73–74.
23. Marlantes, 119.
24. Ibid, 218.
25. Drescher, Kent D., and David W. Foy. "When They Come Home: Posttraumatic Stress, Moral Injury, and Spiritual Consequences for Veterans." *Reflective Practice: Formation and Supervision in Ministry* 28 (2008 2008): 85–102.
26. Litz et al.
27. Worthington, Everett L., and Diane Langberg. "Religious Considerations and Self-Forgiveness in Treating Complex Trauma and Moral Injury in Present and Former Soldiers." *Journal of Psychology & Theology* 40, no. 4 (2012): 274–88.

28. Linehan, Marcia. *Skills Training Manual for Treating Borderline Personality Disorder*. New York, Guilford Press, 1993; Herman, Judith. *Trauma and Recovery: The Aftermath of Violence—from Domestic Abuse to Political Terror*. New York, BasicBooks, 1997.

29. Marlantes, 26.

30. Ibid, 32.

31. Hart, Onno van der, Ellert R.S. Nijenhuis, and Kathy Steele. *The Haunted Self: Structural Dissociation and the Treatment of Chronic Traumatization*. New York: W. W. Norton & Co, 2006, vii.

32. Nakashima Brock and Lettini, 65.

33. Ibid, 5.

34. Ibid, 30.

35. Turner, J. H. *On the Origins of Human Emotions*. Stanford, Stanford University Press, 2000; van der Hart, Nijenhuis, and Steele.

36. Wood, David. "Healing: Can We Treat Moral Injury?" *The Huffington Post*, 2014, March 20. http://projects.huffingtonpost.com/projects/moral-injury/healing.

37. Van der Hart et al, 2006, 16–19.

38. Jung, Carl G. *The Red Book: Liber Novus*. Translated by John Peck, Mark Kyburz, Sonu Shamdasani. Philemon Series. Edited by Sonu Shamdasani. New York: W. W. Norton & Co., 2009.

39. Gray, M. J., Y. Schoor, W. Nash, L. Lebowitz, A. Amidon, A. Lansing, M. Maglione, A. J. Lang, and B.T. Litz. "Adaptive Disclosure: An Open Trial of a Novel Exposure-Based Intervention for Service Members with Combat-Related Psychological Stress Injuries." *Behavioral Therapy* 43, no. 2 (2012): 407–15.

40. Wood.

41. Gray et al.

42. Wood.

43. Ibid.

44. Ibid.

45. Nakashima Brock and Lettini, 89.

Imagining Suicide

1. Cirlot, J. E. *A Dictionary of Symbols*. Translated by Jack Sage. Mineola, NY: Dover Publications, Inc, 1971/2002.

2. Chevalier, Jean, and Alain Gheerbrant. *The Penguin Dictionary of Symbols*. Translated by John Buchanan-Brown. London, UK: Penguin Books, 1996/1969.

When a Woman Leaves Her Batterer

1. Thomas, Kristie A., Manisha Joshi, and Susan B. Sorenson. "'Do You Know What It Feels Like to Drown?': Strangulation as Coercive Control in Intimate Relationships." *Psychology of Women Quarterly* 38, no. 1 (2014): 124–37. https://doi.org/10.1177/0361684313488354.
2. Jacobson, Neil, and John Gottman. *When Men Batter Women: New Insights into Ending Abusive Relationships.* New York: Simon & Schuster, 2007/1998.
3. Keenan, Brian. *An Evil Cradling: The Five-Year Ordeal of a Hostage.* New York: Viking, 1993.

A World without "Narcissists"

1. Beauvoir, Simone de. *The Ethics of Ambiguity.* Translated by Bernard Frechtman. New York: Citadel Press, 1994/1948.

Is It Possible to Recover from Rape and Sexual Abuse? Yes and No

1. Freedman, Karyn L. *One Hour in Paris.* Chicago: University of Chicago Press, 2014.
2. Brison, Susan J. "Surviving Sexual Violence: A Philosophical Perspective." In *Violence Against Women: Philosophical Perspectives*, edited by Stanley G. French, Wanda Teays, and Laura M. Purdy, 11–26. Ithaca: Cornell University Press, 1998.
3. Ross, Colin A. *The Trauma Model.* Richardson, TX: Manitou Communications, Inc, 2000.

Why Do Women Have Sexual Fantasies of Rape?

1. "Facts and Figures: Ending Violence against Women." UN Women, United Nations, Updated November 2021, accessed December 12, 2021, https://www.unwomen.org/en/what-we-do/ending-violence-against-women/facts-and-figures.
2. World Health Organization, United Nations Office on Drugs and Crime, and United Nations Development Programme. *Global Status Report on Violence Prevention 2014.* World Health Organization (Luxembourg: 2014), viii.
3. Brison, Susan J. "Surviving Sexual Violence: A Philosophical Perspective." In *Violence Against Women: Philosophical Perspectives*, edited by

Stanley G. French, Wanda Teays and Laura M. Purdy, 11–26. Ithaca: Cornell University Press, 1998, 24.

4. Critelli, Joseph, and Jenny Bivona. "The Nature of Women's Rape Fantasies: An Analysis of Prevalence, Frequency, and Contents." *Journal of Sex Research* 46, no. 1 (Jan–Feb 2009): 33–45. https://doi.org/doi: 10.1080/00224490802624406.

5. Critelli, Joseph, and Jenny Bivona. "Women's Erotic Rape Fantasies: An Evaluation of Theory and Research." *Journal of Sex Research* 45, no. 1 (Jan–Mar 2008): 57–70. https://doi.org/doi: 10.1080/00224490701808191.

6. Bergner, Daniel. "What Do Women Want?" *New York Times Magazine*, January 22, 2009. http://www.nytimes.com/2009/01/25/magazine/25desire-t.html?pagewanted=all&_r=0.

7. Chivers, M. L., M. C. Seto, M. L. Lalumiere, E. Laan, and T. Grimbos. "Agreement of Self-Reported and Genital Measures of Sexual Arousal in Men and Women: A Meta-Analysis." *Archives of Sexual Behavior* 39, no. 1 (Feb 2010): 5–56. https://doi.org/doi: 10.1007/s10508-009-9556-9.

8. Quoted in Bergner, 2009.

9. Levine, Peter A. *Healing Trauma: A Pioneering Program for Restoring the Wisdom of Your Body*. Boulder, CO: Sounds True, 2008.

10. Ogden, Pat, Minton, Kekuni, and Pain, Clare. *Trauma and the Body: A Sensorimotor Approach to Psychotherapy*. New York: W. W. Norton & Co, 2006.

11. Porges, Steve. *The Polyvagal Theory: Neurophysiological Foundations of Emotions, Attachment, Communication, and Self-Regulation*. New York: W.W. Norton & Co, 2011.

12. Berlatsky, Noah. "When rape is a fantasy. *The Atlantic,* June 17, 2013. https://www.theatlantic.com/sexes/archive/2013/06/when-rape-is-a-fantasy/276933/, Accessed July 26, 2018.

13. Siegel, Daniel J. *The Developing Mind: How Relationships and the Brain Interact to Shape Who We Are* (Second ed.). New York: The Guilford Press, 2012.

14. Yehuda, Rachel. "How Trauma and Resilience Cross Generations." *On Being with Krista Tippett*. July 30, 2015. http://www.onbeing.org/program/rachel-yehuda-how-trauma-and-resilience-cross-generations/transcript/7791.

15. Lyons-Ruth, Karlen, Lissa Dutra, Michelle Schuder, and Ilaria Bianchi. "From Infant Attachment Disorganization to Adult Dissociation: Relational Adaptations or Traumatic Experiences?". *Psychiatric Clinics of North America* 29, no. 1 (2006): 63–86.

16. Stevens, Anthony. *The Two-Million-Year-Old Self*. College Station, TX: Texas A&M University Press, 1993.

17. Quoted in Stevens, 42.

18. Berlatsky, 2013.

19. Young, Iris M. "Throwing Like a Girl: A Phenomenology of Feminine Body Comportment Motility and Spatiality." *Human Studies* 3, no. 2 (April 1980): 137–56.

Intergenerational Transmission of Recovery

1. Regehr, Kaitlyn, and Cheryl Regehr. "Let Them Satisfy Thus Lust on Thee: Titus Andronicus as Window into Societal Views of Rape and PTSD." *Traumatology,* 2012, 18 (2): 27–34.
2. Ibid, 2.
3. Herman, Judith. *Trauma and Recovery: The Aftermath of Violence—From Domestic Abuse to Political Terror.* New York: BasicBooks, 1997.

A Sketch of Societal-Based Obstacles to Transformation after Trauma

1. Foucault, Michel. *The Order of Things: An Archaeology of the Human Sciences.* New York: Random House, 1970, xv.
2. Hillman, James. *Re-Visioning Psychology.* New York: Harper Perennial, 1975, xvi.
3. Jung, Carl G. *Symbols of Transformation: An Analysis of the Prelude to a Case of Schizophrenia.* Translated by R. F. C. Hull. Princeton: Princeton University Press, 1990/1956, 17–18.
4. Levine, Peter. *Waking the Tiger: Healing Trauma.* Berkeley, CA: North Atlantic Books, 1997.
5. Fabrega, Horacio. *Origins of Psychopathology: The Phylogenetic and Cultural Basis of Mental Illness.* New Brunswick: Rutgers University Press, 2002, 311.
6. Levine, 57.
7. The above section on the writings of Horacio Fabrega and Peter Levine appeared in similar form in Kerr, Laura K. "Dissociation in Late Modern American Society: A Defense Against Soul?" M.A. 1486190, Pacifica Graduate Institute, 2010. http://search.proquest.com/docview/753900987?accountid=14026.
8. Mogenson, Greg. *Greeting the Angels: An Imaginal View of the Mourning Process.* Amityville, NY: Baywood Publishing Company, 1992, xv.
9. Smail, Danial Lord. *On Deep History and the Brain.* Berkeley: University of California Press, 2008.
10. This section on René Descartes appeared in a similar form in Kerr, Laura K. "A Phenomenology of Violence." In *Violence in/and the Great Lakes: The Thought of V-Y Mudimbe and Beyond*, edited by Grant Farred, Kasereka Kavwahirehi and Leonhard Praeg. Pietermaritzburg, South Africa: University of KwaZulu-Natal Press, 2014.

11. Davoine, Françoise, and Jean-Max Gaudillière. *History Beyond Trauma: Whereof One Cannot Speak...Thereof One Cannot Stay Silent*. Translated by Susan Fairfield. New York: Other Press, 2004, 91.

12. Ibid, 93–94.

Introducing the Communal Response to Trauma Index (CRTI)

1. Singh-Manoux, Archana, Nancy E. Adler, and Michael G. Marmot. "Subjective Social Status: Its Determinants and Its Association with Measures of Ill-Health in the Whitehall Ii Study." *Social Science & Medicine* 56 (2003): 1321-33.

2. Herman, Judith. *Trauma and Recovery: The Aftermath of Violence—From Domestic Abuse to Political Terror*. New York: BasicBooks, 1997. 77.

3. "Measure of America." Social Science Research Council. Accessed November 2010. https://measureofamerica.org/blog/2010/10/moa-2010-2011-november-launch/.

4. Herman, 9.

Alexithymia, Emotional Neglect, and Capitalism: Are They Related?

1. Aust, S., E. Alkan Härtwig, I. Heuser, and M. Bajbouj. "The Role of Early Emotional Neglect in Alexithymia." *Psychological Trauma: Theory, Research, Practice, and Policy*, 2012. https://doi.org/DOI: 10.1037/a0027314.

2. Linden, David J. *The Accidental Mind: How Brain Evolution Has Given Us Love, Memory, Dreams, and God*. Cambridge, MA: The Belknap Press of Harvard University Press, 2007, 54.

3. Ibid, 75.

4. Liedloff, Jean. *The Continuum Concept*. New York: Da Capo Press, 1985.

5. Ibid, 36.

6. Ibid, 48.

7. Markus, Hazel. "Being Human Conference." San Francisco, CA, March 24 2012.

8. It's important to note that these observations omit the role of culture as well as the role oppression and inequality play in determining socioeconomic status and a person's comfort with individualistic expression.

Are We Hardwired for Avoidance?

1. Maushart, Susan. *The Winter of Our Disconnect*. New York: Penguin Group, 2011.
2. Turner, Jonathan H. *On the Origins of Human Emotions*. Stanford, CA: Stanford University Press, 2000.
3. Ibid.
4. Boehm, Christopher. *Hierarchy in the Forest: The Evolution of Egalitarian Behavior*. Cambridge, MA: Harvard University Press, 1999.
5. Bauman, Zygmunt. "From Pilgrim to Tourist—or a Short History of Identity." In *Questions of Cultural Identity*, edited by S. Hall and R. du Gay. Thousand Oaks, CA: Sage, 1996.
6. Grandin, Temple. Lecture at the Commonwealth Club of San Francisco. June 4 2013. https://www.commonwealthclub.org/events/archive/transcript/temple-grandin.
7. Linehan, Marcia. *Skills Training Manual for Treating Borderline Personality Disorder*. New York: Guilford Press, 1993.

Globalization: The Age of Psychological Neotony

1. Crichton, Michael. *Next*. New York: Harper, 2008.
2. Zimbardo, Philip and Nikita Duncan. *The Demise of Guys: Why Boys Are Struggling and What We Can Do About It*. Amazon Digital Services, Inc, 2012.
3. Marmot, Michael. *The Status Syndrome*. New York: Henry Holt and Company, 2004.
4. Tocqueville, Alex de. *Democracy in America*. New York: Penguin Classics, 2003.
5. Stevens, Anthony. *The Two-Million-Year-Old Self*. College Station, TX: Texas A&M University Press, 1993.

All Those Lingering Lusty Images

1. Dines, Gail. *Pornland: How Porn Has Hijacked Our Sexuality*. Boston: Beacon Press, 2010.
2. Crowley Jack, Dana. *Silencing the Self: Women and Depression*. New York: HarperCollins, 1991.

The Long Shadow of Mass Murder

1. Shamdasani, Sonu. "Introduction." In *The Red Book: Liber Novus, A Reader's Edition*, by Carl G. Jung. Philemon Series. New York: WW Norton & Company, 2009, 18.

2. Jung, Carl G. *Memories, Dreams, Reflections.* Translated by Richard Winston and Clara Winston. Edited by Aniela Jaffé. New York: Vintage Books, 1989.

3. "Breaking Down Mass Public Shooting Data from 1998 through June 2019: Info on Weapons Used; Gun-Free Zones; Racial, Age, and Gender Demographics." 2019. Accessed December 6, 2021, https://crimeresearch.org/2019/07/breaking-down-mass-public-shooting-data-from-1998-though-june-2019-info-on-weapons-used-gun-free-zones-racial-age-and-gender-demographics/.

4. Siegel, Lee. "The Kid's Aren't Alright: Lee Siegel on the Perils of Parenting in the Digital Age." *Newsweek*, December 8, 2012. https://www.newsweek.com/lee-siegel-perils-parenting-digital-age-65335.

5. Levine, Peter. *Waking the Tiger: Healing Trauma.* Berkeley, CA: North Atlantic Books, 1997.

6. Pediatrics, American Academy of. https://www.aap.org/family/tv1.htm. Accessed July 1, 2009.

Dreaming of a Safe America

1. Banks, Russel. *Dreaming up America.* New York: Seven Stories Press, 2008, 6–7.

2. Ferenczi, Sándor. "Confusion of Tongues Between Adults and the Child: The Language of Tenderness and Passion." *Contemporary Psychoanalysis* 24 (1988): 196–206.

3. Mause, Lloyd De. *The Emotional Life of Nations.* New York: Karnac, 2002, 104.

4. Miller, Alice. "The Political Consequences of Child Abuse." *The Journal of Psychohistory* 26, no. 2 (Fall 1998): 573–85.

5. Kaehler, Laura A., and Jennifer J. Freyd. "Borderline Personality Characteristics: A Betrayal Trauma Approach." *Psychological Trauma: Theory, Research, Practice, and Policy* 1, no. 4 (2009): 261–68.

6. Janet, Pierre. *Principles of Psychotherapy.* London: Allen & Unwin, 1925/1919, 663.

7. Kolk, Bessel van der. "Foreword." In *Trauma and the Body: A Sensorimotor Approach to Psychotherapy*, by Pat Ogden, Kekuni Minton, and Clare Pain. New York: W. W. Norton & Company, 2006, xxi.

8. Hart, Onno van der, Ellert R.S. Nijenhuis, and Kathy Steele. *The Haunted Self: Structural Dissociation and the Treatment of Chronic Traumatization.*

New York: W. W. Norton & Company, 2006.

9. Banks, 7.
10. Kalsched, Donald. *The Inner World of Trauma: Archetypal Defenses of the Personal Spirit*. New York: Routledge, 1996, 35.

Need Help Loving Humanity? How to Evolve beyond Us-versus-Them Thinking

1. SoRelle, Ruth. "Like Adults, Black Children Receive Less Pain Relief." *Emergency Medicine News* 34, no. 9 (2012): 1, 32. https://doi.org/doi: 10.1097/01.EEM.0000419511.43102.cc.
2. Coman, Alin, Charles B. Stone, Emanuele Castano, and William Hirst. "Justifying Atrocities: The Effect of Moral-Disengagement Strategies on Socially Shared Retrieval-Induced Forgetting." *Psychological Science* 25, no. 6 (2014).
3. Dunbar, Robin. "The Social Brain Hypothesis." *Evolutionary Anthropology* 6, no. 5 (1998): 178–90, 184.
4. Ibid.
5. Appadurai, Arjun. *Modernity at Large: Cultural Dimensions of Globalization*. Minneapolis, MN: University of Minnesota Press, 1996, 7.
6. Tonglen is a Tibetan meditative practice. On the in breath, hold awareness for the suffering of another sentient being or group of beings. On the out breath, release feelings of compassion.

What to Call "Terror"?

1. Hatzfeld, Jean. *The Antelope's Strategy: Living in Rwanda after the Genocide*. Farrar, Straus and Giroux, 2009.
2. Appadurai, Arjun. *Modernity at Large: Cultural Dimensions of Globalization*. Minneapolis, MN: University of Minnesota Press, 1996, 154–155.

A Meditation on Violence against Women and Nature

1. Griffin, Susan. *Woman and Nature*. San Francisco: Sierra Club Books, 1978, 3.
2. Bosshard, Peter. "The World Bank Is Bringing Back Big, Bad Dams." *The Guardian*, July 16, 2013. https://www.theguardian.com/environment/blog/2013/jul/16/world-bank-dams-africa.
3. Ibid.

4. Quoted in Campbell, Joseph. *Flight of the Wild Gander: Explorations in the Mythological Dimension.* Novato, CA: New World Library, 2002/1951, 113–114.

5. Shepard, Paul. *Nature and Madness.* Athens: University of Georgia Press, 1982, 28.

6. Borgman, Albert. *Crossing the Postmodern Divide.* Chicago: University of Chicago Press, 1992, 33.

7. Campbell, 84.

8. Shepard, 126.

9. Botton, Alain de. *Status Anxiety.* New York: Pantheon Books, 2004, 5.

10. In this discussion, I have left out the development of homosexuality as well as the role of status in women's lives. This is not because they are not important, but they do not seem to drive the violence against women and nature occurring in the Congo the way I believe heterosexual male development does.

11. Hochschild, Adam. *King Leopold's Ghost.* New York: Houghton Mifflin Company, 1998, 34.

12. Ibid.

Shopping Our Way to Extinction

1. Weisman, Alan. *The World Without Us.* New York: St. Martin's Press, 2007.

2. "Measure What You Treasure." 2021, accessed November 17, 2021, https://www.footprintnetwork.org.

3. Freud, Sigmund. *Beyond the Pleasure Principle.* Translated by James Strachey. Seattle, WA: Pacific Publishing Studio, 1920/2010.

4. Ogden, Pat, Kekuni Minton, and Clare Pain. *Trauma and the Body: A Sensorimotor Approach to Psychotherapy.* New York: W. W. Norton & Co, 2006.

5. Shepard, Paul. *Nature and Madness.* Athens: University of Georgia Press, 1982, 15.

6. Jung, Carl G. *The Red Book: Liber Novus.* Translated by John Peck, Mark Kyburz, Sonu Shamdasani. Philemon Series. Edited by Sonu Shamdasani. New York: W. W. Norton & Co., 2009.

Want to Reduce Mental Illness? Address Trauma.
Want to Save the World? Address Trauma

1. Frazier, Patricia A., Margaret Gavian, Sulani Perera, and Samantha Anders. "Prevalence and Effects of Traumatic Life Events among University Students." American Psychological Association, San Francisco, CA, August 17, 2007.

2. McFarlane, Alexander C., and Bessel A. van der Kolk. "Trauma and Its Challenge to Society." In *Traumatic Stress: The Effects of Overwhelming Experience on Mind, Body, and Society*, edited by Bessel A. van der Kolk, Alexander C. McFarlane and Lars Weisaeth, 24–46. New York: The Guilford Press, 1996, 38–39.
3. Kolk, Bessel A. van der, and Alexander C. McFarlane. "The Black Hole of Trauma." In *Traumatic Stress: The Effects of Overwhelming Experience on Mind, Body, and Society*, edited by Alexander C. McFarlane Bessel A. van der Kolk, and Lars Weisaeth. New York: Guilford Press, 1996, 5.
4. Casper, Stephen T. "The History and Future of Neurological Care." *Science* 364, no. 6437 (19 April 2019): 243-44.
5. McFarlane and van der Kolk, 40–41.

Subjectivity and Being Mentally Ill

1. Foucault, Michel. "Technologies of the Self." In *Technologies of the Self: A Seminar with Michel Foucault*, edited by Huck Gutman Luther H. Martin, Patrick H. Hutton. Amherst: University of Massachusetts Press, 1988.
2. Porter, Roy. *Madness: A Brief History*. Oxford: Oxford University Press, 2002.
3. Luhrmann, T. M. *Of Two Minds: An Anthropologist Looks at American Psychiatry*. Second ed. New York: Vintage Books, 2001, 140.

Secrets in Our Silences

1. Davoine, Françoise, and Jean-Max Gaudillière. *History Beyond Trauma: Whereof One Cannot Speak...Thereof One Cannot Stay Silent*. Translated by Susan Fairfield. New York: Other Press, 2004.
2. Ibid, xxvii.
3. Ibid, xiii.

Can DSM Diagnoses Be Other Than Pejorative?

1. Lockhart, Russell. *Words As Eggs: Psyche in Language and Clinic*. New York: Spring Publications, 1983.
2. Cronkite, Kathy. *On the Edge of Darkness*. New York: Delta Publishing, 1994, 3.
3. Lockhart, 90.
4. Ibid, 101.

Does Globalization 3.0 Need DSM 5?

1. Moïsi, Dominique. *The Geopolitics of Emotion*. New York: Doubleday, 2009.
2. Friedman, Thomas L. *The World Is Flat: A Brief History of the Twenty-First Century*. New York: Farrar, Straus and Giroux, 2005, 10.
3. Whitaker, Robert. *Anatomy of an Epidemic*. New York: Crown Publishers, 2010.
4. Gottschalk, Simon. "Escape from Insanity: 'Mental Disorder' in the Post-modern Moment." In *Pathology and the Postmodern: Mental Illness as Discourse and Experience*, edited by Dwight Fee. Inquiries in Social Construction, 18–48. London: Sage Publications, 2000, 21.
5. Woodward, Kathleen. *Statistical Panic: Cultural Politics and Poetics of the Emotions*. Durham: Duke University Press, 2009, 15.

The Red Book: A Primer for Healing Madness in a Mad World

1. Shamdasani, Sonu. "Introduction." In CG Jung's *The Red Book: Liber Novus*. Translated by Mark Kyburz, John Peck, and Sonu Shamdasani. Edited by Sonu Shamdasani. New York: W. W. Norton & Co, 2009.
2. Kerr, John. *A Most Dangerous Method: The Story of Jung, Freud, and Sabina Spielrein*. New York: Vintage Books, 1994.
3. Jung, Carl G. *Memories, Dreams, Reflections*. Translated by Richard Winston and Clara Winston. Edited by Aniela Jaffé. New York: Vintage Books, 1989/1963, 44-45.
4. Ibid, 45.
5. Quoted by Shamsasani, 2009, 196.
6. Quoted by Shamdasani, 2009, 198.
7. Jung, Carl G. *The Red Book: Liber Novus*. Translated by John Peck, Mark Kyburz, Sonu Shamdasani. Philemon Series. Edited by Sonu Shamdasani. New York: W. W. Norton & Co, 2009, "Descent into Hell in the Future," Cap. V.
8. Quoted by Shamdasani, 197.
9. Ibid.
10. Jung, Carl G. *Symbols of Transformation: An Analysis of the Prelude to a Case of Schizophrenia*. Translated by R. F. C. Hull, Bollingen Series. Princeton: Princeton University Press, 1990/1956, 17–18.
11. Shamdasani, 201.
12. Quoted by Shamdasani, 209.
13. Quoted by Shamdasani, 198.
14. Jung, 2009, Liber Secundus, First Day, Cap. viii.

15. Jung, Carl G. *Answer to Job.* Translated by R.F.C. Hull, Bollingen Series. Princeton: Princeton University Press, 2011/1958.
16. Ibid, 33–34.

Leaps of Faith on the Way to Individuation

1. Jung, Carl G. *The Red Book: Liber Novus.* Translated by John Peck, Mark Kyburz, Sonu Shamdasani. Philemon Series. Edited by Sonu Shamdasani. New York: W. W. Norton & Co., 2009.

Dismantling Altars

1. Certeau, Michel de. *The Practice of Everyday Life.* Translated by Steven Rendall. Berkeley: University of California Press, 1984, 35–36.
2. Ibid, 37.

REFERENCES

Appadurai, Arjun. 1996. *Modernity at Large: Cultural Dimensions of Globalization*. Minneapolis: University of Minnesota Press.

Aust, S., E. Alkan Härtwig, I. Heuser, and M. Bajbouj. 2012. "The Role of Early Emotional Neglect in Alexithymia." *Psychological Trauma: Theory, Research, Practice, and Policy*. https://doi.org/ DOI: 10.1037/a0027314.

Banks, Russel. 2008. *Dreaming Up America*. New York: Seven Stories Press.

Bauman, Zygmunt. 1996. "From Pilgrim to Tourist—or a Short History of Identity." In *Questions of Cultural Identity*, edited by S. Hall and R. du Gay. Thousand Oaks, CA: Sage.

Beauvoir, Simone de. 1994/1948. *The Ethics of Ambiguity*. Translated by Bernard Frechtman. New York: Citadel Press.

Bergner, Daniel. 2009. "What Do Women Want?" *New York Times Magazine*, January 22.

Berlatsky, Noah. 2013. "When rape is a fantasy. *The Atlantic*, June 17. https://www.theatlantic.com/sexes/archive/2013/06/ when-rape-is-a-fantasy/276933/.

Boehm, Christopher. 1999. *Hierarchy in the Forest: The Evolution of Egalitarian Behavior*. Cambridge, MA: Harvard University Press.

Bosshard, Peter. 2013. "The World Bank Is Bringing Back Big, Bad Dams." *The Guardian*, July 16. https://www.theguardian.-com/environment/blog/2013/jul/16/world-bank-dams-africa.

Botton, Alain de. 2004. *Status Anxiety*. New York: Pantheon Books.

Brison, Susan J. 1998. "Surviving Sexual Violence: A Philosophical Perspective." In *Violence against Women: Philosophical Perspectives*, edited by Stanley G. French, Wanda Teays, and Laura M. Purdy. Ithaca: Cornell University Press, 11–26.

Bruner, Jerome. 2002. *Making Stories: Law, Literature, Life*. New York: Farrar, Straus and Giroux.

Bubbers, Sally-Anne. "Encounters with the Body: Reflections on the Integration of Trauma Theory and Research into Short Term Therapy." Accessed October 27. https://www.keele.ac.uk /media/keeleuniversity/facnatsci/schpsych/documents/coun-selling/conference/5thannual/EncounterswiththeBody.pdf.

Campbell, Joseph. 2002/1951. *Flight of the Wild Gander: Explorations in the Mythological Dimension*. Novato, CA: New World Library.

Casper, Stephen T. "The History and Future of Neurological Care." *Science* 364, no. 6437 (19 April 2019): 243-44.

Certeau, Michel de. 1984. *The Practice of Everyday Life.* Translated by Steven Rendall. Berkeley: University of California Press.

Chevalier, Jean, and Alain Gheerbrant. 1996/1969. *The Penguin Dictionary of Symbols.* Translated by John Buchanan-Brown. London: Penguin Books.

Chivers, M. L., M. C. Seto, M. L. Lalumiere, E. Laan, and T. Grimbos. 2010. "Agreement of Self-Reported and Genital Measures of Sexual Arousal in Men and Women: A Meta-Analysis." *Archives of Sexual Behavior* 39 (1): 5–56. https://doi.org/doi: 10.1007/s10508-009-9556-9.

Cirlot, J. E. 1971/2002. *A Dictionary of Symbols.* Translated by Jack Sage. Mineola, NY: Dover Publications, Inc.

Coman, Alin, Charles B. Stone, Emanuele Castano, and William Hirst. 2014. "Justifying Atrocities: The Effect of Moral-Disengagement Strategies on Socially Shared Retrieval-Induced Forgetting." *Psychological Science* 25 (6).

Collins, Steven. 2010. *Nirvana: Concept, Imagery, Narrative.* Cambridge, UK: Cambridge University Press.

Crichton, Michael. 2008. *Next.* New York: Harper.

Crime Prevention Research Center. 2019. "Breaking down Mass Public Shooting Data From 1998 through June 2019: Info on Weapons Used; Gun-Free Zones; Racial, Age, and Gender Demographics." Accessed December 6, 2021. https://crimeresearch.org/2019/07/breaking-down-mass-public-shooting-data-from-1998-though-june-2019-info-on-weapons-used-gun-free-zones-racial-age-and-gender-demographics/.

Critelli, Joseph, and Jenny Bivona. 2009. "The Nature of Women's Rape Fantasies: An Analysis of Prevalence, Frequency, and Contents." *Journal of Sex Research* 46 (1): 33–45. https://doi.org/doi: 10.1080/00224490802624406.

Critelli, Joseph, and Jenny Bivona. 2008. "Women's Erotic Rape Fantasies: An Evaluation of Theory and Research." *Journal of Sex Research* 45 (1): 57–70. https://doi.org/doi:10.1080/00224490701808191.

Cronkite, Kathy. 1994. *On the Edge of Darkness*. New York: Delta Publishing.

Crowley Jack, Dana. 1991. *Silencing the Self: Women and Depression*. New York: HarperCollins.

Davoine, Françoise, and Jean-Max Gaudillière. 2004. *History beyond Trauma: Whereof One Cannot Speak...Thereof One Cannot Stay Silent*. Translated by Susan Fairfield. New York: Other Press.

Dines, Gail. 2010. *Pornland: How Porn Has Hijacked Our Sexuality*. Boston: Beacon Press.

Drescher, Kent D., David W. Foy, Caroline Kelly, Anna Leshner, Kerrie Schutz, and Brett Litz. 2011. "An Exploration of the Viability and Usefulness of the Construct of Moral Injury in War Veterans." *Traumatology* 17 (8). https://doi.org/10.1177/1534765610395615.

Drescher, Kent D., and David W. Foy. 2008. "When They Come Home: Posttraumatic Stress, Moral Injury, and Spiritual Consequences for Veterans." *Reflective Practice: Formation and Supervision in Ministry* 28: 85–102.

Dunbar, Robin. 1998. "The Social Brain Hypothesis." *Evolutionary Anthropology* 6 (5): 178–190.

Fabrega, Horacio. 2002. *Origins of Psychopathology: The Phylogenetic and Cultural Basis of Mental Illness*. New Brunswick: Rutgers University Press.

Farlane, Alexander C., and Bessel A. van der Kolk. 1996. "Trauma and Its Challenge to Society." In *Traumatic Stress: The Effects of Overwhelming Experience on Mind, Body, and Society*, edited by Bessel A. van der Kolk, Alexander C. McFarlane, and Lars Weisaeth, 24–46. New York: The Guilford Press.

Ferenczi, Sándor. 1988. "Confusion of Tongues Between Adults and the Child: The Language of Tenderness and Passion." *Contemporary Psychoanalysis* 24: 196–206.

Foucault, Michel. 1970. *The Order of Things: An Archaeology of the Human Sciences*. New York: Random House.

Foucault, Michel. 1988. "Technologies of the Self." In *Technologies of the Self: A Seminar with Michel Foucault*, edited by Huck Gutman Luther H. Martin, Patrick H. Hutton. Amherst: University of Massachusetts Press.

Frazier, Patricia A., Margaret Gavian, Sulani Perera, and Samantha Anders. 2007. "Prevalence and Effects of Traumatic Life Events Among University Students." American Psychological Association, San Francisco, CA, August 17.

Freedman, Karyn L. 2014. *One Hour in Paris*. Chicago: University of Chicago Press.

Freud, Sigmund. 1920/2010. *Beyond the Pleasure Principle*. Translated by James Strachey. Seattle: Pacific Publishing Studio.

Friedman, Thomas L. 2005. *The World Is Flat: A Brief History of the Twenty-First Century*. New York: Farrar, Straus and Giroux.

Global Footprint Network. 2021. "Measure What You Treasure." Accessed November 17. https://www.footprintnetwork.org.

Gottschalk, Simon. 2000. "Escape from Insanity: 'Mental Disorder' in the Postmodern Moment." In *Pathology and the Postmodern: Mental Illness as Discourse and Experience*, edited by Dwight Fee. London: Sage Publications, 18–48.

Grandin, Temple. 2013. Lecture at the Commonwealth Club of San Francisco. https://www.commonwealthclub.org/events/archive/transcript/temple-grandin.

Gray, M. J., Y. Schoor, W. Nash, L. Lebowitz, A. Amidon, A. Lansing, M. Maglione, A. J. Lang, and B.T. Litz. 2012. "Adaptive Disclosure: An Open Trial of a Novel Exposure-Based Intervention for Service Members with Combat-Related Psychological Stress Injuries." *Behavioral Therapy* 43 (2): 407–415.

Griffin, Susan. 1978. *Woman and Nature*. San Francisco: Sierra Club Books.

Hart, Onno van der, Ellert R.S. Nijenhuis, and Kathy Steele. 2006. *The Haunted Self: Structural Dissociation and the Treatment of Chronic Traumatization*. New York: W. W. Norton & Co.

Hatzfeld, Jean. 2009. *The Antelope's Strategy: Living in Rwanda after the Genocide.* New York: Farrar, Straus and Giroux.

Herman, Judith. 1997. *Trauma and Recovery: The Aftermath of Violence—from Domestic Abuse to Political Terror.* New York: BasicBooks.

Hillman, James. 1975. *Re-Visioning Psychology.* New York: Harper Perennial.

Hochschild, Adam. 1998. *King Leopold's Ghost.* New York: Houghton Mifflin Company.

Jacobson, Neil, and John Gottman. 2007/1998. *When Men Batter Women: New Insights into Ending Abusive Relationships.* New York: Simon & Schuster.

Janet, Pierre. 1925/1919. *Principles of Psychotherapy.* London: Allen & Unwin.

Jung, Carl G. 2009. *The Red Book: Liber Novus.* Translated by John Peck, Mark Kyburz, Sonu Shamdasani. Philemon Series. Edited by Sonu Shamdasani. New York: W. W. Norton & Co.

Jung, Carl G. 1989/1963. *Memories, Dreams, Reflections.* Translated by Richard Winston and Clara Winston. Edited by Aniela Jaffé. New York: Vintage Books.

Jung, Carl G. 2011/1958. *Answer to Job.* Translated by R.F.C. Hull. Bollingen Series. Princeton: Princeton University Press.

Jung, Carl G. 1990/1956. *Symbols of Transformation: An Analysis of the Prelude to a Case of Schizophrenia.* Translated by R. F. C. Hull. Princeton: Princeton University Press.

Kaehler, Laura A. and Jennifer J. Freyd. 2009. "Borderline Personality Characteristics: A Betrayal Trauma Approach." *Psychological Trauma: Theory, Research, Practice, and Policy* 1 (4): 261–268.

Kalsched, Donald. 1996. *The Inner World of Trauma: Archetypal Defenses of the Personal Spirit.* New York: Routledge.

Keenan, Brian. 1993. *An Evil Cradling: The Five-Year Ordeal of a Hostage.* New York: Viking.

Kerr, John. 1994. *A Most Dangerous Method: The Story of Jung, Freud, and Sabina Spielrein.* New York: Vintage Books.

Kerr, Laura K. 2014. "A Phenomenology of Violence." In *Violence In/And the Great Lakes: The Thought of V-Y Mudimbe and Beyond*, edited by Grant Farred, Kasereka Kavwahirehi and Leonhard Praeg. Pietermaritzburg, South Africa: University of KwaZulu-Natal Press.

Kerr, Laura K. 2010/2022. *Dissociation in Late Modern America: A Defense Against Soul?* San Francisco: LK Kerr Books.

Kolk, Bessel van der. 2014. *The Body Keeps the Score: Brain, Mind, and Body in the Healing of Trauma.* New York: Viking.

Kolk, Bessel van der. 2006. "Foreward." In *Trauma and the Body: A Sensorimotor Approach to Psychotherapy*, by Pat Ogden, Kekuni Minton, and Clare Pain. New York: W. W. Norton & Company.

Kolk, Bessel A. van der, and Alexander C. McFarlane. 1996. "The Black Hole of Trauma." In *Traumatic Stress: The Effects of Overwhelming Experience on Mind, Body, and Society*, edited by

Alexander C. McFarlane Bessel, A. van der Kolk, and Lars Weisaeth. New York: Guilford Press.

Kudo, Timothy. 2013. "I Killed People in Afghanistan. Was I Right or Wrong?" *The Washington Post*, Opinions. Accessed October 26, 2016. https://www.washingtonpost.com/opinions/i-killed-people-in-afghanistan-was-i-right-or-wrong/2013/01/25/c0b0d5a6-60ff-11e2-b05a-605528f6b712_story.html?utm_term=.d2dfcf51f40d.

Levine, Peter A. 2008. *Healing Trauma: A Pioneering Program for Restoring the Wisdom of Your Body*. Boulder, CO: Sounds True.

Levine, Peter. 1997. *Waking the Tiger: Healing Trauma*. Berkeley, CA: North Atlantic Books.

Liedloff, Jean. 1985. *The Continuum Concept*. New York: Da Capo Press.

Linden, David J. 2007. *The Accidental Mind: How Brain Evolution Has Given Us Love, Memory, Dreams, and God*. Cambridge, MA: Belknap Press.

Linehan, Marcia. 1993. *Skills Training Manual for Treating Borderline Personality Disorder*. New York: Guilford Press.

Litz B. T., Stein N., Delaney E., Lebowitz L., Nash W.P., Silva C., and Maguen S. 2009. "Moral Injury and Moral Repair in War Veterans: A Preliminary Model" *Clinical Psychology Review*. https://doi.org/10.1016/j.cpr.2009.07.003.

Lockhart, Russell. 1983. *Words as Eggs: Psyche in Language and Clinic*. New York: Spring Publications.

Luhrmann, T. M. 2001. *Of Two Minds: An Anthropologist Looks at American Psychiatry*. Second ed. New York: Vintage Books.

Lyons-Ruth, Karlen, Lissa Dutra, Michelle Schuder, and Ilaria Bianchi. 2006. "From Infant Attachment Disorganization to Adult Dissociation: Relational Adaptations or Traumatic Experiences?" *Psychiatric Clinics of North America* 29 (1): 63–86.

Maguen, Shira, and Brett Litz. 2012. "Moral Injury in Veterans of War." *PTSD Research Quarterly* 23 (1): 1–6.

Marlantes, Karl. 2011. *What Is It Like to Go to War?* New York: Grove Press.

Marmot, Michael. 2004. *The Status Syndrome*. New York: Henry Holt and Company.

Mause, Lloyd De. 2002. *The Emotional Life of Nations*. New York: Karnac.

Maushart, Susan. 2011. *The Winter of Our Disconnect*. New York: Penguin Group.

McFarlane, Alexander C., and Bessel A. van der Kolk. "Trauma and Its Challenge to Society." In *Traumatic Stress: The Effects of Overwhelming Experience on Mind, Body, and Society*, edited by Bessel A. van der Kolk, Alexander C. McFarlane and Lars Weisaeth. New York: The Guilford Press, 1996.

"Measure of America." Social Science Research Council. 2010. Accessed November 2010. https://measureofamerica.org/blog/2010/10/moa-2010-2011-november-launch/.

Miller, Alice. 1998. "The Political Consequences of Child Abuse." *The Journal of Psychohistory* 26 (2): 573–585.

Mogenson, Greg. 1992. *Greeting the Angels: An Imaginal View of the Mourning Process*. Amityville, NY: Baywood Publishing Company.

Moïsi, Dominique. 2009. *The Geopolitics of Emotion*. New York: Doubleday.

Morris, David J. 2015. "After PTSD, More Trauma." *New York Times*, January 17. Opinionator Blogs. http://opinionator.blogs. nytimes.com/2015/01/17/after-ptsd-more-trauma/.

Mulhern, Sherrill. 1991. "Embodied Alternative Identities: Bearing Witness to a World That Might Have Been." *Psychiatric Clinics of North America* 14(3): 769–787.

Nakashima Brock, Rita and Gabriella Lettini. 2012. *Soul Repair: Recovering from Moral Injury after War*. Boston, MA: Beacon Press.

Ogden, Pat, Kekuni Minton, and Clare Pain. 2006. *Trauma and the Body: A Sensorimotor Approach to Psychotherapy*. New York: W. W. Norton & Co.

Olin Unferth, Deb. 2006. "Don't Tell It Like It Is." In *Rules of Thumb*, edited by Michael Martone and Susan Neville. Cincinnati, OH: Writers Digest Books.

Porges, Steve. 2011. *The Polyvagal Theory: Neurophysiological Foundations of Emotions, Attachment, Communication, and Self-Regulation*. New York: W.W. Norton & Co.

Porter, Roy. 2002. *Madness: A Brief History*. Oxford: Oxford University Press.

Radin, Paul. 1972. *The Trickster: A Study in American Indian Mythology*. New York: Schocken Books.

Regehr, Kaitlyn, and Cheryl Regehr. 2012. "Let Them Satisfy Thus Lust on Thee: Titus Andronicus as Window into Societal Views of Rape and PTSD." *Traumatology* 18 (2): 27–34.

Ross, Colin A. 2000. *The Trauma Model*. Richardson, TX: Manitou Communications, Inc.

Shamdasani, Sonu. 2009. "Introduction." In CG Jung's *The Red Book: Liber Novus*. Translated by Mark Kyburz, John Peck, and Sonu Shamdasani. Edited by Sonu Shamdasani. New York: W. W. Norton & Co.

Shepard, Paul. 1982. *Nature and Madness*. Athens: University of Georgia Press.

Sherman, Nancy. 2015. *Afterwar: Healing the Moral Wounds of Our Soldiers*. New York: Oxford University Press.

Singh-Manoux, Archana, Nancy E. Adler, and Michael G. Marmot. 2003. "Subjective social status: its determinants and its association with measures of ill-health in the Whitehall II study." *Social Science & Medicine* 56: 1321-1333.

Siegel, Daniel J. 2012. *The Developing Mind: How Relationships and the Brain Interact to Shape Who We Are*. Second ed. New York, NY: The Guilford Press.

Siegel, Lee. 2012. "The Kid's Aren't Alright: Lee Siegel on the Perils of Parenting in the Digital Age." *Newsweek*, December 8.

Smail, Danial Lord. 2008. *On Deep History and the Brain*. Berkeley: University of California Press.

SoRelle, Ruth. 2012. "Like Adults, Black Children Receive Less Pain Relief." *Emergency Medicine News* 34 (9): 1, 32. https://doi.org/doi: 10.1097/01.EEM.0000419511.43102.cc.

Stevens, Anthony. 1993. *The Two-Million-Year-Old Self*. College Station, TX: Texas A&M University Press.

Tocqueville, Alex de. 2003. *Democracy in America*. New York: Penguin Classics.

Thomas, Kristie A., Manisha Joshi, and Susan B. Sorenson. 2014. "'Do you know What It Feels Like to Drown?': Strangulation as Coercive Control in Intimate Relationships." *Psychology of Women Quarterly* 38 (1): 124–137. https://doi.org/10.1177/0361684313488354.

Turner, Jonathan H. 2000. *On the Origins of Human Emotions*. Stanford, CA: Stanford University Press.

UN Women. "Facts and Figures: Ending Violence against Women." UN Women, United Nations. Last modified November 2021. Accessed December 12. https://www.un-women.org/en/what-we-do/ending-violence-against-women/facts-and- figures.

Waal, Frans De. 2005. *Our Inner Ape: A Leading Primatologist Explains Why We Are Who We Are*. New York: Riverhead Books.

Weisman, Alan. 2007. *The World Without Us*. New York: St. Martin's Press.

Whitaker, Robert. 2010. *Anatomy of an Epidemic*. New York: Crown Publishers.

Wood, David. 2014. "Healing: Can We Treat Moral Injury?" *The Huffington Post*, March 20. Accessed October 27, 2016. http://projects.huffingtonpost.com/projects/moral-injury/healing.

Woodward, Kathleen. 2009. *Statistical Panic: Cultural Politics and Poetics of the Emotions*. Durham: Duke University Press.

World Health Organization, *Global and Regional Estimates of Violence against Women*, http://apps.who.int/iris/bitstream10665/85239/1/9789241564625_eng.pdf. For individual country information, see full compilation of data in UN Women, 2012, *Violence against Women Prevalence Data: Surveys by Country*. Retrieved August 31, 2015.

World Health Organization, United Nations Office on Drugs and Crime, and United Nations Development Programme. 2014. *Global Status Report on Violence Prevention 2014*. World Health Organization.

Worthington, Everett L., and Diane Langberg. 2012. "Religious Considerations and Self-Forgiveness in Treating Complex Trauma and Moral Injury in Present and Former Soldiers." *Journal of Psychology & Theology* 40 (4): 274–288.

Yehuda, Rachel. 2015. "How Trauma and Resilience Cross Generations." *On Being with Krista Tippett*. http://www.onbeing.org/program/rachel-yehuda-how-trauma-and-resilience-cross-generations/transcript/7791.

Young, Iris M. 1980. "Throwing Like a Girl: A Phenomenology of Feminine Body Comportment Motility and Spatiality." *Human Studies* 3 (2): 137–156.

Zimbardo, Philip, and Nikita Duncan. 2012. *The Demise of Guys: Why Boys Are Struggling and What We Can Do About It*. Amazon Digital Services, Inc.

ACKNOWLEDGMENTS

I would like to thank the people and organizations that in their various ways supported the writing of these essays. SocialJusticeSolutions.org, AcesTooHigh.com, MadinAmerica.com, DxSummit.org, and HealMyPTSD.com published earlier versions of some of these essays and have supported many writers committed to healing trauma and improving mental health services. The Sensorimotor Psychotherapy Institute, especially under the leadership of Janina Fisher, provided an opportunity to create community around trauma-informed practices and ideals.

I am grateful for an invitation from the Thinking Africa Project of the Department of Political and International Studies at Rhodes University to take part in a colloquium on violence in the Great Lakes Region of Africa and the work of my mentor, Valentin Y. Mudimbe. I appreciate an invitation to speak at the Annual Kaiser National Emergence Medicine Conference on coping with traumatic stress and invitations from John F. Kennedy University VALOR Center and the San Mateo College Veterans Center to speak on the topic of moral injury.

I was fortunate to have opportunities to share versions of some of these essays at the following conferences: Feminist and Women's Association Biennial Conference, Leeds University; Confined Spaces Conference, Cambridge University; Social Pathologies of Contemporary Civilization Conference, University of Hull; CRESC Annual Conference, University of Manchester; United States Association of Body Psychotherapy

Conference, Boulder, CO; After the Crisis Conference, University of Agder; and International Society for Ethical Psychology & Psychiatry Conference, Los Angelas, CA.

I want to thank the readers who found their way to my website where these essays were originally published. I appreciated and enjoyed the enriching correspondences, whether through email or in the blog comments. It was uplifting to be in conversation with so many courageous and spirited people. I felt part of a community brought together through shared traumas and mutual hope for a better world. I remain forever grateful for the connections I made through *Trauma's Labyrinth*.

These essays were written during a time when I was continuing as a scholar while learning the craft of psychotherapy. Joining the divide between these two praxis (and often just moving between them) was facilitated by conversations with Valentin Mudimbe, Larry and Carol Rivers, Katherine Meier, Margaret Cramer, Fran Love, Nicole Livingston, Linda Lawless, Agustina Gallegos, Marilynne Chophel, and Estelle Tham.

Special thanks to Jeff Garmel, who regularly read my essays and gave much appreciated feedback (including catching embarrassing grammatical errors) and Jefferson at FirstEditing who gave the essays the polish they needed. Many wonderful writers have supported my efforts to learn the craft of writing: Gail Ford at the Writer's Studio; BK Loren and James McKean at the Iowa Summer Writing Festival; Dennis P. Slattery's Writing Myths Workshop at Pacifica Graduate Institute; Kathleen McClung at the Writer's Salon; and Jane Ganahl at the Writer's Grotto.

To my sister, Kimberly Kerr: Thank you for taking the journey with me. To my husband, Gus Garmel: Your wholehearted commitment to the success of this project has been the wind in my sails. You make me one of the lucky ones, if not a better person.

ABOUT THE AUTHOR

Laura K. Kerr, PhD is a scholar and former psychotherapist specialized in sensorimotor psychotherapy. Though her primary focus is trauma and its effects, her interests are varied, with degrees in physics, atmospheric and space science, philosophy, counseling psychology, and the philosophy of education and symbolic systems.

Dr. Kerr has published numerous articles, book chapters, encyclopedia entries, and a monograph on dissociation in late modern America. She is currently at work on her next two books: one on the evolution of spirituality and the other on recovery from sexual trauma.

She lives in San Francisco, CA with her husband. When not writing nonfiction, she gardens, paints, writes poetry, practices yoga, and enjoys nature. Visit her at laurakkerr.com.